DIVISION AND THE STRESSES OF REUNION, 1845-1876

DIVISION
and the
STRESSES
of REUNION

<u>1845</u>
1876

DAVID M. POTTER

David M. Potter, Carl N. Degler, Editors
American History Series

Scott, Foresman and Company
Glenview, Illinois   Brighton, England

Cover: Richmond, Virginia, photographed by Matthew Brady. *Reproduced from the collections of the Library of Congress*

Library of Congress Catalog Number: 72-76445
ISBN: 0-673-05786-0
Copyright © 1973 by Scott, Foresman and Company,
Glenview, Illinois 60025.
Philippines Copyright 1973 by Scott, Foresman and Company.
All Rights Reserved.
Printed in the United States of America.

Regional Offices of Scott, Foresman and located in
Dallas, Texas; Glenview, Illinois; Oakland, New Jersey;
Palo Alto, California; Tucker, Georgia; and Brighton, England.

FOREWORD

This book is the fifth title in a series of eight (to be offered alternatively in two large volumes) that will encompass the history of the United States from the first explorations and settlements to the present. Together the series will constitute in general coverage and time span the kind of work that students usually employ as a textbook for a college survey course in American history. Both this book and the series as a whole, however, are intended to be different from the material covered in the usual survey text.

Customarily, a textbook is largely filled with a chronological account of the "essential" facts of the past. Facts and chronology are, it is true, the building stones of historical knowledge, and familiarity with both is essential, but they do not provide the structure of the past by themselves. Rather, it is the framework of an era that the student must grasp if he is to retain and make sense out of the myriad facts that any book—text or other—throws in his path. By framework, however, we are not suggesting a skeleton or outline but the unity or essential thrust of the period—in short, its meaning.

Emphasis falls throughout upon explanation of the past. Why did events turn out as they did? What significance did these developments have for subsequent American history? What importance do they have for the present? How does the American experience compare with that of other countries in similar circumstances? How and why did American attitudes and values alter during the period in question?

The organization and some of the less important facts that are to be found in more conventional textbooks are absent from these pages. It was the conviction of the author and the editors of the series that understanding the relationship among events is more important than just memorizing customarily agreed-upon facts. Therefore, some facts have been omitted simply because they do not contribute to an understanding of the structure of the period.

This book has been written for American college students; that is, readers who have some acquaintance with the history of the United States. While the usual effort has been made to clarify and define obscure or unfamiliar terms and persons, a certain basic familiarity with the subject has been taken for granted. No student who has passed successfully through an American high school need worry about his ability to comprehend what appears within these covers, but it is hoped that his understanding of the direction and the causes behind the movements of American history will be enhanced by reading this book.

Carl N. Degler

PREFACE

When David Potter died suddenly on February 18, 1971, the manuscript for this volume in the Scott, Foresman American History Series was virtually completed. The press of other obligations prevented his filling in a few details or giving the manuscript his usual meticulous final reading. As his fellow editor in this series I have tried to fill in those gaps and to expand one small part of the manuscript. The reader should know that the only place in which I have added anything more than a sentence to Potter's manuscript is in the first chapter where the nature of slavery is briefly discussed. I believe that I have followed the intent of Potter in providing a few more sentences on this subject than he did. I have also written the picture essays. Subheads have been provided by his editor at Scott, Foresman and Company, Nancy Kannappan.

I mention the extent of my own efforts because in fairness to Potter and to his readers it needs to be known that this compact, closely argued, and eminently readable text is Potter's work virtually as he left it and intended it. Because the publishers and I felt strongly that this book should not be tampered with, it does not contain the kind of overview of the cultural developments of the period that other volumes in the series include. Had he lived, Potter undoubtedly would have added such a chapter, for it was his strong conviction from the inception of the series that each volume should include a synthesis of intellectual and cultural history. But since he did not live long enough to write such a chapter, it seemed wrong to have another hand write it, especially when considerations of length would have required cutting some of Potter's completed manuscript if the new chapter were added. Moreover, in the first chapter in particular, and throughout the book, Potter has woven into his tightly knit story a good deal of intellectual and cultural history.

In the opinion of the publishers and the editor, this volume is a model of compression and analysis of the great events that constitute the central period in the evolution of the United States. The book demonstrates particularly well the ways in which slavery became entangled with other issues so that when the war came the central issue was not slavery and the Negro, but quite different concerns, some of which were less important and less realistic. Notable in Potter's interpretation is the clear linkage he establishes between the un-recognized issues of the war and the problems of Reconstruction. As he points out, the central problem of that generation was to reconcile Union and freedom. Not surprisingly, the story of how men of that generation faced up to that problem is not one of unalloyed success, though along the way there were some substantial social gains. Potter's whole approach in this admirable volume is to treat problems rather than events. His success is amazing.

The insights to be found here obviously derive from the larger work on the coming of the Civil War, on which Potter was working at the time of his death. That study, also almost completed, will be published at a later date by another publisher.

The annotated bibliographies following each chapter have been drawn up by the editor. Before Potter's death he had not yet compiled the suggested reading list for his chapters. Without having a special knowledge of the books that he would have included in the suggested reading, I have nevertheless tried to include items related to the subjects covered in each chapter. Neither the items nor the comments are those David Potter would have chosen, but they do include titles that he commented upon and included in other such bibliographies he has written for other publications on this subject.

Carl N. Degler

CONTENTS

DIVISION AND THE STRESSES OF REUNION, 1845-1876

CHAPTER ONE

THE PROGRESS AND PROBLEMS OF A YOUNG REPUBLIC

THIS BRIEF VOLUME attempts to describe and, in part to explain, the important historical developments in the United States in the years between 1844 and 1877. In standard terms this third of a century was first a period of sectional tensions and controversy over slavery, lasting for seventeen years from 1844 to 1861, then a four-year Civil War which was in many ways the costliest war in American history, and finally an eleven-year period of efforts, mostly futile, to develop some constructive social solution out of the northern victory and the abolition of slavery. In underlying terms it was a time when the United States grappled with the long-evaded question of what sort of organization the American union really was, and with the vital problem of the double standard in American society for Negroes and whites. Americans of the mid-nineteenth century approached this latter problem too restrictively in terms of slavery alone, and thus some of the most difficult aspects were left to trouble American society in the twentieth century. Perhaps the nineteenth century was not ready to cope with them in any case, and all that was historically possible was the removal of slavery which exposed a different level of racial discrimination for later generations to deal with. In any event this chapter and the ones that follow will examine the developments of three crucial decades in American history.

In 1844 the American republic was fifty-five years old, counting from the inauguration of George Washington as its first President, or sixty-eight, counting from the declaration of thirteen British colonies that they were free and independent states. Many people were still alive who could remember the beginning.

The Changing World

During these years both the world and the United States had seen some striking changes. At the time of the War for Independence, two of the great political forces of the modern world—nationalism and democracy—were completely unknown in their twentieth-century form, and the technology of generated power, of machinery, and of mass production was in its infancy. Governmental power, in all parts of the world, had been controlled for centuries by small ruling groups of royal dynasties, or by oligarchies which monopolized the ownership of land in economies where land was the most important form of wealth or means of production. Ordinary men and women, subordinate to these ruling groups, remained illiterate, with little awareness of the world beyond their own narrow communities, and bound to the soil not only by traditional ties but even more compulsively by the fact that the existing methods of agriculture were so crude that society had to devote nine tenths of

Life in the South: an idealized view of a cotton plantation on the Mississippi River. *Rare Book Division, The New York Public Library, Astor, Lenox and Tilden Foundations* its manpower to the production of food. Only a small fraction of the energy of society could be devoted to activities other than tilling the soil.

From the time of Columbus until the late eighteenth century, this basic restriction to agriculture had remained primary, but from the fifteenth century onward an important secondary feature had developed. The countries of western Europe had witnessed a steady increase in commerce; an improved technology in shipbuilding, clothmaking, mining, and other productive activities; the growth of towns as centers of trade; and the evolution of a merchant class to operate the new commercial economy. Many middle-class merchants were in fact richer than the land-owning aristocrats. By the end of the eighteenth century, the new middle classes had developed enough social and economic muscle to challenge the primacy of the hereditary ruling class and the system of political and legal privilege by which that class had maintained its ascendancy. Social forces and technological change were already preparing the way for great transformations throughout the nineteenth and twentieth centuries.

At the time of the War of Independence, however, none of these forces had been politically activated. Thus the United States was the first country to base its political system on the clear-cut principle that "governments derive their just powers from the consent of the governed"; some of the American states were the first political entities in the world to choose their government officials by a system approximating universal free manhood suffrage; and the early devotion of the patriots of the American Revolution to their cause was one of the first clear-cut expressions of modern nationalism.

France and Britain. In a limited sense, then, the United States was the scene of some of the world's first important steps toward democracy and nationalism. But while the American republic was still a minor and marginal power in the world, these same forces asserted themselves in more dramatic and more important form in the major countries of western Europe. In 1789 France embarked upon a Revolution which guillotined the king, set up a republic, and invoked a concept of nationalism as a kind of political religion, glorifying *la patrie* and making citizenship a form of spiritual membership in a mystic political community. After a while the Revolution lost its radical zip, as revolutions have a way of doing, and trailed off into a Napoleonic Empire. When Napoleon literally met his Waterloo (1815), the European monarchical powers put a Bourbon back on the throne of France. But before this happened, Napoleon had scattered the seeds of nationalism all over western Europe. Moreover, the liberal idea of elected legislative bodies and of constitutional restrictions upon monarchical power had come to stay.

In Britain the shift toward democracy and nationalism was less spectacular, but more solid. Britain had settled the question of absolute monarchy in the seventeenth century, and since that time the Lords and the elected Commons in Parliament had held the real control. However, when Parliament took power from the crown, it was not a democratic body, but an assembly of great landholders and their agents. Not until the mid-nineteenth century did this oligarchy relax its control, when, by a series of reform bills in 1832, 1867, and 1884–1885, Britain adopted a system of suffrage which was in some respects more democratic than that in the United States. This is not quite the same thing as saying that Britain was a more democratic country, for the upper classes continued to give an aristocratic tone to British society which was conspicuously lacking on the social scene in Jacksonian America.

But if liberalism and nationalism had begun to make their impact felt in the United States and western Europe, the rest of the world was still almost untouched by modernity. In central and eastern Europe, from which so many people would migrate to become Americans in the late nineteenth and early twentieth centuries, the conditions of an earlier age still prevailed. The Hapsburg Empire, the Romanov Empire, and the kingdom of Prussia, surrounded by a patchwork of smaller German principalities, all maintained systems in which monarchs ruled unfettered by constitutions. Economic power was concentrated in the hands of great landed families, and the plain people lived in a semifree condition as serfs, laboring on the land. The industrial and power technology of the modern world had scarcely touched these realms.

The World Beyond Europe. Beyond Europe the world was still an exotic and variegated place, and travel was a supreme adventure for people who crawled slowly over the surface of the oceans in small wooden ships propelled by the wind. Only a few steamboats were in operation, plying the north Atlantic. In Asia the British were rapidly consolidating a hold on India, and the Dutch controlled the rich East Indies, but China was still a "flowery kingdom," living with its own culture and traditions, which had changed very little for many centuries. Japan was as remote and inaccessible as Mars is today. In Africa, from which millions of people had already been brought as slaves to the Americas, European discoverers had still done little more than skirt the edges of the great continent, and had scarcely started the process of exploring it and carving it up into colonies—a process which they would virtually complete by the end of the nineteenth century. In Australia, also, Europeans had barely occupied the eastern rim of the continent, and the vast "outback" was a virtually empty no-man's-land.

In the western hemisphere outside the United States, Canada was beginning an experiment in self-government, started by Britain in 1837, which was to make her in time an autonomous member of the British Commonwealth of Nations. But in Latin America, political appearances did not correspond very closely to living realities. During and after the Napoleonic wars, the colonies which Spain and Portugal had "controlled" for almost three centuries were cut loose from their Iberian ties, and the dominant social groups, which were the great land-holding *encomenderos* of Spanish stock set up republics, together with one brief empire in Mexico and one that lasted for six decades in Brazil. These new governments, in Hispanic America at least, showed considerable instability at the top, where military cliques frequently seized control from one another. But "government" then did not mean what it means today. The men who held public offices and led lives of genteel leisure at the capitals exercised little real influence over the economic and social life of the people, who were of Indian stock, subject to the control of the *encomenderos* and living in a more oppressed status than the serfs of eastern Europe, as semiservile tillers of the soil. For generation after generation, life went on very much the same in this authoritarian, pre-industrial world, and it really did not matter very much which faction of the élite received the military salutes in Mexico City, Lima, Buenos Aires, Santiago, or Caracas. A republic controlled by local grandees could be just as hierarchical as one controlled by grandees in Spain, and though a country might not be a colony politically, it could still be treated as a colony economically. In fact Latin America was to a great extent an economic colony of Britain and a cultural satellite of France and Spain, and these facts had more real meaning for the life of the people than the facts of political independence and republicanism.

The Changing United States

In this mid-nineteenth-century world, so incredibly unlike the world of the late twentieth century, the United States had grown and prospered almost beyond imagination. Beginning with a population in 1790 of a little less than four million, almost all living east of the Allegheny Mountains, it had increased by 1840 to a little more than seventeen million. (The population of the whole country, however, was less than that of either California or New York today.) The original thirteen states had increased to twenty-six by 1844, and more than seven million people were living in the new states. Three of the new states (Ohio, Tennessee, and Kentucky) had larger populations than any of the original states except New York, Pennsylvania, and Virginia.

The territorial growth of the country had been rapid, with the acquisition of the Louisiana Territory in 1803 and of Florida in 1819. Now the western limits of the republic lay along the Great Divide of the Rocky Mountains. Beyond was one of the emptiest areas on the planet in terms of human population—the Oregon Territory which was jointly "occupied" by Britain and the United States, and the northernmost "departments" of the Republic of Mexico, Alta California and New Mexico—which lay sprawling and neglected, far beyond the grasp of the feeble power exercised by the government in Mexico City. The Hispanic population of this whole area probably amounted to less than 50,000 people—44,000 in New Mexico and 4000 in California; the Indian population was perhaps 100,000 in California and only a fraction of that number in the rest of the area west of the Rockies. In Oregon there were, in 1845, about 10,000 Americans, who had migrated to the Willamette Valley since 1834. None was north of the 49th parallel. The Indian population of Oregon south of 49° was about 20,000.

American Social and Economic Success: An Open Society

Even more significant than the physical growth of the country was its apparent success as a social and economic enterprise. At a stage in world history when democracy and nationalism were coming to the fore, and when technology was transforming the patterns of human life, the American society seemed uniquely well adapted, in many respects, to fulfill the goals of democracy and nationalism, and to make the most of a new technology.

The Abundance of Land. Perhaps the primary advantage from which Americans benefited was the fact that the United States enjoyed a very high proportion of resources, and especially of cultivable land, to population. With a population less than half that of France, for example, the United States had an area eight times as great. There was such an acute shortage of labor in proportion to land that land monopoly, which was the traditional basis of social power in Europe and most parts of the world, simply could not be applied in the United States. During the colonial period, some European-style land monopolies had been attempted by privileged grandees, such as the Calvert family of Maryland and the Lords Proprietors of Carolina, but these efforts failed in the face of an abundance of land, and after a time men who had been granted vast acreage were usually content to sell it off for a nominal price per acre. After the American Revolution, the states ceded their western lands to the central government. The government, in turn, gradually evolved a policy of selling this land in small tracts at low prices. By 1820 a person could buy an eighty-acre tract for $100. This was not always the best land, and there was land speculation along with the opening of the public domain, but to an agricultural people, cheap land was the foundation stone of social equality and of political democracy. In a country where the population density was ten persons per square mile, population explosion was no problem.

The Absence of a Privileged Hierarchy. Not only did the abundance of land prevent the exploitation of the cultivators by land monopolists (with one major exception to which we shall come shortly), but it also prevented the development of a social system dominated by a privileged oligarchy, as in Europe. The great difference between the American historical experience and the European experience is that in moving toward fuller democracy America did not have to struggle against an entrenched feudal past, as did Europe. This is the chief reason why the American Revolution was scarcely revolutionary in a basic sense, and was a tame affair indeed compared with the French Revolution ten years later.

This does not mean that America had, as is sometimes asserted, a classless society. In fact it is doubtful that any highly developed society ever existed without class stratification, even in socialist countries. In colonial America social rank had been clearly defined. Wealthy merchants, wealthy planters, well-connected clergymen and lawyers formed a class of "gentle folk" who dressed differently from the "simple folk"—knee breeches, powdered wigs, cocked hats—and whose rank as "ladies and gentlemen" was recognized by all. But social rank in America was not reinforced by vast accumulations of wealth, or by official titles and privilege, or by impassable barriers between different social levels. A person born in poverty might make his own "station" in life, and might rise from humble beginnings to the presidency of the United States as Andrew Jackson and Martin Van Buren had done. An aristocrat might even find it politically advantageous to claim humble circumstances as William Henry Harrison did in the Log Cabin and Hard Cider campaign of 1840. The point was not that America had abolished social status or competitive efforts to acquire wealth as a measure of status. The point is not even that America had literally an equalitarian society, as is so often asserted. But it did have an open society. If this society did not offer broad opportunity for everyone, still it offered opportunity for enough people to make the exclusion of certain others—notably Negroes—all the more discriminatory and ironic.

The Maintenance of Weak Government. The foundations of the open society consisted, as has already been stated, in the ready availability of land and in the absence of a powerful privileged class. But if these conditions had made it open, additional features had been developed to keep it open. One of these was the deliberate maintenance of weak government, to prevent strategically situated families or individuals from concentrating power through political means. Not only the federal government, but also each of the state governments had a written constitution which spelled out a set of controls which the body of citizens imposed upon the governments, restricting them to the exercise of limited powers. Further, the powers of government were separated into executive, legislative, and judicial categories and assigned to three different sets of officials, so that each could serve as a watchdog upon the others. Still further, public officials, except the judges in the federal system and in some of the states, were held accountable to the voters at elections as frequent as every two years.

All these features made for weak government. For instance, it has been a chronic problem in the American political system that from time to time, one of the three branches of the government will get at cross-purposes with another, as President and Congress have often done, with the result that the political system becomes deadlocked, thus paralyzing the operation of government. In a country which is exposed to dangers from other powers, or which depends upon positive and regular government action to maintain the economic and social system in running order, such a deadlock leads to great dangers and dislocations and can scarcely be tolerated. But the loose-jointed American agricultural economy was largely self-regulating, and required only a minimum of governmental attention. As for dangers from other countries, the United States was flanked on the east by an ocean three thousand miles wide, on the west by a trackless expanse of almost empty land, and on the north and south by Canada and Mexico, both too weak to threaten the country's security. Hence a token Army and Navy sufficed, and they were placed under the control of a civilian commander in chief to keep them from getting militaristic ideas. Thus, because the United States had the advantage of what a prominent historian has called "free security," it could afford the luxury of a weak government; it did not have to divert the energies of its young men into military pursuits, as did the nations of Europe; and its economy could expand more rapidly than the economies of countries which were drained by the necessity of devoting money, energy, manpower, and resources to nonproductive military pursuits.

The tradition of weak government reflected the historic experience of ordinary men and women that strong government was usually employed by unscrupulous rulers to oppress the people. To them it seemed that weak government was the only alternative to oppressive government. In the twentieth century, historical experience has shown that democratic control makes it possible to use strong government for democratic purposes, and we have come to accept the positive state to a much greater degree. But to the nineteenth-century mind the principle of limited government seemed a bulwark of democracy.

Encouragement of Public Education. Equality and opportunity were made realities and not mere abstractions by another feature of the American system, which was almost the only field in which American government took a stronger initiative than the countries of Europe: public education. As early as 1642 the Massachusetts Bay Colony passed laws requiring town officials* to ascertain from time to time whether parents, and masters to whom young boys were apprenticed, were attending to their duties in having all children trained in "learning." The motive of this religiously oriented colony was to prepare everyone to read the Bible, and in 1647, the colony went further and ordered every town with as many as fifty households to appoint and pay wages to "a teacher of reading and writing." These laws rank among the most striking innovations in the American experiment, for nowhere in Britain or western Europe at that time did the public authority take the responsibility for assuring the creation of public educational facilities. This did not mean, of course, that the law in Massachusetts was fully met in every case or that every child attended school, or even that education was free. In fact pupils customarily paid fees. But it did mean that education became more public in Massachusetts, and later throughout New England, than anywhere else in the world, with the result that, regardless of whether they read the Bible or not, more of the people were fitted for a greater range of activities.

Public education came later to the states outside New England. In fact state-supported education in the South did not make major strides until after the Civil War. But during the 1830's, some northern cities, including New York, provided for free schools, at which distinctions were abolished between "rate-payers" who paid fees and "paupers" who were obliged to claim poverty

---

*The entire colony was divided into "towns"—not clusters of population, but jurisdictional divisions of the colony. The laws therefore covered everyone in the colony.

in order to qualify for free education. Schools were to be supported by public taxes and not by private fees. In 1834 Pennsylvania, and in 1850 New York, adopted laws under which local school districts could choose between fees and taxes as a basis of support. By 1847, 88 percent of the districts in Pennsylvania had turned to a system of tax-supported free schools. But fees were not totally abolished on a state-wide basis in New York until 1867 or in most other states until after the Civil War.

The story of the development of free, compulsory, tax-supported public education is an intricate one, varying from one locality to another, and involving diverse combinations of fees and taxes. But the important fact is that the United States developed a broad system of elementary education in which an unusually high proportion of the population was involved. By contrast, in England in 1851, scarcely more than half of the children between three and twelve years old were in school, and in 1845, it is estimated that only one sixth of the population could read. This figure, of course, includes many who had grown up before schooling was improved. In France among the young men of age for military service in 1840, the percentage of illiterates was 46.9, and doubtless it was much higher among women. By 1850 the figure stood at 38.9 percent and by 1860 at 32.9 percent. For the United States, the gathering of data on literacy was crudely handled, but the figures indicate that in 1840, only 22 percent of the population was illiterate, and of the white population only 9 percent. The slaves were clearly the chief victims of illiteracy, and in fact, most slave states had laws forbidding the education of slaves. In 1860 overall illiteracy was reported at 19.7 percent, and among whites at 8.9 percent. These data probably underestimated the percentage of illiteracy, but even if liberally discounted, they still show higher levels of public education than elsewhere in the western world. The widespread reading capacity of the American people was reflected in the fact that by 1833, Benjamin Day had established a penny newspaper—the New York *Sun*—as a forerunner of the cheap, mass-market dailies which have been characteristic of American journalism. It was probably the first inexpensive newspaper in the world.

Today literacy is so universal that it requires an effort to realize what important changes resulted when reading and writing ceased to be restricted to those who could afford the extra expense of private instruction. But in the nineteenth century, the educational system was a conspicuously distinctive part of the system which made American society a uniquely open one.

Cheap land, an open social system, democratic government which was restrained from oppressive practices, and universal education all contributed vitally to the great success of the raw young republic. No longer dependent upon landlords who extorted tribute from every crop, the independent farmers of America reaped abundant harvests, built comfortable dwellings, raised their standard of living, and thus avoided becoming a downtrodden peasantry, as so many of their forebears had been in the Old World. Most of this welfare was attributed to the merit of American institutions, and specifically to American democracy. But in fact, Americans benefited also from technological changes which have transformed the entire world in the last two centuries, but which were developed especially in Britain and America, and had such rapid and widespread acceptance and such deeply transforming effects in the United States that they have become identified as an intrinsic part of American culture. When they are introduced into other parts of the world, the process is sometimes spoken of as Americanization.

The Industrial Revolution in America

The sweep of this technological revolution cannot be understood unless one realizes that at the time of the Declaration of Independence, virtually the only sources of power available to provide energy for human activity were the muscle of men and animals, the force of wind on a sail or a windmill, and the force of water turning a wheel or floating a flatboat downstream. Steam power was known chiefly as a scientific curiosity and had only begun to be used in the operation of pumps to remove water seepage from mines. As for the processing of materials and the production of goods—the forging of metal, the cutting of boards, the sowing and harvesting of crops, the making of shoes and clothing—these things were almost all done by hand, and mechanical production was scarcely known except in the spinning of thread and weaving of cloth. Even for these, efficient spinning machinery did not reach the United States until Samuel Slater brought it from England in 1789, and weaving was almost all done on a hand loom until Francis Lowell set up a factory with water-powered looms at Waltham, Massachusetts, in 1814.

Development of Steam Power. But within five decades, the use of steam for power and machinery for processing materials had launched the country upon a revolution in the production and movement of goods. At the time of the constitutional convention, the first experimenters were just beginning to try to propel boats by steam power. But by 1816 a steamboat thrust upriver, against the current, from New Orleans to Louisville. Thus every river deep enough to float a steamboat became a ready-made highway of transportation for a country where the lack of roads had made the movement of bulky crops or other goods impossible and also had isolated not only distant regions but even nearby localities from one another. Before the Civil War 3500 steam vessels were put into operation on the western rivers alone.

The successful use of steam power in turn stimulated revolutionary improvements in the steam engine itself. Beginning about 1805, Oliver Evans of Philadelphia and later of Pittsburgh, devised a high-pressure steam engine, much more efficient than the original low-pressure mechanism. This meant that a much smaller engine could generate as much power as a very heavy and cumbersome one had previously generated. Steam engines could then be used in a wide variety of manufacturing processes, and best of all could be installed in locomotives to draw a train of cars over a roadbed consisting only of two parallel rails laid on wooden ties. And so the first railroad in the country, a 136-mile line between Charleston, South Carolina, and Augusta, Georgia, to divert cotton traffic from the Savannah River, went into operation in 1833 (the Baltimore and Ohio, started in 1828, was completed much later because of legal and physical obstacles). By 1840 the United States had 2800 miles of rail, by 1850, 9000 miles, and by 1860, 30,600 miles.

Effects of the New Transportation Network. During the first generation of steamboats, canal boats, and railroad locomotives, there was not much hauling of manufactured goods, for the rise of factories came later. The major business of the transportation system in its early years was to take crops from the place of growth to the place of marketing. America was still primarily a rural society of small, independent, somewhat isolated farmers who produced for their own use as well as for market, and counted their success in terms of "making a living" rather than of money income. But commercial agriculture offered greater and more varied rewards than subsistence agriculture. The new transportation system enabled many farmers to turn to the production of specialized crops—grain in the West, cotton in the South—and it enabled many others to open up new areas to agriculture which had previously not been worth opening because they lacked access to market.

The network formed by the rivers, canals, and railroads soon broke down the barriers of distance and isolation which had at one time seemed an insurmountable obstacle to real, operative unity within the physically loose-jointed, sprawling, thinly populated republic. Once these barriers fell, they revealed the existence of a new and very large market—perhaps in area and potential capacity the largest single market in the world. This potentiality, in turn, created a challenge to find methods for increasing the production of both agricultural and processed goods. Production had to be increased without very much additional labor, for available workers were few and their wages were high. Therefore mechanical techniques had to be adopted.

Development of Modern Principles of Production: Eli Whitney. The first steps in mechanical production involved no such mass production, assembly lines, and elaborate division of labor as we know in the twentieth century. But the key principles appeared early. In 1798 Eli Whitney, who had invented the cotton gin six years previously, conceived the idea of manufacturing complex mechanisms by breaking down the process and producing the various parts separately, and then assembling the parts. This was possibly the most revolutionary idea in the history of modern technology, for up to that time, a craftsman—for instance, a gunsmith making a gun—would make one barrel, a stock to fit the barrel, a firing mechanism to fit them both, and so on, and would then start over again with his next gun. Whitney recognized that he could (1) use machine tools powered by water wheels to cut out many parts so nearly identical as to be interchangeable; (2) use a metal device, or jig, to hold the parts in place during machining and guide the machine tool with precision; and (3) could then assemble the parts, each with any of the others, since none was a unique part of its own hand-fashioned whole. By this principle of mass production of interchangeable parts, machines could replace craftsmen, productivity per worker could be multiplied many fold, and implements, when broken, could be mended simply by replacing the broken part. The idea as such was not original with Whitney, but he was the man who first made it work in the U.S.

Once this concept was adopted, it could be applied to an infinity of mechanisms—to clocks, to harvesting machines, to steam engines, to guns, during Whitney's lifetime, and later on to typewriters, automobiles, jet airplanes, washing machines, computers, and any number of things.

McCormick's Reaper. One of the earliest and most revolutionary applications was to a machine invented by Cyrus Hall McCormick, and first demonstrated in 1831, for the mechanical reaping of grain. Reaping was the bottleneck of grain production, for the amount of grain that could be reaped controlled the amount that it would pay to plant. Since one man with a sickle could reap only half an acre a day, this was a severely restrictive control on production. But two men with a reaper could reap five or six acres a day. This meant (1) bread could be sold at less than half its previous price because of the reduction in labor costs for producing grain; (2) grain production could be increased five- or sixfold, thus making America a grain producer for Europe; and (3) manpower previously concentrated in agriculture could be diverted into many other forms of productive or distributive activity. The reaper took hold quickly. In 1852 it was estimated that about 3500 new reaping machines were put to work in the fields of the Northwest. McCormick started a factory at Chicago in 1847 for making reapers, and by 1856, despite the rivalry of competitors, he was selling 4000 machines annually.

Roots of American Economic Success. When patriotic spokesmen were called upon to explain the merits which had brought prosperity and rapid progress to the American people, they were likely to reply in political terms, speaking of freedom, democracy, constitutional government, equality before the law, and, perhaps, widespread education and the self-reliance of the Americans. In fact all these features were important: they encouraged initiative; they created an open situation favorable to each man's developing his potentialities; and they were conducive to the widespread distribution of the fruits of social progress. But along with these were other features, not so clearly recognized at the time, which gave immense advantages to American society. In a world whose inhabitants still lived mostly by tilling the soil, it was an immeasurable advantage to have a vast surplus of fertile land which had never been brought under the plough. In a world where the techniques of production were so primitive that all the able-bodied adults, in a regime of unremitting labor, could barely produce enough food, clothing, and shelter for society's basic needs, it was a new feature in the history of man to command technological devices which enabled a single worker to do the work which six or eight or ten workers had done before.

All these advantages, leading to rapid growth, quick solution of physical problems, and widespread material comfort for the American people generated a spirit of optimism and confidence in progress, and even a smug, complacent conviction of the superiority of all things American. Americans of the mid-century were notorious for boasting immoderately about the perfection of their society.

The Anomaly of Individualism in a Changing Economy

Yet with all the genuine merits and assets of society in the United States, there were three great anomalies which lurked dangerously beneath the surface of the American system. The first of these was the fact that Americans had lived for two centuries, during the colonial and early republican periods, in circumstances where individual welfare was best promoted by leaving people on their own, to accomplish what they could for themselves by private action. As a result, they had come to believe in a kind of unrestricted individualism in which private persons were left free to seek their personal advantage regardless of the social consequences, and to do as they pleased with the physical environment, despoiling the landscape, depleting the soil, and, in short, looting the resources of a richly endowed continent.

In this situation, control by citizens acting through their government, for purposes of regulation in the interests of the social group, was scarcely available. Jefferson's concept of the ideal government was widely accepted: it should be "wise and frugal" . . . it should "restrain men from injuring one another . . . leave them otherwise free to regulate their own pursuits of industry and improvement, and . . . not take from the mouth of labor the bread which it has earned." Each of these features, it is worth noting, was a negative one—what government should not do, rather than what it should do. For a republic of small farmers, living in isolation from one another, and producing goods for their own consumption, this may have been an idyllic formula. But (1) when steamboats, railroads, and canals created a national market which destroyed the protective isolation within which local markets had been sheltered; (2) when advances in mechanized technology made workers dependent upon access to machines rather than upon their own craft skills; (3) when the growth of commercial agriculture made farmers dependent upon the transportation by which they reached their markets; and (4) when power machinery made possible the rapid extraction of resources—when these things happened, a concentration of economic power began to occur which was out of balance with the carefully arranged decentralization, even neutralization, of political power. This lack of adjustment of the political system to the rapidly changing economic system was to present increasingly acute problems in American society from the formation of the first great trusts or economic monopolies in the 1870's until and beyond the New Deal of Franklin D. Roosevelt. But the roots of the problem extended back to a far earlier period.

The Anomaly of Federalism

A second anomaly involved the question whether the American Union was an integrated nation, in which the states were essentially political subdivisions, or whether it was a pluralistic association of member states each retaining its own integral separateness and its own ultimate autonomy. This anomaly existed because the nationalists had found that the people of the states in 1787 were not ready to make the great decision in favor of nationhood and the best they could do was to accept an ambiguous answer which might, in time, develop into an affirmative answer.

Constitutional Background. This ambiguity went back to the time when the colonies revolted against Britain. At that point they had no formal or legal ties with one another, except through their common membership in the British Empire, and the Declaration of Independence severed that tie. When they became independent, therefore, there were theoretically thirteen separate sovereignties. When in 1781 they ratified the Articles of Confederation, which formed the framework of a loose union, they specified first of all that "each state retains its sovereignty, freedom, and independence." In the treaty of peace with Britain, in 1783, each state was named separately as a party to the treaty.

But whether or not the American states formed a nation legally or politically, there were many people who felt strong nationalist loyalties psychologically. Many Americans of the Revolutionary generation, of whom George Washington was foremost, had focused their loyalties on the Union, and they believed that the shared sacrifices of the Revolution had joined the colonies together in a single union. They tried to translate this solidarity of spirit into political form at Philadelphia in 1787 by voting, in the first days of the Constitutional Convention, "that a national government ought to be established, consisting of a supreme Legislature, Judiciary and Executive." But the opposition was so strong that the national-minded members soon recognized that their plan could not win ratification by enough of the states and they retreated from their original purpose, realistically deciding to settle for a system that would be, in the words of James Madison "mixed . . . partly national and partly federal." Thus they left in uncertainty the question whether the United States formed a single nation.

A Mixed System. This "mixed" structure in the Constitution provided that in some features the American people were treated as a collective whole, as in the House of Representatives and in that the laws enacted by the central government operated directly upon the whole people. But in other features the states retained an intact identity—for instance in amending the Constitution, which required ratification by three fourths of the states, regardless of whether or not a popular majority approved the amendment. To resolve the ambiguity of this mixed system, many critics from Daniel Webster to the present have argued that the American people were fused into one whole and that the fusion is shown by the language of the Preamble, which states that, "We the people of the United States . . . do ordain and establish this Constitution." But the phrase "we the people of the United States," was not intended to distinguish between all the people *collectively* and the separate populations or peoples of the various states *separately;* it was intended instead to distinguish between ratification by the *people* of the states acting in their sovereign capacity as citizens and ratification by the *governments* of the states acting as agents for the people*—the framers did not want an association of member governments like the U.N.; they wanted an association of member peoples. By the act of ratification the bodies of citizens in the various states vested certain political powers in a central government and certain other political powers in their state governments, and it remained unclear whether they had formed themselves into one single political body. Among the framers, not only were the men who tried to insert an affirmation of unitary nationalism voted down, but others who tried to insert explicit guarantees of the sovereignty of the several states were also voted down. As Elbridge Gerry realistically remarked, "we were in a peculiar situation. We were neither the same nation nor different nations." It was because of this dualism that the framers finally proposed and the states accepted an arrangement which was, as James Madison said, "neither a national nor a federal constitution, but a composition of both."

The Evolution of a Nation. Instead of creating a nation, the framers had created a situation in which a nation could evolve. In a sense this forbearance was an act of supreme wisdom, for the cohesion of a democratic nation depends upon the voluntary loyalty (a psychological attitude) of its citizens more than upon formal legal devices. The framers could not enact a psychological attitude; they could only encourage its development.

As time passed it became unmistakably clear that a nation was developing. For instance, in 1821 Chief Justice John Marshall handed down a Supreme Court decision (*Cohens* v. *Virginia)* in which he declared "the United States form for many and for most important purposes a single nation." In 1817 John C. Calhoun, later to become the great champion of state sovereignty, urged the appropriation of federal money for the development of improved transportation, and in urging it, exclaimed, "Let us then bind the republic together with a perfect system of roads and canals. Let us conquer space. . . . The more enlarged the sphere of commercial circulation—the more extended that of social intercourse—the more strongly we are bound together—the more inseparable are our destinies." Within fifty years after the ratification of the Constitution the central government had created thirteen new states to balance

*In *Federalist,* No. 39, James Madison wrote, "In order to ascertain the real character of the government, it may be considered in relation to the foundation on which it is to be established . . . On examining [this] on one hand, that the Constitution is to be founded on the assent and ratification of the people of America, given by deputies [at state conventions] elected for the special purpose; but, on the other, that this assent and ratification is to be given by the people, not as individuals composing one entire nation, but as composing the distinct and independent States to which they respectively belong. It is to be the assent and ratification of the several States, derived from the supreme authority in each State—the authority of the people themselves. The act, therefore, establishing the Constitution, will not be a *national* but a *federal* act."

the thirteen original states which had created it. By the 1840's, the United States had a national anthem, a national flag, a cult of the Constitution and the Union which was characterized by an attitude of worship toward both, and a national holiday (July 4) which was universally observed with extravagant nationalistic glorification of the American Union.

So long as everyone accepted the Union by universal consent, the ambiguity of the legal or formal underpinnings of national strength did not seem to matter especially. The republic grew uninterruptedly in area and population; it gained in cohesion as internal commerce multiplied, as roads and canals broke through isolating barriers, and as rapid communication enhanced the strength of a network of information and ideas, shared by the American people. Political parties, church bodies, and other institutions organized on a national basis.

A Latent Threat to the Nature of the Union. As the actual degree of cohesion of the American people increased in response to physical and dynamic circumstances, the psychological spirit of nationalism increased with it. Thus, in one sense, the problem of nationality was working itself out naturally and painlessly by an evolutionary process. Yet in another sense, the static stipulations of 1787, with their emphasis upon the power and perhaps even the sovereignty of the states, remained unchanged and provided a legal basis for resistance to national power. So the gap widened between functional reality and legal theory, and the question of what kind of union existed among the American people remained unsettled at a theoretical level. Seldom in history have people lived in such tranquillity, prosperity, and concord as the Americans lived for seventy years without any basic agreement as to the fundamental nature of their political system.

In the first half of the nineteenth century, the American people were able to gloss over this vital question because they shared a broad range of common values and social attitudes, and were perhaps a more homogeneous people than they have ever been, before or since. Overwhelmingly English in speech, Protestant in religion, middle class in social status and outlook, agricultural in occupation, and rural in their social conditioning, they believed in the middle-class virtues of thrift, self-denial, and hard work, and in the distinctively American value of equality, with its corollary that the individual must accept the manners and morals of the majority of his equals, or in other words must be a conformist. The small, independent farmers who made up the bulk of the American population were self-reliant, naive in their social ideas, dogmatically moralistic, suspicious of luxury and wealth as leading to corruption, intensely practical in their ideas about almost everything, including education, and distrustful of intellectual virtuosity.

So long as they shared these qualities, lived in a prosperous and comfortable economy, and escaped the heavy hand of taxation and government controls, they could conduct public affairs with very few really divisive issues to cause friction among them. But there were certain more or less latent forces of divisiveness from the beginning, and when these divisions became focused upon the gap between theory and practice concerning the nature of the Union, a crisis ensued which led to the worst failure the democratic process has ever experienced in the United States.

The Underlying Division. The basic divisiveness can be and has been stated in several ways—in economic terms, in social-cultural terms, in terms simply of the issue of slavery. It has been analyzed as a strictly moral contest between freedom and slavery, and as a simple rivalry for power between conflicting interest groups. But no matter how it is analyzed, the divisiveness appeared along geographical lines, following roughly the Mason-Dixon boundary and the Ohio River, thus placing Pennsylvania, Ohio, Indiana, and Illinois on one side, and Maryland, Virginia (including what is now West Virginia), and Kentucky on the other. Economically the area south of these lines engaged primarily in the production of staple crops, especially cotton, which was sold on the world market. The northeastern area had been oriented much more heavily toward commerce, and by the 1840's was turning to industrial production of iron, textiles, shoes, and other finished goods, while the northwestern area, with substantial industry of its own, concentrated on the production of grain crops which fed urban industrial workers both at home and abroad, and were also shipped south to feed the workers in the cotton fields.

The Northwest and the South were both agricultural, but their agriculture was different. Much northern grain was sold to commercial and industrial centers in the Northeast, so the grain farmers were natural allies of their customers and were willing to accept northeastern manufactured articles in exchange for their produce, within the confines of a national market. But southern cotton was sold mostly to textile producers in Britain, and southern planters, producing for a world market where they sold at unprotected prices, had no incentive to put up tariffs which would give artificial protection to northern industry. A more fundamental difference lay in the fact that the grain crops had a short growing season, could be harvested by machine, and did not need a regular year-round work force, but the staple crops, including tobacco, rice, and sugar as well as cotton, had so long a season between planting early in winter and harvest fairly late in the autumn, that a permanent labor force was almost essential.

The Anomaly of Racial Inequality

Because of these circumstances, the South had begun during colonial times to draw a supply of laborers from Africa—either directly or by way of the West Indies—with consequences which were portentous for American history and which presented a third anomaly—the greatest one faced by the young republic in the 1840's. This anomaly was that one person out of six in the United States belonged to an ethnic group to whom the equality and opportunities available to all other persons were denied, and one person in seven was legally a slave—a thing rather than a person.

Geographical Distribution of Negroes. The geographical distribution of the Negro population of the United States in the 1840's was very different from what it has become in the last third of the twentieth century. By the 1970's a majority of American Negroes lived outside the South; they were concentrated in the great urban centers (New York, Chicago, Washington, Los Angeles, Cleveland, Detroit) in one of which, Washington, they constituted a majority of the population. But throughout the nineteenth century, the Negro population was overwhelmingly concentrated in the rural districts of the South. In 1840 about 94 percent of all Negroes lived in the southern states (including Missouri), and more than 90 percent of those who lived in the South were slaves (though there were more free Negroes in the slave states than in the free states—the condition of freedom in the free states sometimes seeming to mean an absence of Negroes rather than the presence of a significant proportion of free Negroes).

Slavery and Prejudice. Because of these concentrations, many writers have treated the condition of Negroes in the period before the Civil War as if it were synonymous with the condition of slavery, and as if it were purely a southern phenomenon. In view of the statistics just cited, it is easy to see why they do this, but looking at the matter in this way obscures a crucial historical fact, namely that the condition of American Negroes was partly determined by slavery, but it was also partly determined by racial discrimination or prejudice against Negroes, slave or free. Slavery, after 1804, was completely sectional, being confined to the southern states, but racial prejudice was national. Slavery was abolished in 1863 and 1865 by the Emancipation Proclamation and the Thirteenth Amendment, but racial prejudice was not abolished by either. It may be argued—and has been—that slavery caused the basic difficulty, and that it was the stigma of slavery becoming associated with Negroes, which led to anti-Negro prejudice. This is to say that the ethnic status was tainted by its association with an inferior legal status. But it may also be argued that racial prejudice was the basic problem, resulting in the subordination of Negroes, of which slavery was just one manifestation—though the severest and historically most important manifestation. This is to say that the harsh legal status was imposed only upon individuals with an ethnic status which was the object of prejudice. Without doubt public attitudes toward Negroes and toward slaves reinforced one another, and also, without doubt the repression of the slaves prevented them from developing their capabilities in a way which might have overcome some of the prejudice against Negroes.

Whichever of the two is regarded as primary, both were much older than the United States or even the American colonies; and both had been brought to America in an already developed form.

Origins of Modern Slavery. Europeans and Africans had their first modern confrontation in the fifteenth century when the Portuguese, pushing their explorations down the African coast, encountered in numbers the people of tropical West Africa. In a number of respects, the West Africans presented a sharp contrast to the Portuguese. They were not Christians but pagans, and this at a time when the term Christendom was used by Europeans as a synonym for the civilized world. Technologically, they were not as advanced as the Portuguese, and though Africa had produced impressive civilizations, the Africans lacked a written language, and hence lacked all the advantages which literacy offers in the way of keeping records, communicating, and transmitting learning. Furthermore, in their hair texture and their black skins, their physical differences from Europeans, though not biologically significant, were notice- able enough to appear significant. The Portuguese skirmished with some of these people, made them captives, and enslaved them, as often happened to captives throughout history, both ancient and modern. This seemed almost the "natural" thing to do, since the Africans were pagans, were inferior in their technology, were captives, and were so readily distinguishable from Europeans in their appearance that most Europeans did not fully recognize human kinship with them. Once the Africans were enslaved, their inferior status was illogically confused with a condition of innate inferiority. Thus, Europeans began to adopt the tragic historical fallacy which regards the impairment caused by oppression as proof that the oppression is justified. Slavery made men inferior, and since the men enslaved were Negroes, the inferiority of slaves was taken as a justification for the subordination of Negroes.

It would be a mistake to say that this is how racism was born, for in fact human history is full of cases where societies form in-groups, which reject members of out-groups, develop stereotypes about them, and treat them as inferior. But it is accurate to say that this is how the race tensions of the twentieth-century United States were born.

New World Abundance Encourages Slavery. Soon after the Portuguese explorations, Columbus discovered America. Here were two vast, rich con- tinents, thinly populated by Indians with primitive technologies. It was a supreme opportunity for the Europeans to exploit great windfalls of land and mineral wealth—but to do so, they needed labor, and it had to be labor which they could control. In Europe the mastery over labor was maintained through land monopoly: that is, land was so scarce in proportion to population that land owners could control the cultivator by dictating the terms on which they would allow him to use the land. But in America land was so plentiful that land monopoly was impossible, and control of labor could be attained only by direct mastery over the cultivator himself—in other words by holding him as an unfree worker. Consequently the unique economic bounty of the New World led to the institutionalization on a vast scale of the slavery practiced on a very limited basis by the Portuguese.

Thus, by the first of a number of bitter paradoxes, the abundance of land which contributed so much to fulfill the potentialities of freedom for the Europeans in America—this same abundance caused the revival of a dying, archaic system of slave labor which destroyed the opportunities of freedom for Africans in America.

The African Slave Trade. During the sixteenth, seventeenth, eighteenth, and even nineteenth centuries, one of the most important human and economic developments in the world was a vast commercial traffic in human beings, which is known in history as the African slave trade. Estimates of the number of men, women, and children taken from the coast of Africa during these centuries have ranged between five and fifteen million. The most recent effort at an estimate places it at slightly less than ten million. After being bought from other Africans who had captured them, they were packed in small sailing vessels and transported across the Atlantic to be sold as slaves in the West Indies, Brazil, other parts of Central and South America, and eastern North America. Like all large operations, this traffic ramified out in many ways. In Africa the chieftains along the coast engaged in tribal wars ranging far into the interior, to capture other Africans whom they sold to "blackbirders" frequenting the Guinea coast. In Europe powerful countries, especially France, Holland, and Britain vied with one another for control of the trade; British cities such as London, Bristol, and Liverpool measured their commercial greatness by their leadership in the trade. In America itself relatively few slaves were carried into the colonies north of Chesapeake Bay, but some shipowners and merchants of Massachusetts, Rhode Island, Connecticut, and New York prospered by supplying the slave markets farther south. During the seventeenth and eighteenth centuries, far more Africans than Europeans crossed the Atlantic, and it was only in the nineteenth century that the population of the Western hemisphere became ethnically more European than African.

Differences Between Indentured Servants and Slaves. The fact that the Africans came to America as a result of capture and coercion rather than of contract also had far-reaching consequences. Servants coming from Europe came under indentures (contracts) which legally assured them of the restoration of their freedom at the expiration of their term of service. But the Africans, as captives, had no protection against lifetime servitude either for themselves or their posterity. Further, since the Africans did not come of their own free will, as the indentured servants did, they could not maintain any kind of group cohesion, and since they were completely under the control of whoever bought them, they could not follow a pattern of life which perpetuated their own African culture—their speech, their religion, their pattern of social relationships, their modes of work and play. West Africa has many languages and many cultures rather than a single one, and a slave, newly arrived in America, was not likely to find a fellow slave who shared his culture. Thus the Atlantic crossing was a wholly different affair for Europeans and for Africans. Physically it was an ordeal for both, and the servants suffered many of the same hardships experienced by the slaves. But for the Europeans, even the servants, it was a transit of culture—they brought with them their church, their mother tongue, their system of law, their ways of living, their family structure, and their social lore. All of these have tremendous value as psychological supports. But for the Africans it was a traumatic stripping of culture—they were reduced to the bare physiological fact of human existence, and had to be resocialized, as it were, and to reconstitute their identities and their personalities from the ground up.

Conditions of Life Under Slavery. This process of adjustment had to be carried out in circumstances of complete dependence upon an owner who could do almost as he willed with his slaves. In the nineteenth century, to be sure, there were laws that prescribed minimum conditions of life for slaves and sometimes maximum hours of work for them, just as there were laws forbidding masters to teach slaves to read or write or to hire themselves out. But in all such instances the laws were ineffective for at bottom the master determined the life of the slave. The master could sell, flog, even starve his slaves, though willful killing of a slave by a master was murder under the law in some states and illegal in all. No law, however, even tried to protect the slave against separation from family or from sexual exploitation. Punishment, which was the sovereign prerogative of the master, could therefore be just or unjust, yet in neither case had the slave any appeal except to the master's conscience and concern for public opinion. Conversely, masters could bestow favors and some masters did, such as permitting their slaves to keep extra earnings, or

Surplus slaves were chained together in groups and marched to southern slave markets. *Courtesy of The New-York Historical Society*

RAFFLE

Mr. Joseph Jennings respectfully informs his friends and the public that, at the request of many acquaintances, he has been induced to purchase from Mr. Osborne, of Missouri, the celebrated

DARK BAY HORSE, "STAR,"

Aged five years, square trotter and warranted sound; with a new light Trotting Buggy and Harness; also the dark, stout

MULATTO GIRL, "SARAH,"

Aged about twenty years, general house servant, valued at *nine hundred dollars,* and guaranteed, and

Will be Raffled for

At 4 o'clock P. M., February first, at the selection hotel of the subscribers. The above is as represented, and those persons who may wish to engage in the usual practice of raffling, will, I assure them, be perfectly satisfied with their destiny in this affair.
The whole is valued at its just worth, fifteen hundred dollars; fifteen hundred

CHANCES AT ONE DOLLAR EACH.

The Raffle will be conducted by gentlemen selected by the interested subscribers present. Five nights will be allowed to complete the Raffle. BOTH OF THE ABOVE DESCRIBED CAN BE SEEN AT MY STORE, No. 78 Common St., second door from Camp, at from 9 o'clock A. M. to 2 P. M.
Highest throw to take the first choice; the lowest throw the remaining prize, and the fortunate winners will pay twenty dollars each for the refreshments furnished on the occasion.
N. B. No chances recognized unless paid for previous to the commencement.

JOSEPH JENNINGS.

This poster gives an indication of the value placed on slaves in the southern economy. *Reproduced from the collections of the Library of Congress*

making agreements whereby the slaves could buy their freedom, or freeing them as a reward or gift. For most of the four million slaves held in the South by 1860, however, life was harsh, as it was under all systems of plantation slavery. Work was ever present and the incentive was generally the lash or some other punishment. Food was coarse and monotonous, but generally adequate. Housing and clothing were minimal, usually varying with the master's economic circumstances. Throughout it all, the slaves managed to make a life for themselves, as their folktales, songs, and the very endurance of the Negro people today make clear.

There has been a great deal of controversy among historians about the conditions of life under slavery and it may be, as some contend, that the physical cruelties have been exaggerated. Life was extremely cruel in some respects in Africa, too. The Africans transplanted to America did not necessarily suffer more. The fact that slaves reproduced themselves in the United States at a rather steady rate after the closing of the foreign slave trade in 1808, suggests, for example, that the physical circumstances under which the slaves lived were not excessively harsh. No other system of Negro slavery in the New World was able to expand on the basis of reproduction alone, once the importations from Africa were closed. It is evident, too, that many slaveholders clearly felt goodwill toward their slaves and showed a sense of basic responsibility for their physical welfare. The worst feature of slavery therefore may not have been the cruelty of the lash and the auction block, but rather the impairment of personality and the prevention of the fulfillment of human potentialities which were built into the slave system.

Reaction Against Slavery. Apparently these grim features little troubled the European-American mind until the latter part of the eighteenth century. Until then, southern planters felt no compunction about exploiting the labor of slaves, and northern merchants joyously reaped the profits of the African trade. But, finally, for reasons not easy to understand, a great change in attitudes began to occur. This change is somehow related to the philosophy of the Age of Reason, which questioned on rational grounds the artificial distinctions of rank or status which prevailed between different categories of mankind—kings, nobles, freemen, serfs, slaves—the rulers and the ruled. It is also related to the great religious revivals of the eighteenth and nineteenth centuries, which questioned on spiritual grounds, whether it was not a sin for one of the children of God to claim property ownership in another of God's children. This intellectual and spiritual reaction against slavery was so strong that by the 1770's, British reformers were trying to abolish the African slave trade to the West Indies, and were hopefully asserting that slavery itself would wither away if the supply of new slaves from Africa were cut off.

Abolition in the North. The leaders of the American Revolution were disciples of the Enlightenment, and most of them condemned slavery in theory even when, like Thomas Jefferson, they continued to hold slaves in practice. In 1787 when the Congress of the Confederation organized the region north of the Ohio River into the Northwest Territory, it excluded "slavery or involuntary servitude" from the territory. In the same year, the delegates to the Constitutional Convention from the northern states tried to write the abolition of the African trade into the Constitution, and though they were blocked by the Southerners, they did secure an agreement that Congress could abolish the trade after twenty years—which it proceeded to do in 1808.

Meanwhile, a number of the northern states were abolishing slavery within their own borders. This was done during the Revolution by judicial decisions in Massachusetts and New Hampshire, and by legislation in Pennsylvania. After the Revolution, Connecticut and Rhode Island acted in 1784. New York waited until 1799 and New Jersey until 1804, and a number of these states provided for gradual, rather than immediate, action. But after 1804 the legal division between slave states and free states was strictly sectional, just as the actual concentration of slaves in the South had been sectional from the outset.

The Cotton Gin and Slavery in the South. During the Revolutionary and post-Revolutionary period, there was sentiment against slavery in the South also (especially in Virginia), and optimists believed that the wave of emancipation which had swept the North would be extended to cover the South as well. But the South's stake in slave property was immense. Further, in 1792, Eli Whitney's invention of the cotton gin made possible the profitable cultivation of short-staple, green seed cotton in the interior districts of the South (long-staple, black seed, sea island cotton could be grown only near the coast), and this economic windfall suddenly increased the profitability of slave workers and invigorated what had been a static labor system. Soon cotton and slavery began advancing together across the lower South, and by 1830, southern spokesmen were defending slavery as a socially justifiable institution, good for the slaves as well as the free men.

The Roots of Conflict

The Conflict of Cultures and Economies. By the 1830's, the North and the South were moving in opposite directions, not only in their attitudes toward slavery, but also in the life style of their societies. In analyzing these opposites, some historians have seen slavery as the factor which polarized into a lethal conflict other differences which would have remained mere dissimilarities if the slavery issue had not expressed itself indirectly through them. Others have argued that the sectional difference was much broader, involving a conflict between two civilizations: one based on agriculture and directed toward maintaining a static, traditional, somewhat conservative pattern of rural living, with ownership of a plantation as the highest social goal; the other based on commerce and industry, and committed to mobility, rapid change, social dynamism, and the attainment of financial wealth rather than land ownership.

Those who emphasize the broader differences regard staple-crop agriculture rather than slavery as basic to the diagnosis of the southern position. They point out that such agriculture produced only narrow margins of profit, and therefore required a fixed supply of unskilled, low-cost labor which the slavery system happened to provide. If the workers in the cotton fields had been free, their economic life would have remained very much the same. Advocates of this view note that great sectional differences between the cotton-growing South and the rest of the country continued for many decades after slavery was abolished, and they contend that the northern majority was never prepared to force a showdown on the abolition of slavery, but was prepared to fight for the adoption of economic policies compatible with the continued growth in power of its industrial interests.

The Conflict over Slavery. Those who focus on slavery, on the other hand, emphasize that the practice of slavery was a total violation of basic ideals of freedom and equality which formed the creed of many Americans, and that divergent views about slavery fatally impaired the goodwill and mutual confidence that had existed between the sections during the times when both of them engaged in slave holding or the African trade, or later when the North hoped for a voluntary abandonment of slavery by the South. Further, it is argued that slavery shaped the whole pattern of southern culture. The South feared slave insurrection, and it valued conditions which would keep the slaves from getting out of hand. It did not welcome social innovations, economic change, and dynamic conditions, but preferred to maintain a hierarchical, authoritarian social system. It did not want an economy which needed skilled labor, but favored instead plantation agriculture which kept the workers unskilled and toiling under supervision in a relatively settled system. In this sense slavery, or rather the emphasis upon subordination of the Negroes, perpetuated and reinforced all the characteristic features of the southern economy, and all the values and attitudes of the southern culture.

The Conflicts Intensified Each Other. While it is interesting from a theoretical standpoint to ask whether sectional friction was generated by the slavery issue and the southern compulsion to use slavery as a means of race control, or by the broad divergence between southern culture, which was based on a system of staple-crop agriculture, and northern culture, which was not, the important fact is that the two differentials converged in a way which intensified the divisive effect of each. As the two aspects merged, Northerners opposed the spread of slavery not only as a violation of the creed of freedom, but also as an aristocratic menace which obstructed policies favorable to industry and which threatened the welfare of small farmers who did not want to compete with slave (or Negro) labor. Southerners, on the other hand, supported slavery not only as a property stake in two and a half million valuable chattels, but also as an indispensable feature of an idealized social system in which the human relationships were not determined by such social considerations as profits and wages, but by the personal sense of responsibility of the planter for "his people" and by the personal loyalty of slaves to their master. This concept was partly a way of sentimentalizing a relationship which could only appear as brutal if viewed in objective terms. It was partly an attempt, sometimes successful in a limited way, to impart humanity by idealistic justification to a system that had no inherent humanity. And it was partly a realistic recognition that the wage-slavery of some theoretically free industrial workers, including small children laboring underground in the mines, was sometimes more exploitative and harsh and coldly impersonal than the chattel slavery of workers in the cotton fields. But regardless of the degree of moonshine in their idealized picture of plantation life, belief in it made Southerners fierce defenders of their land and their traditions.

Thus the tensions of the slavery issue imparted vital importance to sectional dissimilarities which might otherwise have seemed marginal, and sectional dissimilarities made the slavery issue much more than a financial question of a property interest or an economic question of a labor system.

The Ironic Plight of the Free Negroes. Viewed from the perspective of the late twentieth century, perhaps the most inexplicable thing about the deepening division between the North and the South is that while the issue of slavery was discussed endlessly, scarcely anyone recognized that slavery was only one aspect of the denial to Negroes of rights claimed by all other Americans. Apparently, the status of being a chattel, subject to being bought or sold or mortgaged or flogged or separated from one's family or tracked by blood-hounds—this status dramatized the evil of slavery so much that many people who failed to see Negroes even potentially as fellow Americans could still sympathize with the slave and urge his emancipation. But there was nothing dramatic enough in the indirect oppression of the free Negro to make people equally responsive to his plight. As a result northern states, which had abolished slavery within their own borders, and which sent to Congress men who denounced slavery and fought against its extension—such states denied to their own Negro residents many essential rights of citizenship. In 1844 there were thirteen free states, and five more were admitted between then and the Civil War. Five of the thirteen and none of the subsequent five permitted Negroes to vote. The states with Negro suffrage were New York, Maine, Vermont, New Hampshire, and Massachusetts. In 1850 they had a total population of 19,500 free adult male Negroes. It is only a slight exaggeration to say that Negroes could vote where there were none to cast a ballot, but could not vote where there was actually a Negro population to be found. No state before 1860 permitted Negroes to serve on juries. Seventeen free states either segregated Negroes in separate public schools or excluded them from public education; but in some parts of Massachusetts after 1855, they were enrolled on an unsegregated basis. Four states—Ohio, Indiana, Illinois, and Oregon—adopted laws to prevent Negroes from coming within their borders. Everywhere, Negroes were segregated in residence and employment, were excluded from places frequented by genteel society, and were held at the bottom levels of income.

The great irony of the Civil War era is that during the generation between 1844 and 1877, the United States passed through a supreme crisis, during which it paid the immense price exacted by a major war, in an effort to solve fundamental problems. One of these problems concerned the nature of the Union; it was solved. Another concerned what forces should dominate the American economy; it too was solved, and six decades of southern agricultural ascendancy were brought to an end. A third was the problem of the place of Negro Americans in American life. But it was not even recognized in its broader, more inclusive sense, except by a few people. Instead it was seen restrictively and incompletely as a problem of slavery; the solution, bought at so great a cost, was as restrictive and incomplete as the recognition of the problem had been.

Sectional Frictions Threaten the Union, 1820–1844

When sectional frictions which were immeasurably intensified by slavery exerted their stress upon a union whose very nature still remained ambiguous and whose strength depended upon voluntary loyalty by everyone, the danger of disruption was obviously serious. By 1844 the American people had already experienced a number of episodes which signaled this danger.

The Missouri Compromise. In 1820 the application of Missouri for admission as a slave state, at a time when the number of slave and free states was evenly balanced, had led to northern efforts to impose restrictions upon slavery as the price of admission, and this in turn had led to a dangerous confrontation between the sections. The crisis was eased by the admission of Maine to balance Missouri, and by the imposition of a geographical line at 36° 30′ north latitude to divide the remaining area of the Louisiana Purchase, with a provision that slavery should not be admitted north of the line.

Abolitionists Turn Militant. In 1830 the antislavery movement in the North, which up to that time had been a mild-mannered affair, politely beseeching slaveholders to emancipate their slaves, suddenly took a militant, activist turn, castigating slaveholders as sinners and demanding immediate federal legislation against slavery. In 1831 William Lloyd Garrison launched his antislavery weekly, *The Liberator,* with a promise never "to think or write, or speak with moderation"—a promise which he faithfully kept. In 1834, in Ohio, an ardent young evangelist, Theodore Dwight Weld, organized a band of theology students who withdrew from the Lane Theological Seminary and moved to Oberlin in order that they might devote themselves more fully to the antislavery cause; soon they were carrying a message of antislavery, in flaming words, to pulpits throughout the Middle West.

The Nullification Crisis. In 1832 South Carolina, angered by failure to repeal the tariff of 1828, threatened to prevent the enforcement of the tariff law within the state, thus bringing on the nullification crisis. Although the tariff was the immediate issue in this conflict, Carolina was clearly impelled fundamentally by a belief that the welfare of the whole socioeconomic system of the state was at stake, and slavery lay, of course, at the base of the system. In 1836 the Southerners in Congress pushed through adoption of a so-called gag rule by which antislavery petitions would automatically be tabled without opportunity for consideration or discussion. This was the beginning of a contest which continued intermittently for ten years before the gag was repealed.

The Question of Texas. Also in 1836 the Anglo-American inhabitants of Texas declared their independence of Mexico, proclaimed a republic, and sought admission as a state of the American Union. Southern Congressmen would have welcomed Texas as a state, but the leaders of the antislavery movement denounced the plans for annexation as a conspiracy to increase the strength of what they called "the slave power"—an evil and malevolent force. For the first time in its history, the United States refused an opportunity for territorial expansion, and persisted in this refusal for eight years, even after Britain and France had recognized Texas as a republic, thus showing that they no longer regarded Mexico's claim as valid.

In the light of all these developments, it is clear that the slavery question became an increasingly inflammatory issue from 1820 onward. But during this first phase of slavery controversy, certain features prevailed which held the disruptive force of the question in check.

Forces Restraining Conflict

Importance of Preserving the Union. For one thing, while most Northerners did not like slavery, and had shown their dislike by abolishing it within their own borders and by placing legal obstacles in the way of slaveowners who tried to reclaim fugitive slaves, the majority of people in the free states clearly regarded the preservation of the Union as more important than the emancipation of slaves in the South. They regarded the agitation of the slavery question as a danger to the intersectional harmony on which union was based, and therefore they disapproved of it. During the 1830's, mobs of conservatives consistently hounded and harassed abolitionist speakers. In 1840 when anti-slavery activists entered a candidate in the presidential elections, they carried less than four votes in 1000 even in the free states. Four years later, with a greater effort, they polled only 32 votes in 1000 in the free states. This hostility of the northern public to the abolitionists may have reflected in part a conservative reaction to an attack on property rights, and in part a racial prejudice against Negroes, but apparently it reflected most of all a violent dislike of men who disturbed the tranquillity of the Union. Most Americans, like Abraham Lincoln, recognized that the Constitution had grudgingly accepted slavery without naming it (e.g., in the fugitive slave clause and the three-fifths clause); they felt that this was a pledge which had been given in exchange for the pledges given by the South, and that they were in honor bound by the agreement. Some Northerners seemed even to welcome this idea of constitutional obligation as something which relieved them of the necessity for making a difficult moral decision.

Slavery a State, Not National, Issue. But perhaps the chief tranquilizing factor in the situation was a belief which may be hard to understand in the twentieth century, but which quite genuinely dominated political thought during the first seven decades of the republic. This was simply the view that many matters were the business of the states and not of the central government, and the legality or illegality of slavery was one of these matters. This idea had been accepted from the time of the Revolution, and it had worked to the advantage of antislavery, for seven states had abolished slavery by their own action, within their own limits, and at different times. Many people apparently felt that if their own states had done away with slavery, their moral duty had been fulfilled, and they had no obligation and indeed no right to force abolition on the southern states, any more than they had an obligation to force it upon Cuba. As they conceived the division of responsibility between the central government and the states, the question of slavery did not arise directly in the federal sphere, but came in only indirectly, in connection with the District of Columbia, or the rights of slaveowners to recover slaves who had fled into free states, or the laws for enforcement of the prohibition on the African trade. But for most of the United States the question was regarded as settled. In the states, each state determined the status of slavery for itself. In the area not yet admitted to statehood Congress controlled (though some Southerners challenged the constitutionality of this control). Thus in the part of the Northwest Territory which had not yet been admitted to statehood (namely the Wisconsin area and part of what is now Minnesota), slavery was forbidden by the

Ordinance of 1787; in the part of the Louisiana Purchase not yet admitted to statehood, slavery was excluded north of the line 36° 30′ by the Congressional Act of 1820 (the Missouri Compromise). These arrangements covered all the land in the United States and left nothing to quarrel about except the District of Columbia.

Expansion Precipitates Conflict

But if there were new land, concerning which no understanding had been reached, then the slavery issue would arise as a federal question, and would produce the dreaded confrontation between North and South in Congress. The flare-up over the region of the Louisiana Purchase had shown how abruptly and violently such a situation could convulse the Union. After the Missouri Crisis, during Monroe's second term and during the administrations of J. Q. Adams, Jackson, Van Buren, Harrison, and Tyler, no such situation arose.

Texas and Oregon. As the Presidential election approached in 1844, the leading Whig and Democratic candidates intended to maintain a situation in which no such question would arise. Both Henry Clay and Martin Van Buren made carefully worded announcements that they would not regard the question of Texas annexation as a campaign issue. But the forces of expansion were strong. Many Northwesterners wanted to terminate the joint occupancy by which Britain and the United States shared Oregon, and to bring the Oregon territory completely under the American flag. Many Southerners wanted to annex Texas. Some of the more astute Democratic politicians recognized that the chief obstacle to each of these acts of expansion was the fear of Southerners, in the case of Oregon, or of Northerners, in the case of Texas, that the other section would gain an advantage by the acquisition. But if the two acquisitions could be linked with one another, the republic as a whole would gain by a two-pronged expansion, while neither section would gain at the expense of the other.

Polk and Manifest Destiny. Following this strategy, the expansionist Democrats blocked the nomination of Van Buren at the Democratic convention in 1844, and brought forward a man who had not even been regarded as a candidate, James K. Polk of Tennessee. They nominated Polk on a platform which called for the re-annexation of Texas (*re*-annexation on the flimsy argument that Texas had been part of the Louisiana Purchase, foolishly bargained away to Spain in the Adams-Oñis Treaty of 1819) and the re-occupation of Oregon (*re*-occupation on the claim that an American naval vessel commanded by Robert Gray had occupied the mouth of the Columbia in 1792). With expansionism thus cut loose from the sectional jealousies which had blocked it for the preceding eight years, Polk ran slightly ahead of Henry Clay in both the North and the South, and won the Presidency.

His victory impelled the expansionists to move fast. Without waiting for his inauguration on March 4, 1845, they set about annexing Texas, and when they discovered that they could not get the two-thirds majority necessary to ratify a treaty of annexation, they resorted to a joint resolution of the House and the Senate to vote annexation in January and February. When Polk became President in March, he was interested in more than just completing the annexation of Texas. The whole southwestern region of what is now California, Nevada, Utah, Arizona, and New Mexico seemed a possible realm for the fulfillment of American "Manifest Destiny" to expand to the Pacific. There were enough Anglos in California to make the possibility of a Texas-style revolution on the Pacific coast quite likely. Also, war with Mexico loomed as a possibility when, shortly after Polk's inauguration, Mexico broke diplomatic relations with the United States in protest against the annexation of Texas, which Mexico still claimed as a part of her territory. This act was mostly a face-saving gesture by a proud people, and did not indicate any purpose to take warlike steps against Texas annexation. But Polk chose to treat it as a threat of war, and four months after becoming President he sent an American army under Zachary Taylor to Texas. Even before he did this, his Navy Department had given naval officers on the Pacific coast secret instructions about what to do in the event that Mexico should declare war—they were to seize what is now San Francisco. In November, Polk sent a minister plenipotentiary to Mexico City to try to buy New Mexico and California. The Mexicans might have been willing to receive a special envoy, but after having broken diplomatic relations, they refused, quite logically, to receive a regular minister. But as soon as Polk learned of the rejection of his minister, he ordered General Taylor to advance from the Nueces River to the Rio Grande. Historically, the Nueces had been the southern boundary of Texas, and in moving to the Rio Grande, Polk was not

The dramatic expansion of the 1840's took the United States from one ocean to the other. It also aggravated some of the underlying tensions in American society.

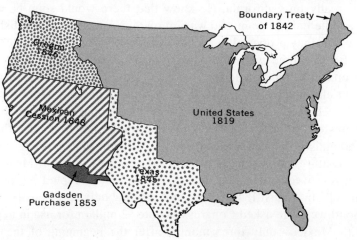

WESTWARD EXPANSION OF THE UNITED STATES

only claiming Texas, but was using military force to assert a boundary claim which was at best debatable, and at worst trumped up.

Declaration of War Against Mexico. Taylor remained on the northern bank of the Rio Grande from January until May 1846. By April Polk, who clearly wanted war with Mexico, began making plans to ask Congress for a war declaration on the ground that Mexico had rejected the American minister and had failed to pay certain claims. But late in the month the Mexicans gave him a better pretext for war. A detachment of Mexican troops crossed the Rio Grande, skirmished with American dragoons, and killed and captured a number of them. As soon as Polk learned this in May 1846, he sent Congress a message calling for a declaration of war.

Opposition and Oregon. By a series of steps, from March 1845 to May 1846, Polk had turned the Texas question into a question of the acquisition of the whole Southwest, and by some very sharp maneuvering he had pushed the Mexicans into a war. Some of his actions were not known to the public, but enough was evident to arouse opposition in Congress. Northern representatives especially were reluctant, and many of them voted against the war declaration. They regarded it as a move by the "slave power" to gain the whole southwestern empire.

Their opposition was soon further aroused by Polk's failure to take an equally aggressive attitude on Oregon. This region extended north to latitude 54° 40′, and when Polk first became President, he had boldly affirmed that the United States would make good its claim to all of the Oregon Territory. But in July 1845, just when he was sending Taylor to Texas, he made an offer to the British to divide Oregon at latitude 49°. The British rejected this offer, and when Congress met, Polk recommended that the United States give the British notice that the arrangement for joint occupation would terminate in one year. This looked as if he meant to force the issue. Northwestern expansionists jubilantly voted approval and waited expectantly for him to compel the British to back down. Polk served the expected notice in April, but by that time, his mind was really on California. He knew that there would soon be war with Mexico, and he did not want two wars at one time. In June the British offered him a way out; they proposed to accept latitude 49°, which they had previously rejected. By this time war with Mexico had actually begun. Polk sent the British proposal to the Senate for "advice." The Senate debated very angrily but very briefly and voted approval, over violent protests from Northwesterners who claimed that the program of bisectional expansion had been betrayed. Instead of annexing Texas for the South and Oregon for the North, the Polk administration had settled for half of Oregon while pushing to promote the Texas venture into a seizure of no-one-knew-how-much of Mexico.

Only a few weeks after the Oregon Treaty was accepted by the Senate, President Polk, in August 1846, for the first time publicly revealed his intentions for the Southwest. He asked Congress to vote $2 million for use in negotiating peace with Mexico—only three months after the beginning of the war. He stated his hope that "a cession of territory may be made" by Mexico, for which the United States ought to pay "a fair equivalent."

The Wilmot Proviso—1846. This brought the question of slavery expansion out into the open, and it gave all the northern Democrats who were dissatisfied with the administration a chance to strike back. Friends of Van Buren who resented his defeat for the nomination in 1844, Oregon expansionists who resented the compromise at latitude 49°, high-tariff men who resented Polk's successful efforts to get a tariff reduction enacted, spoilsmen who were disaffected by his veto of a fat rivers and harbors appropriation, and anti-slavery men who feared a great new slave empire extending from Texas to California—all these were ripe for a move to challenge Polk's leadership. At this point a freshman Democrat, Representative David Wilmot of Penn-sylvania, offered an amendment to the proposed appropriation of $2 million stipulating that if land were acquired from Mexico, "neither slavery nor involuntary servitude shall ever exist in any part of said territory, except for crime whereof the party shall first be duly convicted." This was the famous Wilmot Proviso.

The House of Representatives voted for the amendment; the Senate refused to accept it; and both the appropriation and the amendment failed of adoption in the deadlock between the two chambers. But the Wilmot Proviso was crucially important: it had brought the slavery question into national politics, and made it impossible to defuse the question by leaving it to the states. Other aspects of slavery could be pushed out of the federal arena, could be spread out and localized. But when it was a question of whether the advance of the American flag would extend slavery over areas previously free, no one could any longer keep the issue out of national politics.

Slavery in the Territories a National Issue. Thus the territories became, for political purposes, the focus of the slavery question. For fifteen years, from 1846 to 1861, instead of discussing the situation of several million real, living slaves in the slave states, Congress debated the future situation of imaginary slaves in an unsettled wilderness. The great battles of the fifties turned upon issues which were only marginal to the practice of slavery in the United States, and fierce contests were waged over fine-spun metaphysical questions concern-ing the true meaning of "popular sovereignty," the constitutionality of the 36° 30' line established in 1820, and whether slavery could be abolished by a territory (a local government authorized by Congress preliminary to state-hood).

All these disputes and others like them gave a curious, indirect quality to the slavery controversy, as Chapter Two will show. But they also had a further distorting effect, for they separated the question of slavery even further from the broader question of racial discrimination, of which, to repeat, slavery was only an aspect. So long as the debate centered on real slaves, it was difficult to ignore the fact that these slaves were Negroes and to recognize that the question of where slaves stood in American life was also a question of where

Negroes stood. To recognize this link would have been realistic. But when the debate centered on imaginary or fictitious slaves in places where there were neither Negroes nor slaves, it was easy to deal with the slavery question so abstractly that its real meaning as an aspect of the race question never penetrated the public mind. Thus, in the years between 1846 and 1861, the United States traveled down a road that would lead to the emancipation of four million Negro Americans, but it did this in such a way that the question of the future place of these Americans in the life of the republic was not clearly visualized, and received a minimum of realistic consideration.

SUGGESTED READING (Prepared by Carl N. Degler)

A short general volume which deals with the whole prewar period and which also follows the modern emphasis upon slavery as central to any explanation is Elbert B. Smith, *The Death of Slavery: The United States, 1837–1865* (1967). Arthur C. Cole, *The Irrepressible Conflict, 1850–1865* (1934) emphasizes the social and economic history of the period. The best general book on the nature of slavery is Kenneth M. Stampp, *The Peculiar Institution* (1956), but Ulrich B. Phillips, *Life and Labor in the Old South* (1929), older and rather pro-South, still is useful for putting the institution into a broad economic framework. Stanley Elkins, *Slavery, A Problem in American Institutional and Intellectual Life* (1959) has sparked a whole series of studies reinterpreting and rethinking the nature of the institution, but the book needs to be used with caution. A good compendium of recent writings on slavery since Elkins' book is Allen Weinstein and Frank Otto Gatell, eds., *American Negro Slavery* (1968). For the most recent views on the extent and nature of the international slave trade, see Philip Curtin, *The Atlantic Slave Trade. A Census* (1969).

Like slavery itself, the antislavery movement has seen important new interpretations. Gilbert H. Barnes, *The Anti-Slavery Impulse, 1830–1844* (1933) emphasized the middle-western wing of the movement at the expense of New England, but William Lloyd Garrison has been reestablished as highly important by John L. Thomas, *The Liberator* (1963), a critical and informed biography of Garrison, and by Aileen Kraditor, *Means and Ends in American Abolitionism* (1969), which brilliantly defends Garrison against the familiar charges of fanaticism. The essays in Martin Duberman, ed., *The Anti-Slavery Vanguard* (1965) defend the abolitionists as a group against charges of unwarranted extremism. A balanced general study of the antislavery movement is Louis Filler, *The Crusade Against Slavery, 1830–1860* (1960). Dwight Lowell Dumond, *Antislavery Origins of the Civil War in the United States* (1939) links opposition to slavery and the North's growing hostility toward the South, while recognizing that concern for Negroes was not always at the root of opposition to slavery. The best general study on northern hostility toward blacks during these years is Leon F. Litwack, *North of Slavery: The Negro in the Free States, 1790–1860* (1961). A similar important point is made about the western states in Eugene H. Berwanger, *The Frontier Against Slavery: Western Anti-Negro Prejudice and the Slavery Extension Controversy* (1967).

The best general study of the nature of southern society is Clement Eaton, *The Growth of Southern Civilization, 1790–1860** (1961). Eric McKitrick, ed., *Slavery Defended: The Views of the Old South** (1963) is a handy collection of proslavery writings. An important, if controversial interpretation of the old South's economy is by Marxist Eugene D. Genovese, *The Political Economy of Slavery* (1965). Important for the politics of the period is Arthur C. Cole, *The Whig Party in the South* (1913), which is old, but unsuperseded. More modern, and relying on statistical analyses is Joel H. Silbey, *The Shrine of Party: Congressional Voting Behavior, 1841–1852* (1967). Thomas B. Alexander, *Sectional Stress and Party Strength* (1967) examines Congressional roll calls between 1836 and 1860 to test sectional versus party allegiances. Clement Eaton, *Henry Clay and the Art of American Politics** (1957) is a brief, but knowing introduction to the life of one of the most important statesmen of the period, while Charles G. Sellers, *James K. Polk* (2 vols., 1957–1966) is now the best biography of the man and President. Leonard D. White, *The Jacksonians: A Study in Administrative History 1829–1861* (1954) studies the structure and operation of the federal government. Chilton Williamson, *American Suffrage: From Property to Democracy 1790–1860** (1960) traces the spread of universal, white male suffrage.

*Available in a paperback edition.

Industrialization Before the Civil War/Pictorial Essay
by Carl Degler

Although the industrialization of the United States is generally associated with the post-Civil War era, the work of recent economic historians demonstrates that the 1850's saw the development of industry on an important and ever increasing scale. The accompanying pictures make clear something of the quality, if not the quantity, of that early industrialization. The picture of the Du Pont powder mills, for instance, not only shows one example of northern military and industrial power during the Civil War, but also one of the ways in which the new industrialization was brought about. That was to multiply or to bring together a number of manufacturing establishments in close proximity rather than to leave them widely scattered and under separate management and control. The picture of the Singer Sewing Machine factory, on the other hand, is a good example of the new, large-scale factory, in which many male workers were brought together in a single place—usually a large, barnlike structure. The hoopskirt factory illustrates the same organizational principle, though this time the employees were all women. By 1860 women workers—almost all of whom were young unmarried women, as this picture shows—made up about 20 percent of the labor force in manufacturing. Many of the women were immigrants.

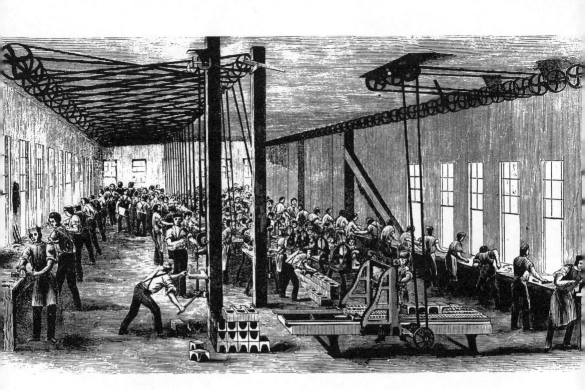

STRIVE TO EXCEL.

W. S. & C. H. THOMSON'S SKIRT MANUFACTORY.

PATENT INDESTRUCTABLE

Left: DuPont Mills. *Courtesy E. I. Du Pont de Nemours and Company*
Top: Singer Sewing Machine Factory. *Frank Leslie's Illustrated News, Supplement, July 23, 1853. Owned by the Henry Ford Museum*
Bottom: Hoopskirt Factory. *Reproduced from the collections of the Library of Congress*

Perhaps the most striking aspect of both pictures of factories is the large number of workers as compared with the small number of machines or labor-saving devices. That disparity points up the fact that in the early days of the Industrial Revolution, labor remained, as in preindustrial days, the central component of production. Power and machines were used, to be sure, but principally for large, gross tasks, while hand labor was still needed for any kind of complicated, skilled work. And as the picture of the iron foundry in Paterson, N.J., makes clear, even when power and machines were used, sheer muscle on the part of the workers was still required in many industries. Notice how the workers are expected to push heavy carts or to hold up one end of heavy pipes that are being raised by crude hoists. Although all of these lithographs presented idealized, rather than realistic, depictions of life in contemporary factories, it is evident that working conditions were hardly pleasant or relaxed. Workers were crowded together to take advantage of every inch of space as in the Singer Sewing Machine or hoopskirt factories. They were subjected, too, as the Paterson Iron Foundry shows, to intense and prolonged heat, as well as dust, heat, and smoke. Safety regulations or devices were hardly thought of.

The picture of Davenport, Iowa, which was located far from the center of industrialization, nonetheless depicts some of the sources and consequences of industrialization. The picture, for one thing, gives an idea of how urbanization appeared in the pre-Civil War era. Cities generally did not have buildings much higher than five stories and often they were lower than that. The skyline was usually broken only by church steeples. The Otis elevator, which was invented in 1852, did not affect the height of buildings until long after the Civil War. The steamboats on the river and the railroads along the banks suggest the importance of new methods of transportation in providing wider and therefore bigger markets for the goods now being produced in ever larger quantities by the factories of the industrializing east.

Far left: Iron Foundry. *Reproduced from the collections of the Library of Congress*
Left: Otis Elevator. *Courtesy Otis Elevator Company*
Below: Davenport, Iowa. *Courtesy Chicago Historical Society*

Above: Sleeping Car. *Frank Leslie's Illustrated Newspaper, April 30, 1859*
Right: Advertisement for McCormick's Reaper. *State Historical Society of Wisconsin*

Railroads and steamboats carried people as well as goods. Indeed, prior to the Civil War, railroads were more important as passenger carriers than as transporters of goods. And given the distances in the United States it is not surprising that sleeping cars came on the scene in 1859, thanks to the ingenuity of George Pullman, whose name has since been applied to that type of car. The interior of a sleeping car during the day, which is shown here, makes evident that one hundred years ago railroad cars had already achieved substantially the design that they still exhibit. The beds for sleeping, in this particular car, were let down from the ceiling, while the backs of the floor seats were lowered to provide a lower berth, as can be seen in the adjacent contemporary drawing in which the size of the car is grossly exaggerated.

Finally, the advertisement for McCormick's reaper illustrates the influence of industrialization upon agriculture—for the reaper became one of the major sources of increased agricultural productivity during the Civil War, thanks to McCormick's ability to turn out reapers in large numbers. The drawing also shows that even at that early date advertising was a part of the American industrial way.

MᶜCORMICK'S PATENT VIRGINIA REAPER.

CHAPTER TWO

EXPANSION AND CONFLICT

FROM 1846 TO 1861 the United States grew in population, wealth, territorial extent, and in all the factors of economic and cultural interdependence which made the republic a cohesive unit. During these years, more than in any preceding, the United States took on the qualities of a nation. Yet at the very same time, sectional rivalries and animosities also grew in a way which challenged the unity of the republic and which led to a revolt against the strong centralizing tendencies and against the inevitable features of life in an industrialized society. Through the fabric of this contest, the thread of slavery was always visible, and it always diverted attention from the more fundamental—but less easily recognized—issue of race.

The War with Mexico

California and New Mexico. This fifteen-year span began with a two-year period of war with Mexico. In its details the course of the war was curious, and like some other American wars, this one had theaters of combat and consequences which bore little relation to the point of origin or the causes. Some fifty years later, the United States went to war with Spain over the island of Cuba and the first fighting took place in the Philippines. In 1846 the United States went to war over Texas and the first action took place in California. This was not as odd as it appeared, since President Polk had wanted California from the outset, had sent Colonel John C. Frémont there on an exploring expedition, and had instructed the American consul at Monterey to give encouragement to any Texas-style revolution that might spontaneously break out in California. Perhaps such instructions were scarcely necessary to trigger the gringoes—800 more or less—in California, who were sensitively tuned to the rather clear signals that were being sent from Washington. Thus it happened that about a month after the war began, but before news of it reached the remote and isolated shores of California, American residents, stimulated by the presence of Colonel Frémont, proclaimed a republic and raised a flag with a grizzly bear on it as a visible sign of their "Bear Flag" republic. This theatrical production ran for three weeks, until reliable information that war had been declared reached the Pacific Coast, whereupon Commodore John D. Sloat of the United States Navy landed at Monterey and claimed California for the United States. Meanwhile Colonel Stephen W. Kearny, with ten regiments of volunteers, mostly from Missouri, made an extraordinary march from Fort Leavenworth, Kansas, down the Santa Fe trail, and captured the capital of New Mexico without firing a shot, in August 1846. Thus the areas which Polk hoped to gain by the war were in American possession before the fighting began.

Bloodless victory in the Southwest: U.S. Marines raise the American flag at Monterey, California, on July 7, 1846, while Commodore John D. Sloat's Pacific squadron fires a salute in the background. *U.S. Marine Corps Museum*

Invasion of Mexico. At this point a less martial administration might have considered the advisability of simply sitting down in California and New Mexico and waiting for the Mexicans to make the next move. Mexico's hold on its northern districts had been extremely weak, and the government in Mexico City would have had great difficulty in sending and supplying a military expedition as far north as California or the upper Rio Grande. But by the autumn of 1846, Polk's military program was in full career. In September General Zachary Taylor marched south from bases on the Rio Grande, and captured Monterrey, in the state of Nuevo León (not to be confused with Monterey, California). In the following February, he won a decisive battle against Santa Anna at Buena Vista. While Taylor was near Saltillo, Colonel Alexander Doniphan, one of Kearny's Missourians, led a force of about 900 men against the town of Chihuahua. After an epic march of more than a thousand miles, he met and shattered a substantial Mexican force thirty miles outside of Chihuahua, and triumphantly entered the town. Taylor's greater victory and Doniphan's smaller but no less brilliant one had great significance defensively, for they secured California, New Mexico, and Texas against any counterstrokes by Mexico. But for offensive purposes, the American operations had reached a dead end. The barren desert wastes of northern Mexico made it impossible for Taylor to advance farther south, for supply lines could not have been maintained and Doniphan's force was too small for major operations in any case. Taylor might have been transferred to another command, but President Polk, who recognized that the "Hero of Buena Vista" would be a wonderful presidential candidate for the Whigs (whom he hated worse than Mexicans), refused to give the hero a chance to win more laurels. As a result Taylor settled into his base at Monterrey and the fighting in the north virtually ended.

Defeat of Mexico City. Taylor believed, in fact, that the war could be terminated at this point merely by holding the line he had already established. But Polk was determined to force Mexico promptly to terms, and he decided to send another Whig, but one who was less politically oriented, General Winfield Scott, to strike at no less an objective than the Mexican capital. Mexico City was a formidable objective, protected by encircling mountains and physical obstacles which might terrify any invader. Scott had a pompous manner and a naive mind, but he knew the art of military operations, and he conducted a brilliant campaign. Landing at Vera Cruz in March 1847, he advanced quickly to the mountains and fought his way through them in a campaign in which he won six hard-fought battles. Though his army numbered only six thousand men, he had enough bold decisiveness to abandon his line of supplies on August 7 and live off the country until he could fight his way into Mexico City on September 17.

The Treaty of Guadaloupe Hidalgo. Scott scored such a complete victory that his success left Mexico without a government which could negotiate peace. His triumph also led to demands in Congress that the United States annex all of Mexico, or at least the northern part of the present Mexican Republic. Peace negotiations ran into further complications when President Polk lost confidence in his peace commissioner, Nicholas P. Trist, and recalled him to the United States; but Trist, who felt that Polk did not understand the situation (communications took several weeks each way), decided to disregard his instructions and complete the negotiation which he had begun. The result was the treaty of Guadaloupe Hidalgo, by which the United States would acquire an area of more than 500,000 square miles, including the present states of California, Nevada, and Utah, all of New Mexico and Arizona except a strip at the south acquired five years later by the Gadsden Purchase, and part of Wyoming and Colorado. Polk hated to settle for these terms, but he recognized that the war was unpopular in the North and that the treaty provided for a settlement which he had previously approved. If he repudiated it now, Congress might refuse to support the war any further, and he might then lose California and the Southwest. Polk recognized that he really had no choice, so he sent the treaty to the Senate. There the Whig opposition members found themselves in the dilemma that a vote for the treaty would support expansion, which they opposed, and a vote against would support continuation of the war, which they also opposed. At the moment of decision, they regarded expansion as the lesser evil and gave enough affirmative votes to accept the settlement. Thus the United States rounded out its continental domain, acquired what is now a vital part of its area, and became a two-ocean, transcontinental republic. It accomplished these great steps in a situation where, ironically, hardly anyone was really satisfied with the settlement.

Long-Range Consequences of the Mexican War

Physical and Psychological Results. In physical terms the Mexican War virtually completed the series of territorial acquisitions by which the Atlantic seaboard colonies of 1776 grew to control land and natural resources which would bring the United States in the latter half of the twentieth century to the peak of world power. In psychological terms results are harder to assess, but the spectacular victories with very small loss of life did much to strengthen the self-confidence of Americans and their belief that they could meet any test of courage, ingenuity, or endurance. This faith of Americans that there is nothing which they cannot accomplish—that "We do what is difficult at once; the impossible takes a little longer"—has had a very positive value in releasing great psychological drives of energy, endurance, and initiative. (It is worth noting that Alexander Doniphan's men marched six thousand miles and the American armies in Mexico repeatedly defeated superior forces in adverse and extremely perilous circumstances.)

Repercussions of Overconfidence. But on the negative side, the Mexican War greatly encouraged a complacency in the American character: a dangerous illusion that there are no problems which are insoluble, a naive conviction of what has been called "American innocence"—that is, a belief that Americans have been endowed with a special virtue and an immunity to the corruption and evil of the human condition. It is, of course, but one step from this belief to the further idea that other people—foreigners, dissenters, or the like—are inferior and need not be taken quite seriously as human beings. More than a hundred years later, after this conviction had prevailed unchallenged for most of our history, the dissenters and the minorities struck back fiercely with wholesale denunciations of almost all accepted American values and attitudes. But the intensity of this reaction itself reflects the excess of complacency and thoughtless self-satisfaction which had previously prevailed. Moreover, the impatience of American dissent has reflected the belief of Americans in the possibility of instant remedies for all social ills, quite as much as the complacency of conservatives has reflected the belief that all the real social problems have already been solved and that any remaining problems can be cleared up by superficial remedies which will not affect our basic social, economic, and commercial arrangements.

In this kind of discussion of what is called "national character" there is a great risk of oversimplifying, for generalizations are made about millions of persons, no two of whom are exactly alike. Also, observations are made about people of one nation with the implication that the qualities noted are peculiar to just one national group, whereas they may in fact be common to all mankind. Certainly Americans had no monopoly on the conviction that they were better than other peoples, for it seems to be a psychological compulsion of all ingroups, and especially national groups, to regard all outgroups as inferior in one way or another. But it may be argued that a certain amount of defeat and failure will give to a society an awareness of the tragic dimension of life and the shared imperfections of man and society. American society, collectively, never experienced defeat or failure and never learned the universality of the gap that always separates human realities from human ideals. This limitation in the experience of Americans made American conformists bland and complacent in their blindness to the shortcomings of their society; and it made American dissenters intolerant and self-righteous in their demands for instant perfection.

Perhaps these qualities should not be mentioned without again noting that all satisfied people, everywhere, are likely to be complacent, and reformers everywhere are likely to be self-righteous. Some of the traits frequently attributed to Americans as if they were unique exist to varying degrees in all mankind. Also, they are far too general to be traced to any single experience, especially a limited one such as the Mexican War. But the one-sided and relatively bloodless victories of that war, and the ineffectiveness of the Mexicans in resistance doubtless reinforced and confirmed an impulse, already well-developed among Americans, to regard themselves as providentially endowed with personal virtues and institutional values superior to those possessed by any other of the earth's peoples.

Political Significance of the War. In fact, however, analysis of the long-range significance of the Mexican War has been almost beyond the capacity of historians. The war, in fact, has been reduced to a minor place in American history, and a recent historian has described it as "America's forgotten war." Perhaps in view of the ruthless fashion in which territory was seized from Mexico, Americans would prefer not to remember it too clearly. Yet the territory seized was mostly empty, and the Mexican War resembles the earlier colonial-imperial wars such as the French and Indian War in that it was primarily a process by which the political spheres of potential growth were brought into realistic alignment with the dynamic forces of physical growth which were projecting an energy of their own, regardless of political boundaries. Concretely, this means that by 1869, the United States connected California with the Atlantic Coast by railroad, and by 1969, it put a population into California which was 40 percent of the population of all of Mexico. Mexico could have developed (which also means exploited and despoiled) California at only a fraction of this rate, and the imagination can hardly conceive what the United States might be in the late twentieth century without Texas, California, and the Southwest, or what Mexico might be if it still held them. Perhaps the migration of restless and enterprising Anglos into these regions was inevitable; perhaps these lands would inevitably have gravitated into the orbit of the United States; and perhaps the exact process by which they did so is only a matter of detail. But the fact remains that the combined Spanish-American area of Texas and the Southwest, including California, to which the Mexican War secured control by the United States, was greater than the area of the Confederate States of America for which the Union fought a far more famous, costly, and unforgotten war thirteen years later.

Immediate Consequences of the Mexican War: the Slavery Issue Erupts

Whatever the long-range consequences of the Mexican War may have been—and they were perhaps more favorable than those of any other war in American history—the immediate consequences were to bring the slavery controversy to a point where it could no longer be contained. Efforts at containment began before the Treaty of Guadaloupe Hidalgo, and such efforts continued, sometimes with apparent success, until 1861, but no real meeting of minds was ever attained after 1846.

Basis of Earlier Containment of Slavery Issue. Before then, as has already been stated, the slavery question could still be contained because enough Americans agreed that in the states, each state determined the question for itself; local autonomy enjoyed constitutional sanctions which even men who hated slavery felt bound to respect. In the areas not yet admitted to statehood, Congress exercised control, and when Congress organized a new territory as the step preliminary to statehood, it decided in each individual case whether to exclude slavery (as in the Northwest Territory in 1787) or to sanction it (as in various southern territories). After the uproar over Missouri in 1820, Congress attempted to settle the question for the future by the 36°30' line. For a while thereafter the slavery question came to Congress only on narrower issues such as the right of petition and the enforcement of laws against the African slave trade. The question of the admission of Texas raised the slavery question in a much more important context, but even this was a limited issue, for Texas was admitted directly to statehood (as a slave state) and Congress did not have to make any decision about the status of slavery in Texas as a territory.

Oregon and Mexican Cession Precipitate Confrontation. But once Oregon south of 49° and the Mexican cession were added to the map of the United States, the slavery question took a form which made confrontation unavoidable. Northern leaders, already angry that claims for Texas had been pressed hard enough to force an expansionist war with Mexico, while the Oregon claim was being compromised, were resolved not to let the South convert the Mexican cession into a slave empire. Mexico had abolished slavery in 1829, and though the northern leaders had been outmaneuvered on the Texas question, they were determined that the Stars and Stripes, the flag of freedom, should not carry slavery back to a land that was already free. (The semifree condition of Mexican agricultural labor actually blurred the clarity of this high moral distinction, but men are guided by what they believe and want to believe rather than by what they do not know and do not want to know.)

Southern leaders, on the other hand, felt that soldiers from the South had really won the war, for all the troops except a tiny nucleus of standing-army regulars were volunteers (there was no conscription), and a disproportionately high share of these volunteers came from the South. Southerners felt, in short, that they had done the fighting which won this domain, and they would not now turn their victory over to the abolitionists. Even if New Mexico and Arizona did not offer appropriate opportunities for the use of slave labor, as many astute men like President Polk declared to be the case, the Southerners still did not intend to see slavery stigmatized by an act of the Congress, and did not propose to be told that a basic southern institution could not go into lands which southern blood and southern valor had won. This was not a controversy which could be negotiated like tariff rates, by moving them up a little or down a little.

Northern and Southern Positions Harden. In short, North and South suddenly found they had reached an impasse. Northern Congressmen, who were a majority in the House, followed the free-soil principle of the Wilmot Proviso and would not vote for the organization of territories open to slavery; southern Congressmen, who dominated the Senate, were equally determined to prevent the exclusion of slavery. Even in an area like Oregon, where the question had no living significance, deadlocks still occurred because Southerners were determined not to give a green light to any free territories while the North was holding a red light on slave territories. As a result Polk, who had begun his presidency with a burst of accomplishments, failed to achieve anything during the last three Congresses of his administration except the enactment of a bill to organize the Oregon territory without slavery, and even this required a titanic struggle.

Meanwhile, the sectional leaders were hardening their positions. Antislavery men affirmed the constitutional right as well as the moral duty of Congress to exclude slavery from the territories, and cited Article IV of the Constitution: "The Congress shall have Power to dispose of and make all needful Rules and Regulations respecting the Territory or other Property belonging to the United States." Proslavery men, on the other hand, took up an argument first put forward by John C. Calhoun—a contention much weaker logically than some of the other arguments of that currently unpopular but formidable thinker. According to Calhoun, the owners of the territories were the states collectively rather than the central government, the central government managed the territories only as a kind of agent or trustee for the owners (the states), and the agent could not make regulations which would favor one of the owners (a free state) at the expense of another owner (a slave state). In other words, it was unconstitutional for Congress to prevent citizens of a state from carrying property (i.e., slave property) which was legal under the law of the state in question into the territories.

Compromise Proposals

Extension of 36°30' Line. Despite the legal vulnerability of this argument, Southerners supported it vehemently. They took a position directly opposite that of the antislavery men. Meanwhile, as always happens in situations of intense friction, other leaders anxious to avoid a crisis came forward with compromises. One of these was a proposal to extend the 36°30' line to the Pacific. This was, of course, purely an expedient; the 36°30' line was intrinsically no better than any other line, and if what it established on one side of the line was right, presumably what it established on the other side was wrong. Moreover, it had the considerable operative disadvantage of cutting California in two. Since it would have left the Southerners with claims to less than a fourth of the remaining territory, it would have meant that, in the long run, the South must lose in the race to create new states. Perhaps the principal merits of the plan were, first, that it followed a respected precedent, and second, that it was clear enough for everyone to tell what it meant.

Cass' Political Solution. But political leaders do not always value clarity. Southern Congressmen did not want to go home and admit that they had conceded everything north of New Mexico and Arizona to antislavery; northern Congressmen did not want to admit that they had forced Mexico to give up free lands and then had opened these lands to chattel bondage. Consequently, both sides proved more receptive to a second compromise formula, first put forward by Senator Lewis Cass of Michigan and later championed by Stephen A. Douglas of Illinois. Cass argued, most persuasively, that the people of the new territories should be permitted to decide the question of slavery for themselves. This, he said, was the democratic way. If the citizens of the states could be trusted to settle the question in their states, the citizens of the territories, who were in no way inferior to those of the states, could settle it for their territories. This would get the whole tearing, rending question out of Congress and would localize and diffuse an explosive issue.

But there was a joker in Cass' formula, and it had probably been placed there on purpose and with ingenuity. Cass did not say at what point in time a territory could decide the question of slavery. Could it decide as soon as Congress passed a bill organizing it as a territory, in which case slavery might be kept out from the very beginning? If so, antislavery men might accept it. Or, on the other hand, would the territory have to wait until it was presenting an application for statehood to make its decision? If the decision came at the time of statehood, slavery might exist for a long period before exclusion would be possible. (New Mexico existed as a territory for sixty-two years, from 1850 to 1912, before attaining statehood.)

Senator Cass dodged this question most artfully, saying that the courts would have to decide, and not saying what he thought the court decisions would be or ought to be. (After 1850 Stephen A. Douglas finally said flatly that the territories could decide at the time of organization, only to be told by the Supreme Court's Dred Scott decision in 1857 that he was wrong. But for several happy years northern Democrats could endorse popular sovereignty, construing it to mean local power to exclude slavery as soon as the territory was organized, while southern Democrats could endorse it, construing it to mean local protection for slavery in the territories, at least until statehood.) With their differences thus papered over, the two factions could then work together in the serious business of winning elections against the Whigs.

Stalemate and Southern Efforts Toward Consolidation

The double meaning of the original Cass formula offered a way to conceal the impassable political gap that had opened between the sections as early as 1846. Yet both sides recognized what a tricky weapon it was, with possibilities of losing as well as gaining by it. For the latter half of the Polk administration, no territorial governments except the one in Oregon were organized. The need for organization, however, became progressively more acute. New Mexico already had a substantial population, and after gold was discovered in California, its population leaped ahead. Sectional rivalries sharpened; Congress skirmished bitterly over the status of slavery in the District of Columbia; and by the end of Polk's term John C. Calhoun was attempting the always difficult task of getting southern Democrats and southern Whigs to unite in a "Southern Address" or manifesto.

Few of the many thousands of gold seekers became rich, but prospectors such as these at Auburn, California, continued to try. The sluice box was so placed in a stream that when a miner shoveled dirt into the box, the water would carry the dirt away, leaving the gold. *Courtesy California State Library*

Calhoun's first efforts failed, primarily because the southern Whigs regarded Calhoun's operation as a Democratic party maneuver, and by the time Calhoun was well started, the Whigs had already won the presidential election.

Election of 1848. As the election of 1848 approached, James K. Polk had stepped aside, and the Democratic convention nominated Lewis Cass. But the free-soilers among the Democrats, who recognized the element of doubletalk in Cass' "Popular Sovereignty," and who also resented his role in defeating Van Buren four years earlier, withdrew from the convention and soon after formed a Free-Soil party with Van Buren as its nominee.

With the Democrats thus divided, the Whigs saw their opportunity to win, and nominated another military hero, as they had done in 1840. This one was the "Hero of Buena Vista," Zachary Taylor, a man with no political record and no known political views. Northern Whigs hesitated to accept him, for he was a Louisiana planter who owned more slaves than any person who had ever been President.* Southern Whigs were ecstatic at the thought of electing such a man—a native of Virginia, a military officer, a southern planter—and they were ready to take him with no questions asked. The Whig convention nominated him and did not even adopt a platform. In the election that followed, Taylor ran strong in both North and South, with even antislavery Whigs like Abraham Lincoln supporting him. He carried a majority of both northern and southern

*The slaveholding Presidents were Washington, Jefferson, Madison, Monroe, Jackson, Tyler, Polk, Taylor, and Andrew Johnson.

states and was triumphantly elected. That was why the southern Whigs in the winter of 1848, waiting for Taylor to be inaugurated in March, were frigidly indifferent to proposals to join the Democrats in a "united South" combination.

But when Taylor took office, the Southerners received a traumatic disappointment. It turned out that Taylor held unexpectedly independent political views and, though he believed in slavery, he did not believe in the corollary widely accepted in the South, that expansion was indispensable to the slave system. Further, he formed close ties with the antislavery Senator from New York, William H. Seward. In the nine months between his inauguration and the meeting of Congress, it gradually dawned upon the Southerners that Taylor was not their man and that their apparent victory had been a disastrous defeat. When they realized this, Calhoun's "united South" movement took on a new vitality. Two months before Congress met, the Mississippi legislature invited all the southern states to meet in a convention at Nashville in June 1850.

The Nashville Convention. The purpose of the proposed Nashville convention was to enable the South to present a solid front—no southern state should be left isolated as South Carolina had been left at the time of nullification in 1832—and the united action intended by a good many of the sponsors was southern withdrawal from the Union. Many Southerners had claimed, ever since the Virginia and Kentucky Resolutions of 1798, that the states were sovereign, that the Union was a voluntary association, and that any state which believed its constitutional rights to be violated might secede from the Union. For many years strong patriotic feelings had imposed a kind of taboo on the discussion of disunion as a political remedy, but in the winter of 1849–1850, loud, defiant threats of secession became commonplace. Men who cared deeply about the Union were discouraged and alarmed.

President Taylor's Response. President Taylor believed that the way to meet this crisis of union was as Andrew Jackson had met the nullification crisis—by firmness and a show of readiness to use force. (Taylor perhaps overlooked the fact that Jackson had, at the same time, encouraged substantial concessions to South Carolina.) In his annual message to Congress, he announced that he had already taken steps to organize California politically on a basis that would lead directly to statehood, without passing through a territorial phase. Everyone knew this would mean a free state. Further, he added that he would encourage a similar process for New Mexico. As for the Union: "Whatever dangers may threaten it, I shall stand by it and maintain it in its integrity."

Some historians believe that Taylor's firmness was the highest statesmanship; that the South, if confronted with force, would have backed down; and that the tragic Civil War which came eleven years later might have been forestalled in 1850.

Significance of the Crisis for the South. But the evidence indicates that many Southerners regarded this as a supreme crisis, in which the preservation of the slave system and with it the whole social structure of the South was at stake. If slavery could be excluded from California and New Mexico, it could probably be excluded from all of the many future states which were certain to follow. For the South this prospect held grim implications. First, it would destroy the precarious political balance of sectional power which still existed in the Senate, although northern numerical superiority had already upset the balance in other parts of the political system. (Zachary Taylor was the last resident Southerner whom voters have sent to the White House—Harry Truman of Missouri and Lyndon Johnson of Texas got there by way of the vice-presidency.) Second, by preventing the expansion of slavery, it would destroy the economic dynamism of the institution and reduce it to a static and perhaps declining condition. Third, it would threaten the South ultimately with a preponderance of free states great enough to attack slavery directly by constitutional amendment. Southerners recognized all these dangers to their system, and their reaction to Taylor's message seemed so grim and resolute that many alarmed Unionists, both in and out of Congress, felt desperately anxious for some kind of compromise.

Clay's Compromise of 1850

One man who recognized the opportunity created by the emergency was the seventy-two-year-old, silver-tongued orator, Senator Henry Clay, who had already made a name for himself as the "Great Pacificator" at the time of the Missouri Compromise and whose role as the representative of a border state, Kentucky, was strategic. Clay came forward with a full-scale proposal to settle all aspects of the slavery question once and for all. For the North, he would abolish the buying and selling of slaves in the District of Columbia, but for the South, he would guarantee the right to hold slaves in the District and would enact a stronger law to secure the return of fugitive slaves. For the North, he would admit California as a state without slavery, but for the South he would organize the two territories of Utah and New Mexico without any restrictions on slavery in the organizing act. This did not quite mean that these territories would be open to slavery; it meant only that Congress would not exclude slaves. There was still a possibility (a) that the territorial legislature might exclude them, if the federal courts construed the federal Constitution to allow the territories such power, or (b) that the courts themselves might do so by a judicial ruling that the Mexican law of freedom still applied. In short, the most crucial provision of the compromise was wrapped in ambiguity, and Clay refused to let the ambiguity be resolved because he knew that an unequivocal provision could not pass Congress. The cohesion of the American Union was thus already so badly impaired that a crisis could be averted only by concealing the depth of the division rather than by closing it.

The Failure of the Giants. During the winter and spring of 1850, Congress —especially the Senate—considered the Clay proposals in one of its most famous debates. The atmosphere of emergency and the oratorical talents of the speakers added to the drama of the occasion. Clay, famous for his magic as a speaker, was at his silver-tongued best; Calhoun, so ill that he would die before the vote was taken, made a tremendously impressive voice-from-the-grave appearance to sit in his senatorial seat while his farewell speech was read for him; and Webster, heightening the suspense by his silence, finally came out in favor of the compromise in a technically brilliant speech arguing that slavery was not adaptable to California and the Southwest in any case, and that it was insane to convulse the country over an abstract question. It has been said that Clay tried to float the compromise to adoption on a tide of stately speeches, and the speeches were indeed superb productions. Hopes for compromise grew accordingly, and these hopes attained such strength that when nine southern state delegations finally gathered at Nashville in June, the disunionist momentum had been lost and all they could do was to vote to adjourn temporarily and reassemble after the fate of the compromise had been decided.

Despite the optimism of the Unionists, however, major obstacles still stood in the way of compromise. President Taylor was apparently ready to veto Clay's New Mexico bill which would have wrecked the entire compromise plan, and, as events were soon to show, there was not a clear majority in either house of Congress in favor of the compromise as a whole. The prospects appeared very negative, and on July 31 the opposition maneuvered the proponents of compromise into an intricate parliamentary trap which enabled them, in a series of votes, to cut the compromise to pieces, bit by bit. At that point it seemed that the mighty effort for compromise had failed.

Douglas Engineers Victory. But, in fact, the tide had already turned in its favor. On July 4 Zachary Taylor fell ill of what today might be called gastroenteritis, and on July 9 he died. His Vice-President, Millard Fillmore of New York, although a Northerner, supported the compromise as vigorously as Taylor, the Southerner, had opposed it. Soon the power and the influence of the administration began making themselves felt in rounding up votes in support of the compromise. Further, after the debacle of July 31, Henry Clay, worn out with months of strenuous effort, gave up the leadership of the compromise forces. A hard-hitting, resourceful, adroit, young Democratic Senator from Illinois—Stephen A. Douglas, the "Little Giant," the "steam engine in breeches"—became the manager for the compromise.

Douglas clearly grasped the essence of the situation. There was not a majority in favor of the compromise as a whole, and therefore it could not be adopted as one package, which is what Clay had attempted. However, a crucial minority supported it as a whole, and there were northern and southern sectional blocs. If the compromise group voted with the northern bloc for the parts of the compromise favorable to the North and with the southern bloc for the parts of the compromise favorable to the South, majorities could be secured for all parts of the compromise and it could be enacted.

So the great quest for a compromise entered a second phase, very unlike the first. Calhoun was dead, Clay had gone to Newport for a rest, Webster had left the Senate to become Secretary of State, and there were no more immortal speeches. Fillmore had replaced Taylor in the White House. Having discovered the winning formula, Douglas wasted little time in putting it into effect. In less than six weeks he steered every item of Clay's original plan through both Senate and House. Fillmore signed the measures as fast as they were adopted, and in September the battle of the giants came to an end. The crisis had been passed.

Significance of the Compromise. This settlement has been designated in history as the Compromise of 1850. Men at the time regarded it as a tremendous accomplishment, averting the worst danger the American Union had ever faced. But even at the time, and without any historical perspective, the compromise betrayed some flimsy and vulnerable features. For one thing, if a compromise is an agreement between two parties, this was not a compromise at all. Majorities of Northerners consistently voted against majorities of Southerners and *vice versa;* it was only the swing vote of a minority of compromisers which saved Clay's plan. Further, the organization of Utah and New Mexico territories without any decision as to the power of the territorial legislatures to regulate slavery left still unresolved a bitter dispute which had raged for four years. This meant that peace was built on ambiguity. Further still, no ultimate question had been settled: the North had given up its insistence on the Wilmot Proviso, but had not modified in the slightest degree its conviction that slavery was morally repulsive and that the South was responsible for this repugnant institution in American society; the South had decided not to exercise its alleged right to disrupt the Union, but it was more united than ever before in insisting upon the validity of this right to secede.

In historical perspective, of course, we know that the disunion crisis came back again eleven years later. While this relapse was not necessarily the fault of the political physicians who pulled the patient through in 1850, it still appears that what the settlement of 1850 did was to buy eleven years of time.

The question how much this time was worth to the Union in the long run is, of course, speculation, because no war was fought in 1850, and history does not tell us the results of wars which are not fought. But history does show that the North had a greater margin of physical superiority over the South in 1861 than in 1850—population, productivity, resources, wealth. Technology had advanced in certain ways, such as the building of railroads, which made it possible to carry military operations hundreds of miles into hostile territory in a way that would have been almost impossible in 1850. The Union grew in cohesiveness which better prepared the people to resist disruption in 1861 than they might have been in 1850. Although certainties cannot satisfactorily be balanced against speculation, it may be worth observing that no one can be sure either how serious or how successful an effort to disrupt the Union would have been in 1850; we know with certainty that a most formidable effort was made in 1860–1861, and that, at the cost of a great and closely contested war, it was defeated. This did not mean, of course, that all the problems of the Union were solved, nor should an objective historian automatically assume that the preservation of the Union was a good thing, regardless of what the Union did after it was preserved. But its preservation certainly changed the course of world history, as well as of the history of the American people, and it probably changed the course of the history of democracy in the modern world.

SUGGESTED READING (Prepared by Carl N. Degler)

The westward expansion of the United States has been studied in great detail. A good entry into the literature is Ray Allen Billington, *America's Frontier Heritage** (1966) and his textbook on *Westward Expansion* (2nd ed., 1960), which provides a good summary of the story of expansion. The classic and indispensable study of ideology is Albert K. Weinberg, *Manifest Destiny** (1935). More recently the leading authority has called into question the view that Americans wanted to expand; see Frederick Merk, *Manifest Destiny and Mission in American History: A Reinterpretation** (1963). Merk is also the primary authority on the issue of the Oregon territory; see his *The Oregon Question: Essays in Anglo-American Diplomacy and Politics* (1967). Norman Graebner, *Empire on the Pacific: A Study in American Continental Expansion* (1955) argues that trade with Asia and the acquisition of Pacific ports were more important in sparking the occupation of California than mere territorial gains. Another manifestation of American expansionism is discussed in Donald F. Warner, *The Idea of Continental Union: Agitation for the Annexation of Canada to the United States, 1849–1893* (1960). The American propensity for filibustering abroad is treated at length in Edward S. Wallace, *Destiny and Glory* (1957).

The lure of California is explained in two books by Rodman W. Paul, *California Gold** (1947) and *Mining Frontiers of the Far West, 1848–1880** (1963), the second being a fine study of the technology of mining as well.

The standard and fullest study on the Mexican War—that fruit of American expansionism—is Justin H. Smith, *The War with Mexico* (2 vols., 1919). A more recent and compact study is Otis A. Singletary, *The Mexican War** (1960). Glenn W. Price, *Origins of the War with Mexico: The Polk-Stockton Intrigue* (1967) is distinguished by its hostility to Polk and the United States. A convenient compendium of articles and interpretations is Ramon Eduardo Ruiz, ed., *The Mexican War—Was It Manifest Destiny?* (1963).

The fullest and most recent study of the Compromise of 1850 is contained in Holman Hamilton, *Prologue to Conflict** (1964). Allan Nevins, *Ordeal of the Union* (vols. I and II, 1947–50) also treats the Compromise and the years preceding it in depth and with insight. A brief, but informed biography is Richard N. Current, *Daniel Webster and the Rise of National Conservatism.** Calhoun is sympathetically portrayed in Charles M. Wiltse, *John C. Calhoun* (3 vols., 1944–51). Less friendly is Gerald Capers, *John C. Calhoun, Opportunist* (1960).

---

*Available in a paperback edition.

Reformers / Pictorial Essay

by Carl Degler

For three decades before the Civil War, a variety of so-called reform movements subjected the established institutions of the country to critical analysis, with many suggestions for improvement. Best known was the antislavery movement. It is worth noting, though, that not all reforms were necessarily critical of society or its institutions in the same way or degree that antislavery was. Many were essentially individualistic in spirit, seeking freedom for fulfillment of individual potentialities—a progress to perfectibility. For example, the interest in religion, which was epitomized by the Church of Jesus Christ of Latter Day Saints, also called Mormons, did not seek to change men except by individual conversion. The Mormons, on the other hand, were themselves often the object of attack from their neighbors. Indeed, so severe were the physical attacks upon the Mormons in their city of Nauvoo, Illinois, in the late 1840's that they decided to migrate to Mexican territory, where they would be beyond the reach of the hostility of other Americans. This was the origin of the great trek to Salt Lake in Utah. That area, however, soon came under United States jurisdiction anyway, as a result of the Mexican war. In the accompanying picture the famous handcart part of the migration to Utah is shown. The Mormons were undoubtedly the most highly organized of all the westward migrants. Some advance units actually planted crops along the way to be harvested by later contingents. The handcart migration was a measure of the determination as well as the ingenuity of the Mormons, for it enabled even those families too poor to own oxen and a wagon to make the trip to Utah.

The temperance movement, which began like Mormonism in the years before 1848, became a political movement in the 1850's. Like the Mormons, too, the opponents of liquor were more concerned with individual conversion than with changing the existing society. The illustrations from *Six Nights With the Washingtonians* show one of the means used to convert readers to

From *Six Nights With the Washingtonians. Reproduced from the collections of the Library of Congress*

James Latimer persuades his wife to drink.

Latimer has lost his job, so Mrs. Latimer pawns clothes to buy more bottles.

Mormon Hand Carts. *The Church of Jesus Christ of Latter-Day Saints*

abstaining from drink. The results of indulgence were starkly spelled out: poverty, madness, and delinquent children. Apparently, however, this effort to reform individuals was not effective or persuasive enough for by the 1850's the opponents of liquor were seeking to prohibit the sale and consumption of liquor by state law. Although some states passed such laws in the 1850's, they were virtually all repealed by the time of the Civil War. "Prohibition," however, would return in the twentieth century, but this time through the use of federal power.

Having lost most of their possessions, Latimer kills his wife in a drunken quarrel.

Locked up in a madhouse, Latimer is visited by his delinquent children.

Left: Walt Whitman. *The Granger Collection*
Above: Ralph Waldo Emerson. *George Eastman House Collection*

As one might expect in an age of individualistic reformers, some writers eloquently praised individuality and personal independence. Certainly two of the best known of such men were Walt Whitman and Ralph Waldo Emerson. In the 1850's Emerson was an elderly man, though he would live for another thirty years, while Whitman was just beginning his famous career as poet and believer in democracy and in America. In 1855 he published his great book of poems *Leaves of Grass*, which marked a new era in poetry in the English-speaking world. Despite the novelty of Whitman's style and language, Emerson praised the book upon its appearance, though he himself was one of the leaders of the traditional poetry. Emerson believed one should perfect both one's own nature and that of society. His individuality was demonstrated at the time of the execution of John Brown, when he commended Brown for his efforts to end slavery. Most white Americans thought Brown a madman and a menace because he sought to rouse the slaves to rebellion in Virginia in 1859. The hanging of Brown is shown here in a contemporary sketch; its continuing impact is measured in the opposition to keeping his memory alive. The disruption of the Boston meeting honoring Brown in 1860 illustrates another aspect of the antislavery reform movement: the involvement of blacks in public affairs on a large scale for the first time. Frederick Douglass was an escaped slave who became a nationally known antislavery editor and orator. Although he had been interested in Brown's scheme to lead a slave insurrection, at the last moment Douglass wisely recognized the inadequate preparations Brown had made as well as the extreme danger involved and the small chance the raid held for helping the slaves to throw off their bondage. As a result, Douglass did not participate in Brown's raid. The long-term impact of Brown's raid and execution is measured, too, in the famous Civil War marching song, "John Brown's body lies a-moldering in the grave...."

Execution of John Brown. *Frank Leslie's Illustrated Newspaper, December 17, 1859*

Mob disrupts meeting in honor of John Brown at Tremont Temple in Boston. Frederick Douglass was thrown down the staircase. *Harper's Weekly, December 15, 1860*

Sojourner Truth.
Sophia Smith Collection, Smith College

Almost as famous as Douglass was Sojourner Truth. She was also born a slave but was freed when the state of New York, where she was born, abolished slavery. She devoted her considerable oratorical gifts not only to opposing slavery, but to campaigning for women's rights as well. Unlike Douglass, Sojourner Truth (a name she took at the beginning of her reform activities) never learned to read or write. Yet her speeches reached eloquence when uttered in her deep, compelling voice. Her well-known answer to men who asserted women could not work was to tell of her labors as a slave and worker, and then bare her arm or breast and say "And ain't I a women?"

Although the number of blacks who actually used "the underground railroad" as a way of escaping bondage was very limited—probably no more than 60,000 blacks escaped to the North over a thirty-year period—for those who did, it was a dangerous and difficult path to take. In the accompanying picture, runaways are being put up at the home of an abolitionist for the night. Only with such way stations was it possible for a slave to escape in winter, but the really dangerous part in running away occurred long before the slave reached the North on his way to Canada, that is when he was traversing slave territory. And along that path there was no underground railway; for those miles the runaway was entirely on his own.

The Underground Railway by C. T. Webber. *Cincinnati Art Museum*

Akin to the antislavery movement in its opposition to entrenched power and privilege was the women's movement, which had its beginnings in 1848 at a small meeting at Seneca Falls, New York. The accompanying cartoon entitled "The Discord" sums up some of the concerns, symbolic and otherwise, that grew out of women's demand for equality. Notice how the children are depicted as siding with the parent of the same sex and how the man who drew the cartoon interprets women's aspirations for equality as really a demand for dominance. The emphasis upon pants as a symbol of power may be a reference, also, to the attempt on the part of some women to wear pants because they thought the skirts of the period inhibited women's physical mobility and, therefore, the jobs or work they could do. This was the era of the beginnings of dress reform for women, too. But as the picture of women on strike in 1860 makes evident, even with long, hobbling skirts some women not only worked in the new factories, but could also participate in demands for better working conditions. All this does not exhaust the impetus to reform, which expressed itself in a further variety of ways: in the abolition of imprisonment for debt, in prison reform, in humane care for the mentally ill, in campaigns for a ten-hour working day, and in programs for training the blind.

Left: Who Wears the Pants? *Courtesy of The New-York Historical Society*
Above: Women Shoemakers Strike. *Reproduced from the collections of the Library of Congress*

CHAPTER THREE

STEPS TOWARD SEPARATION

ISTORY TENDS to focus on public issues, and especially controversial public issues, rather than upon general developments or the affairs of everyday life. Thus history has concentrated on the slavery controversy as if it were uppermost in the minds of every man, woman, and child in the United States for a full decade before the Civil War. Yet, in realistic terms, probably most Americans thought about slavery only occasionally, while all sorts of other matters also engaged their attention. Aside from the ordinary personal and domestic problems of family life and earning an income, Americans lived with the preoccupations of a rapidly growing country: a high rate of immigration, great mobility of population, and rapid technological change. This meant that Americans were busy building railroads and factories; many were moving from the farm to the city; and many more were moving west to Iowa, Missouri, Wisconsin, Minnesota, Oregon, and California. While many Americans were mobile, many Europeans were also mobile in coming to America. During the decade of the 1840's there was a higher proportion of immigrants to resident citizens than in any other decade of American history. All the while, the rate of productivity was rising, and with it the standard of living. Even in the field of reform, the quest for the abolition of slavery did not stand alone. Other reformers gave their ideals and their energy to the development of public education, the achievement of women's rights, the temperance movement, the improvement of care for the mentally ill, the improvement of prisons, and other activities to improve the quality of human life. Americans were not as obsessed with the question of slavery as one might suppose from reading books of history (even this history). Perhaps they were not obsessed enough. But slavery had a way of involving itself with all sorts of other questions so that, even in an issue which appeared to have nothing to do with slavery, it often turned out in the end that the slavery question swallowed up the other issue.

The Slavery Issue and Expansion

This was true, for instance, in connection with territorial expansion. From the beginning of the nineteenth century, the United States had shown a steady impulse to increase its area, through the Louisiana Purchase, the seizure of West Florida during the War of 1812, the attempt (unsuccessful) to conquer part of Canada during the same war, the acquisition of East Florida by treaty with Spain in 1819, the annexation of Texas, the campaign in 1844 for the acquisition of all of Oregon north to 54°40', and the acquisition of California and the Southwest in the Mexican War. Americans had adopted a mystic idea of "Manifest Destiny" to justify almost unlimited expansion in the Western

Quantrill's raid on Lawrence, Kansas: a pencil sketch based on interviews with survivors. The town was virtually destroyed in the Kansas-Missouri border war; Quantrill, a ruthless southern sympathizer, was dominant among the many marauders who desolated the area. *The Kansas State Historical Society, Topeka*

Hemisphere, and as early as the Jefferson administration they had begun to covet the rich and strategically located island of Cuba. In the earlier stages of expansionism, relatively little sectional rivalry was involved, so growth had proceeded with a broad basis of support throughout the Union.

Today many Americans would question whether the whole process of expansion did not involve unjustified aggression upon the Indians and upon relatively weak neighboring countries. But in the 1850's expansion was still generally accepted, and the process was actually halted because of jealousies between the sections as to which of them would gain most by any given new territory. This sectional obstacle to expansion became very apparent during the administration of Franklin Pierce, who succeeded Fillmore as President in 1853.

Election of 1852. In the election campaign of 1852 the northern Whigs, who had never accepted the Compromise of 1850, who were more vigorously antislavery than the northern Democrats, and who especially detested the Fugitive Slave Act, got their revenge on President Fillmore by blocking his nomination, which was strongly supported by southern Whigs. After a long deadlock, the Whig convention nominated Winfield Scott, a good general but a pompous and clumsy political candidate. Meanwhile, the Democrats proclaimed the "finality of the Compromise" as a permanent solution of sectional antagonisms, and nominated Pierce, the governor of New Hampshire. Pierce was young, attractive, and dynamic, but as it later turned out, not very bright and not able to make up his mind. In the election Pierce won by what appeared to be a landslide, carrying all but four states, two in the North and two in the South. On closer scrutiny the victory was less overwhelming than it seemed, for the combined vote of the Whigs and of the Free-Soil party in the free states was slightly more than Pierce's vote in that area. But his triumph appeared to give a nationwide sanction to the Compromise. With the slavery question "out of the way," as the Democrats hopefully supposed, they could now get on with other business.

The Gadsden Purchase. Part of this other business was expansion and when Pierce was inaugurated, he announced "my administration will not be controlled by any timid forebodings of evil from expansion." The new President's appointments made good on this promise, for he sent James Gadsden of South Carolina to Mexico with instructions to buy the northern part of the five Mexican states which bordered the United States, plus all of Lower California. To Spain he sent Pierre Soulé of Louisiana, with instructions to buy Cuba. But both projects resulted in fiascoes, and in both the expansion question was promptly converted into a slavery question. Mexico was simply not interested in bargaining away the whole northern segment of her domain, and Gadsden had a hard time inducing the Mexican government to sell that part of the valley of the Gila River which lies at the southern edge of New Mexico and Arizona. The Gadsden Purchase was important because, from an engineering standpoint, it provided a feasible route for a railroad across the southern part of the United States. But the most significant development occurred when Pierce sent the treaty to the Senate. Northern senators opposed the acquisition, and its supporters were able to save it only by cutting out 9000 square miles of the area that Mexico had agreed to sell. Never before had the United States refused to accept land ceded to it by treaty.

Pierce's Cuban Scheme. If Pierce's Mexican scheme was a failure, or at best a narrowly limited success, his Cuban scheme was a disaster. It failed partly because Pierce and the expansionists could not decide whether to try to buy Cuba from Spain, to encourage a local revolution like the Bear Flag revolt in California, or to permit private operators known as filibusters, with headquarters in New Orleans, to organize an invasion of Cuba under the pretext of aiding a Cuban revolt against Spain. Pierce tentatively tried all three, but the firmness of Spanish refusal prevented purchase negotiations and the intensity of northern opposition forced the President to abandon his encouragement of the filibusters, who had developed full plans for an invasion of Cuba, to be led by ex-Governor John A. Quitman of Mississippi. In June 1854, Pierce issued a proclamation warning that the neutrality laws, which forbade filibustering activities, would be strictly enforced. This was the most decisive step Pierce ever took as President. It ended the possibility of annexing Cuba, and it should have ended proslavery efforts to acquire Cuba, with its large slave population.

The Ostend Manifesto. But the proslavery expansionists would not give up. They persuaded the Secretary of State to permit a meeting in Europe of the American ministers to Britain, France, and Spain to discuss the Cuban question. The three met at Ostend in October 1854, and there prepared a statement which was "intended" to be a private memorandum to the State Department, but which was soon leaked to the press and therefore appeared to be a public challenge to the world. This "Ostend Manifesto" indiscreetly declared that "Cuba is as necessary to the North American republic as any of its present members," that the United States should attempt to buy Cuba, and that if Spain should refuse to sell and should pursue policies that endangered American peace (such as, presumably, emancipating Cuban slaves) then, "by every law, human and Divine, we shall be justified in wresting it from Spain if we possess the power."

All efforts of Pierce and Secretary of State Marcy to disassociate the administration from this statement by its three principal foreign envoys were, of course, in vain. Pierce became forever tarred with the stigma of proslavery expansionism and of hostile aggression against a peaceable neighbor. This fate befell him five months after he had effectively put a halt to plans of aggression. But the "Ostend Manifesto," although mere reckless talk about a matter already settled, completed the process by which the issue of expansion was converted into an issue of slavery.

The Slavery Issue and a Transcontinental Railroad

This tendency of all sorts of matters to gravitate toward the slavery controversy also showed up in the question of opening up the western plains and building a railroad to the Pacific coast. Desire for a transcontinental railroad developed even before the United States became a transcontinental republic. As early as 1844 a New York merchant, Asa Whitney, brought forward a grandiose scheme for such a railroad, which had considerable appeal. But after the acquisition of California and the discovery of gold there, the need for a railroad became far more urgent. At the end of the Mexican War, the United States was in the curious position that the republic extended unbroken from the Atlantic to the Pacific, but much the best way to get from the east coast to the west coast was to sail around South America. (The shorter Panama route was very dangerous because of unchecked tropical diseases on the Isthmus.) Everyone agreed that there must be a railroad.

Scarcely anyone agreed, however, about the route of the road or its eastern terminus. While patriots saw the necessity of creating a link between east and west, promoters saw a chance to get rich on building contracts and real estate speculations. At one time it seemed that every town in the Mississippi Valley aspired to be the eastern terminus. Chicago, St. Louis, Memphis, Vicksburg, New Orleans, and lesser towns competed fiercely for the prize, and all the rivals were constantly ready to gang up on any single competitor which seemed about to snatch the prize. It was part of the pattern of all this local rivalry that Southerners tended to favor a southern terminus—New Orleans or Memphis, perhaps—while Northerners wanted a terminus in the North, with Chicago the favored choice.

Douglas and the Northern Route. In 1853 Congress voted funds to conduct engineering surveys of several possible routes. That was why President Pierce sent James Gadsden to Mexico to buy the land strategic to a southern route. It was clear by this time that the rivalry was approaching a climax, and all competitors seemed to redouble their efforts. One of the principal combatants was Stephen A. Douglas. As Senator from Illinois, Douglas automatically supported Chicago, and as a long-time chairman of the Committee on Territories, which had drafted all the bills for organizing new territories, Douglas had a special interest in western development.

Douglas' railroad and territorial interests converged, for a railroad could scarcely be built without federal grants of land, which of course had to be surveyed first; and land could scarcely be surveyed until the surrounding area had been politically organized as a territory. This link between territorial organization and railroad promotion gave considerable advantage to the South for, after 1850, the whole area from New Orleans to San Francisco lay within the states of Louisiana, Texas, and California, and the organized territory of New Mexico (which included what is now Arizona). Farther north, however, there was an immense gap, an unorganized region extending from the western edge of Missouri and Iowa all the way to the Utah territory. The advocates of a northern route needed to get this area organized. Douglas introduced a bill to organize it but he was defeated by a solid bloc of southern votes in 1853.

As Douglas analyzed his situation at the end of 1853, he saw that there were some conservative eastern interests which would always oppose him because they objected to the expense and to the increase in federal power which a railroad would involve. Combined with the kind of southern opposition which he had just encountered, his adversaries would always have a majority, as he clearly perceived. Tactically, he had to get some southern votes and to do so he had to give the Southerners some inducement to vote for his measure. But this would be almost impossible, for under the terms of the Missouri Compromise of 1820, slavery would be excluded from the territory which he proposed to organize. Southerners simply had no motive to vote to organize territories which would both be closed to slavery and would aid the drive for a northern route for the railroad. Douglas had to give them a motive.

The only motive he could give them was to remove the slavery exclusion and let them hope to get another slave territory. Personally, Douglas regarded slavery as an outdated, inefficient institution, not in good repute, and unsuited to as progressive a country as the United States, but he felt no moral fervor about it. Politically he regarded the issue as a nuisance which generated disruptive tendencies in an otherwise harmonious Union and got in the way of his own political plans.

The Kansas-Nebraska Act. At this crucial moment in 1854 he knew that it might be dangerous to tamper with the Compromise of 1820—in his own words it would raise "a hell of a storm. . . ." But he felt that he had to have the southern votes so he made up his mind to eliminate the exclusion of slavery. First he tried to do this in an indirect, unobtrusive way by advancing a very tricky argument that the Compromise of 1820 had already been replaced by the Compromise of 1850. The latter applied to the Mexican cession, the former to the Louisiana Purchase, and one did not necessarily have any bearing upon the other; certainly no one in 1850 had contended that the compromise of that year repealed the earlier Missouri settlement. But some southern members insisted that the Act of 1820 could not be repealed by indirect action. Under severe pressure, Douglas finally yielded by placing an explicit repeal of the Act of 1820 in his bill for the organization of two new territories, Kansas and Nebraska.

To antislavery men the Missouri Compromise had dedicated the northern part of the Louisiana Purchase to freedom forever and the Douglas proposal was a wanton violation of a solemn covenant. To Douglas himself the bitter conflict which burst out at once was a needless uproar about a fictitious question—no slaveowners would be foolish enough to try to take slaves from the profitable cotton fields of the South to the plains of Nebraska, and if any did, the territorial legislature could pass laws to keep them out. To the Southerners it was an issue which they had not raised, but which they would not concede once Douglas had raised it. With all the abolitionists denouncing the proposal as an evil plot by the slave power, Southerners rallied to support the bill. From January through May 1854, a savage battle raged in the Senate and the House—perhaps as bitter as any before or since. Douglas, who had really lost control when he was maneuvered into proposing repeal of the Act of 1820, and who was bitterly assailed by powerful opponents, fought with immense energy and resourcefulness. Using to the utmost his extraordinary parliamentary skill and the influence of the administration, he forced the measure through both houses. By the time it was adopted, it had long since ceased to be part of a railroad project and had become part of a renewed slavery conflict, waged with more bitterness than ever before. Whatever slight chance the Compromise of 1850 had ever had of being final was now destroyed.

Ironically the man who had saved the Compromise of 1850 after Clay failed was the man who destroyed it a little less than four years later. And by a further irony, he also lost the fruits of the measure for which he had sacrificed so much of his own influence and popularity: in the ensuing session of Congress he brought in a railroad bill which passed the Senate, the only transcontinental railroad bill to pass either chamber before the Civil War. This bill was modified in the House and was once voted, but was later reconsidered and then defeated. Thus the Kansas-Nebraska Act did not lead to the Pacific Railroad bill which was its intended sequel, but it did lead to a deeply intensified renewal of the slavery contest, which was not intended.

The Consequence of Kansas-Nebraska: Rivalry for Kansas

Kansas-Nebraska had two profoundly disruptive consequences. One of these was that it invited the proslavery and antislavery parties to engage in a contest for the control of Kansas. This was not a contest of ideas, speeches, or appeals to reason, but a physical contest—a rivalry of manpower, guns, and armed forces. As such it kept national bitterness at white heat. A second consequence was that it precipitated the collapse of one of the national political parties which was already badly weakened, namely the Whigs, and caused the restructuring of the other national party, the Democrats, so that in fact no truly national parties remained. First let us examine the conflict in Kansas.

When Stephen A. Douglas introduced his bill to repeal the slavery exclusion of 1820, he by no means intended to hand Kansas over to the "slave power"—though some of his southern allies may have supposed he was delivering Kansas to them. What he did intend was that the people in the territory should decide the slavery question just as the people in the states decided it. Why, he asked, was a citizen living in a territory less competent to handle this question than a citizen living in a state? This was what he meant by "popular sovereignty." State action by citizens had abolished slavery earlier in the New England states and in New York, Pennsylvania, and New Jersey. Why could not the same kind of local action keep slavery out of Kansas without convulsing the country, keeping Congress in an uproar—and interfering with the Pacific Railroad? The Douglas argument had a certain persuasiveness but, as we shall see, it eventually fell afoul of the Supreme Court's Dred Scott decision, and as Abraham Lincoln later argued with great effectiveness, it treated the slavery question as a local question when it was inescapably a national question. But the most immediate fallacy in Douglas' plan was that it assumed that the emigrants to an empty territory would behave like the settled citizens of a populated state. Because of circumstances on the frontier this was simply not true. What the passage of the Kansas-Nebraska Act did was not to settle a contest but to intensify it while transferring it from the halls of Congress to the plains of Kansas.

The Race for Voters and Arms in Kansas. If the slavery question in Kansas was going to be settled by the voters there, then the proslavery and the antislavery parties were both challenged to get voters into Kansas. What should have been a gradual process of farmers filtering in to settle down became a race between competing factions in which the land-hungry farmers, who for the most part cared very little about slavery, were forced to take sides with one faction for the sake of protection against the other. Instead of organizing their supporters to debate and vote in Congress, both sides now organized supporters to go to Kansas and win in a contest there.

Given the circumstances, the conduct of both sides seems easy to understand. In New England, Emigrant Aid Societies were organized to help finance the migration of free-state sympathizers to Kansas; ultimately these societies gave financial assistance to about 2000 men, but they exaggerated their own operations and talked of a fund of $5 million. This kind of talk led proslavery men in Missouri, whose homes were separated from Kansas only by an invisible surveyor's line, to fear that they were about to be overrun by swarms of wild-eyed, fanatical abolitionists. They reacted by forming secret Blue Lodges and preparing to use armed force against the Yankee emigrants. Later, when the Missourians did use force, the antislavery organizers quite logically concluded that there was no point in sending defenseless men at considerable expense to Kansas just to leave them at the mercy of the "Border Ruffians" of Missouri; so the New Englanders shipped several hundred rifles to their supporters. Soon Kansas was gripped in the throes of a minor arms race.

A Fraudulent Election. Perhaps worse was the fact that when the first territorial legislature was elected, no registration was required as a preliminary to the voting. Both sides, therefore, rushed in supporters at the last moment in an effort to build up an electoral majority. When the contending forces started playing this game, the proslavery men held an immense advantage, for their supporters were within a day's ride in Missouri, while the antislavery reinforcements were hundreds of miles away. Ironically, when the election was held the proslavery faction had a legitimate majority, but feeling uncertain of their own strength they brought over swarms of Border Ruffians from Missouri. These transients stole an election which could have been won without it. Over 6000 votes were cast in an election where there existed about 3000 eligible voters.

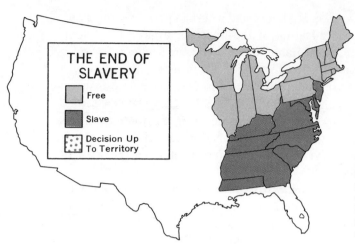

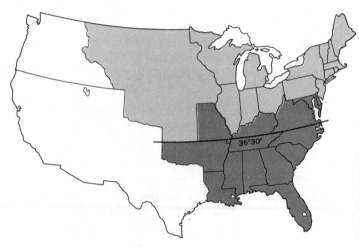

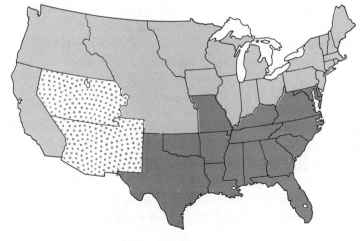

THE END OF SLAVERY

- Free
- Slave
- Decision Up To Territory

1800

Between Independence and 1800, most of the northern states either abolished slavery or adopted gradual emancipation laws. Congress had also prohibited slavery in the Northwest and Indiana territories.

1820

The Missouri Compromise prohibited slavery north of 36°30′ latitude in all Louisiana Purchase territory except Missouri. To balance Missouri, Maine (formerly in Massachusetts) was admitted as a free state.

1850

Expansion fed discord over territories. Slavery was prohibited in Oregon in 1848. The Compromise of 1850 admitted California as a free state and left to popular sovereignty a decision in Utah and New Mexico.

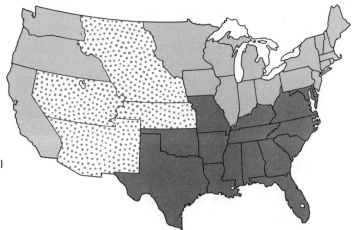

1854
Designed to win southern support for organizing Kansas and Nebraska (for a transcontinental railroad), the Kansas-Nebraska Act opened these territories to popular sovereignty, and repealed the Missouri Compromise.

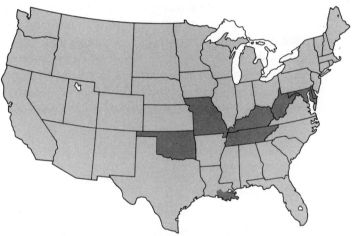

1863
In 1862 Congress had forbidden slavery in all organized territories, and in 1863, the Emancipation Proclamation ended slavery in all those parts of the Confederacy still in rebellion.

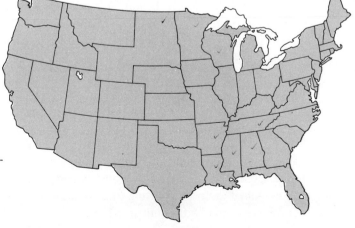

1865
The Thirteenth Amendment abolished the last surviving slavery in Kentucky and Delaware and in the unorganized territory that became Oklahoma. The other border states had already abolished it.

The territorial governor, inhibited by some genuine legal technicalities, made the fatal mistake of failing to declare the whole election void.

Two Rival Governments. The bogus legislature, thus elected, met and made the situation even worse by extreme and repressive legislation. It passed a law, for instance, making it a felony to question the right to hold slaves in Kansas and it expelled the few antislavery legislators who had been elected. The antislavery men, victimized by a fraudulent election, outraged by the bigoted behavior of the proslavery group, and denied even the representation which they had won, denounced the territorial government as a fraud. They proceeded to organize a new government, drawing up a state constitution, and electing a governor and a legislature of their own. Kansas now had two governments, one legal but not honest, the other honest but not legal.

The antislavery or Topeka "government" had to decide whether merely to deny the validity of the laws of the regular government or actually to violate them. This question arose in various forms, such as whether taxes should be paid to the regular government, and it forced almost everyone, including many who wanted only to get on with their farming, to take sides. The people of Kansas thus divided into hostile camps and were virtually forced to arm for their own protection. Acts of individual violence were inevitable in a situation where land titles were uncertain. Delays in the surveying of Kansas land made this condition worse. Such land disputes occurred on every frontier, even where there was no slavery issue. But the presence of this issue meant that large organized forces were at hand to support any member of one faction, even in a personal fight, if it was against a member of the other faction. Under the circumstances, escalation was inevitable: for instance, a proslavery man killed an antislavery man in a quarrel; other antislavery men retaliated by threatening the life of the proslavery man and burning the dwellings of two of his witnesses; the sheriff arrested one of the arsonists; a band of antislavery men intercepted the sheriff and rescued the prisoner; the sheriff then collected a posse of 3000 men to go to arrest the rescuers. Later the sheriff was shot, though not fatally.

Lawrence and Pottawattomie Creek. This kind of disturbance was chronic in Kansas from 1855 until 1857. Armed bands roamed the prairies; Border Ruffians made their incursions. Although very few people were killed, no one was safe and terror reigned in Kansas. Only twice, however, did the situation get completely out of control. Once, in 1856, the proslavery sheriff marched into the antislavery stronghold of Lawrence with a posse which threw printing presses in the river and engaged in a certain amount of burning and looting. A proslavery man was killed accidentally by a piece of a wall which fell on him. Three days later, however, one of the antislavery faction, John Brown by name, led a detachment of seven men to a proslavery settlement on Pottawattomie Creek. In the dead of night they took five unarmed men from their cabins, killed them by splitting their skulls with broadswords, and in one case, cut off the hands of the murdered man.

Hostilities Are Stopped in "Bleeding Kansas." The antislavery faction did not approve of the Pottawattomie massacre and joined in denouncing it, though not in bringing Brown, who was the known perpetrator, to justice. In fact, despite the atmosphere of hostility and the chronic episodes of shooting which led to the term "Bleeding Kansas," the lack of any large-scale violence was perhaps the most significant aspect of the situation. Bloodthirsty threats of extermination were commonplace, and on several occasions hostile armies faced one another ready for battle, but they always avoided large-scale combat. The fact was that most Kansans did not want to fight and they armed themselves and went marching and countermarching only because they lived in fear of the opposite faction. Probably both factions were secretly relieved when President Pierce sent out a new territorial governor, John W. Geary, who forced both to behave peaceably, though each made a great show of reluctance and boasted that it was gaining its objectives by Geary's settlement.

Geary put a stop to violence in Kansas. Some of the most militant members of both factions ceased their strife and even joined together in the kind of land speculations and fastbuck operations which were a chronic part of the opening of any new American frontier. "Bleeding Kansas" ceased to bleed. But though hostilities ended, strife did not. The antislavery faction continued to maintain its shadow "government" and to refuse to recognize the legitimacy of the regular government by voting in its elections. The proslavery faction continued to take advantage of the fact that the antislavery group let the elections go by default. Everyone recognized that matters would never settle down until the question of statehood had been put to the test.

The Lecompton Constitution. James Buchanan, whose election to the presidency will be discussed later in this chapter, recognized that the statehood question must be faced. When he came to office in 1857 he made a major effort to settle it by sending a leading Democrat, Robert J. Walker, to be governor of Kansas; he promised Walker that when a state constitution was drafted it would not be accepted, whether slave or free, "unless a majority of the people shall first have fairly and freely decided this question for themselves by a direct vote on the adoption of the Constitution." In June 1857, Kansas elected delegates to a convention to draw up a constitution. With the free state faction still distrustfully abstaining, the proslavery element won an overwhelming majority of delegates. In October this convention met at Lecompton, Kansas, and proposed a constitution which guaranteed the rights of the owners of the slaves already in Kansas (perhaps 200 in number) to hold their property in perpetuity, but which gave the voters an option between clauses (a) allowing or (b) forbidding the introduction of additional slaves in the future.

At once a violent dispute broke out as to whether the Lecompton proposal represented either a fair application of the principle of popular sovereignty or, even more, a fulfillment of Buchanan's promise. To advocates it was perfectly fair: it gave the voters a chance to exclude all slaves, except for a few in whose cases the property rights of Kansans were already involved. In fact, they argued, this was fairer than a vote on a proslavery constitution, for such a vote would force opponents of slavery to lose statehood as the price of rejecting slavery; the Lecompton plan would enable them to vote against bringing in new slaves, and they would still get statehood no matter which way they voted. But antislavery men saw the matter in an entirely different light: Buchanan had promised they could vote on the adoption of a proposed constitution, accepting or rejecting any provisions which it contained on slavery; now they were told that they could not vote against the permanent enslavement of about 200 Blacks, the permanent presence of slavery in Kansas—they could vote only on whether more slaves might be brought to Kansas in the future.

Although Buchanan contended that the Lecompton plan fulfilled his promise and represented a true application of the principle of popular sovereignty, Governor Walker and Stephen A. Douglas insisted that the plan was a betrayal of and travesty on popular sovereignty. Buchanan tried to get Congress to approve it and admit Kansas as a state. Douglas fought like a tiger to defeat it, and the country was treated to the ironical spectacle of Douglas working in close alliance with antislavery Congressmen who had denounced him as a Judas when he was sponsoring the Kansas-Nebraska Act.

In many ways the situation was like the one four years earlier. Again, there was a spectacular parliamentary battle. Again, the Democratic party was torn apart. Again, the Administration exerted immense pressure to secure votes in a contest where only a few votes would separate victory from defeat. And again the suspense and drama gave to this marginal aspect of the slavery question an excitement which, unfortunately, the question itself did not command.

Defeat of the Lecompton Constitution and Its Significance. Finally, neither side could win a clear-cut victory. Congress neither accepted nor rejected the Lecompton Constitution, but introduced a new question, and on this question sent the Constitution back to Kansas to be voted on again. This new question was to reduce the unusually large amount of federally held land in Kansas which the Lecompton plan had provided should be given to the state. If the voters accepted it they got statehood, with continuing slavery for the resident slaves, exclusion for future slaves, and a reduction of the public land area of the state. If they rejected it they lost statehood and could not apply again until the territory attained a population of 90,000—which meant not again soon. Supporters of the Administration accepted this formula in the hope that Kansans would tolerate a small number of slaves rather than lose the advantages of statehood. But in August 1858, the Kansans defeated this modified form of the Lecompton plan by a vote of approximately 11,000 to 2000, and Kansas remained a territory until the Civil War.

Neither proslavery nor antislavery had won a decisive victory, but the Buchanan Administration had been ruined at its beginning by the Lecompton battle just as the Pierce Administration was ruined at its beginning by Kansas-Nebraska. Douglas did not have his railroad; Kansas did not have statehood; and the American public had spent four years watching with

The assault on Senator Sumner occurred the day after the attack on Lawrence, Kansas. *Frank Leslie's Illustrated Newspaper, June 7, 1856*

hypnotized fascination a battle which purported to be about slavery—yet which never really focused on the realities of slavery and did not prepare the public to grapple with these realities in a realistic way. The epic battle about Lecompton hinged on about 200 slaves in Kansas. There were many individual planters throughout the South who owned more than 200 slaves. And even the Free-Soil party in Kansas was as much anti-Negro as it was antislavery, for it had voted laws to prevent free Negroes from coming into the territory. But in spite of these anomalies, and in spite of the Kansans' reluctance to do real battle with one another, even while engaging in warlike gestures, the Kansas struggle had done more than anything else to embitter relations between the North and the South, and to prepare them both for a real war on a large stage over an issue still curiously undefined.

The Assault Against Senator Sumner. The nature of this bitterness had been dramatically illustrated in the summer of 1856 when Charles Sumner, Senator from Massachusetts, made a speech, "The crime against Kansas," in which he denounced slavery in rhetoric dripping with bitterness, and at the same time made some personally insulting remarks about the elderly Senator Andrew P. Butler of South Carolina. Under the southern code of honor a deliberate verbal insult of one gentleman by another called for physical retaliation, usually on the dueling ground. But Representative Preston Brooks, a cousin of Butler's, knowing that Sumner would refuse a challenge to duel, went to the Senate when it was not in session, found Sumner at his desk, and beat him severely with a cane, while he was still seated. The extent to which Sumner's injuries were physical, as against psychological, is still disputed, but he was certainly injured and did not return to full activity for over three years. Also, regardless of the injuries, it seemed the opposite of honorable to beat with a stick a defenseless, seated man. But Southerners praised and toasted Brooks and sent him souvenir canes, while Northerners concluded that southern honor was a fraud. Sumner's bitter words and Brooks' bitter deed made it easier for each section to form an ugly stereotype of the other. This was just one more aspect of the poison generated by Kansas-Nebraska.

The Consequence of Kansas-Nebraska: Political Polarization

The second disastrous consequence of Kansas-Nebraska was the effect which it had on the system of political parties in the United States. At the time of Pierce's election there were two parties, both of which might be called national, in the sense that each had a strong northern wing and a strong southern wing, each wing dependent on the other to give it strength. In presidential elections, the winner, whether Whig or Democrat, usually won both in the North and in the South. This situation had an immensely moderating influence on sectional extremism in either party, for each wing needed allies in the other section to win against adversaries in its own section who belonged to the opposite party. In 1852 this delicate sectional balance began to weaken, and with the Kansas-Nebraska Act it almost collapsed.

The Whigs and Immigration. The breakdown of the Whig party began visibly with the deep split in 1852 between the southern supporters of Fillmore and the northern supporters of Scott, who fought each other for forty-two ballots. The disastrous defeat of Scott, who carried only four states, caused northern Whigs to blame southern Whigs for saddling Scott with a platform which endorsed the compromise and thus made victory impossible in the North. Southern Whigs blamed northern Whigs for forcing the party to nominate Scott and then failing to carry any free states except Vermont and Massachusetts for him.

Further, the entire party was under a deep pall of gloom, because the stream of immigration was steadily increasing, and the mostly Irish Catholic immigrants affiliated overwhelmingly with the Democrats. Just why the Democratic party won the support of such a large proportion of the immigrants cannot be told with certainty. Probably, at the outset the Whigs, who were concentrated most heavily in New England, had a stronger Puritan tone than the Democrats. Puritanism was traditionally hostile to Catholicism; the Irish immigrants sensed this hostility among the Whigs and gravitated toward the Democrats. The Whigs, then, seeing that the immigrants were the allies of their political antagonists, began to demand laws unfavorable to immigrants, such as statutes requiring many years of residence before voting. The process then became cumulative: the more the immigrants became Democrats, the more the Whigs opposed them; and the more the Whigs opposed them, the more they became Democrats. By 1852 some Whigs had reached the conclusion that all Irishmen were Democrats, which was not far from the truth. This was a grim conclusion to reach because the stream of immigration was a flood in 1851.

As late as 1842, total immigration had never reached 100,000 in a single year, but in the late 1840's—the "hungry forties" as they have been called—Ireland experienced almost total failures of her potato crops, followed by acute famine and widespread starvation. Immense numbers emigrated—more to the United States than anywhere else. Three times in the four years between 1851 and 1855, total immigration to the United States exceeded 400,000. Later, in the decades around the turn of the century, the United States had considerably greater total immigration, but it never had so high a proportion of immigrants to the resident population, nor half so high a proportion from one country. In a decade when the population, excluding slaves, was 27 million, more than 1,200,000 immigrants arrived from Ireland. Total immigration in the four years preceding Winfield Scott's defeat in 1852 exceeded the total of Scott's popular vote.

After 1852 most Whigs felt that Whiggery was a losing proposition. Each sectional wing felt that its alliance with the other sectional wing—North or South as the case might be—cost more locally than it was worth nationally; and all recognized that continued immigration would be fatal to a party which failed to attract the immigrants and was rejected by them. Some wanted to fight the immigrants openly; some wanted to bail out of a party that had hopelessly antagonized them. All were ready for new allies. But they were still a bisectional party—Scott had carried 43 percent of the vote in the free states and 44 percent in the slave states. And they had no one to ally with. The victorious Democrats certainly wanted no affiliation with them.

Kansas-Nebraska offered the northern Whigs a way out, for it bitterly antagonized northern antislavery Democrats. The intensity of this opposition was shown by the losses sustained by northern Democrats because of Kansas-Nebraska, which the southern Democrats supported 57 to 2 in the House of Representatives. At the time of the vote northern Democrats held ninety-one seats; after the storm of opposition that swept the North in 1854, only twenty-five free state Democratic Congressmen survived after the November elections.

New Alignments. As the antislavery Democrats swarmed out of the Democratic party, the northern Whigs recognized the potential allies whom they so badly needed. But they knew the Whig label, already a liability, would be an obstacle to alliance. Hence they abandoned the Whig organization, and in the elections of 1854 and 1855, an astonishing array of new parties appeared, varying from state to state.

IMMIGRATION TO THE UNITED STATES

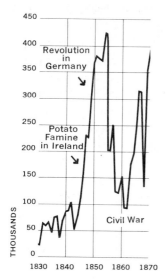

Irish immigrants often remained in seaboard cities as workers in the mushrooming factories. The Germans, more likely to settle in midwestern cities, were sometimes middle-class professionals. From many northern European countries came smaller numbers, generally young and single, but sometimes in religiously inclined family groups that settled into self-segregated communities.

Besides the old names, there were such new names as Anti-Nebraskaites, Peoples Party, Republican Party, Temperance Party, Rum Democrats, Hard Shell Democrats, Soft Shell Democrats, Half Shells, Know Nothings, and Know Somethings.

The Know Nothings and the Republicans. In all this medley, two focal points began to emerge. Antislavery sentiment began to concentrate in the Republican party; anti-immigrant sentiment concentrated in a nativist organization that was partly a political party and partly a secret society; the Order of the Star Spangled Banner, whose members were called Know Nothings, because they were pledged to say, "I know nothing," if questioned about the society's secrets.

If the Know Nothings had been strictly a political party they would, of course, have consistently competed with other parties, including the Republican, and every political candidate or officeholder could have been classified as a Republican, a Know Nothing, or as the member of some other party. But since the Know Nothings were partly a secret order, it was possible for a person to be both a Know Nothing and a Republican. Not only was it possible, but in the Congress elected in 1854, a majority of the free state members were both Know Nothings and Republicans. There were almost enough to form a majority of the House. On one flank were twenty-odd Know Nothings who were not Republicans, and on the other twenty-odd Republicans who were not Know Nothings.

Historians since then have not recognized this curious dualism, perhaps in part because it was a complex and unconventional situation, perhaps even more because the tradition of antislavery is an honored one and the tradition of nativism is despised. Historians have been at a loss to deal with a situation where men who opposed the oppression of Negroes at the same time were ready to discriminate against Catholics and immigrants. They have been reluctant to see that there was even a certain affinity between the psychology of many of the abolitionists and many of the nativists. Both had a paranoid tendency to suspect an evil conspiracy against the republic, by the "slave power," or by the popish church. In an age when sexual inhibition prevented the expression of a direct interest in sex, both abolitionists and Know Nothings rationalized that they were exposing "moral evil" to justify an indulgence in fantasies about the sexual depravities practiced by priests with nuns or by southern planters with beautiful quadroon slave girls. To recognize this fact is not to deny that there was certainly sex exploitation in slavery; it is only to say that the injustice of this exploitation was not the only reason why antislavery men took such an excited interest in it. At any rate, regardless of any psychological kinship between antislavery and nativism, or of the profound philosophical differences between them, the fact is that a great number of people were sympathetic both to antislavery and to a nativism which was directed especially against Irish Catholic immigrants. Nativism was so strong that many observers expected the Know Nothings rather than the Republicans to become the second party in the two-party system and to win the election of 1856.

The Republicans Win Out. The Republicans, of course, became the major party instead, and the Know Nothings faded away. The fact that the slavery question thus, in the long run, was uppermost, suggests that more people cared more deeply about it. But it must be added that in 1855 and 1856 the Republicans used some very adroit and even unethical tactics to gain the upper hand. First, in choosing a Speaker for the House of Representatives which was elected in 1854, they knew that they would have to accept someone who was both a Know Nothing and a Republican, as were a majority of the members, but they planned to bring about the election of a candidate whose nativism was secondary and whose commitment to antislavery was primary. For this purpose they chose Nathaniel P. Banks of Massachusetts. After inducing the Know Nothings to delay choosing a nominee for the Speakership, they moved to make Banks a nominee and manipulated the situation so that the candidate favored primarily by the Know Nothings was set aside. So, after a fierce struggle against the Democrats, Banks won the Speakership.

Later the Republicans completed their maneuver in the presidential campaign of 1856. They faced a dilemma because the Know Nothings had scheduled a nominating convention to precede the Republican convention. If the Know Nothings nominated first, the Republicans would either have to accept the Know Nothing nominee, which would make them appear disadvantageously to be junior partners in an alliance dominated by nativists, or they would have to choose a different nominee, which would split the anti-Democratic vote and almost assure a Democratic victory. They escaped this dilemma neatly by arranging for Banks to be nominated by the Know

Nothings, for him to double-cross them by delaying his acceptance until the Republicans had made a nomination, and then for him to decline the Know Nothing nomination. This would force the Know Nothings to accept the Republican nominee or to make another nomination which would split the anti-Democratic vote. In short, with Banks playing a double game, they turned the tables completely on the Know Nothings and chose John C. Frémont, who was not a Know Nothing at all but who was reluctantly accepted by a majority in the Know Nothing convention. Thus the Republicans went into the election with the advantage of receiving Know Nothing votes, but without the stigma of being a nativist party. The details of this maneuver may seem excessive in a general history such as this one, but in fact it was a critical transformation point in the history of American political parties. It meant that Republicans rather than Know Nothings replaced Whigs as the second major party in a two-party system which has never had more than a temporary place for third parties. It meant also that the Republican party received a nativist infusion which has continued to make itself felt for more than a century, for the Democratic party has consistently had a disproportionate share of supporters who were Catholic in religion and of immigrant stock, while the Republican party supporters have been disproportionately Protestant and of British stock. Yet the Republican party has avoided any explicit or complete identification with nativism.

The Election of 1856. In 1856 the Democrats nominated James Buchanan, with forty years of public service in the Cabinet, the Congress, and the diplomatic corps, to run against Frémont, with no public service except as an explorer of the Rocky Mountains and the Far West. The southern branch of the Know Nothing party nominated Millard Fillmore, and those who still clung to the Whig Party nominated Fillmore also.

The election almost resolved itself into two contests, with Buchanan running against Fillmore in the slave states and against Frémont in the free states. Buchanan won by carrying every slave state except Maryland (won by Fillmore) and five free states—Pennsylvania, New Jersey, Illinois, Indiana, and California. But Buchanan lost eleven free states to Frémont—all of the New England states, New York, Ohio, Michigan, Wisconsin, and Iowa.

What had happened was that, in place of two national political parties with bisectional wings and national strength, there were now two parties which were polarizing very heavily to become strictly sectional. The Democratic party drew two thirds of its strength from the slave states and in the House of Representatives, the southern Democrats usually outnumbered the northern Democrats by two to one (58 to 25 in 1854; 75 to 53 in 1856; and 68 to 34 in 1858). This meant that Southerners controlled the party caucus, the committee chairmanships, and the Congressional leadership. The Democratic party became and remained until Franklin Roosevelt's New Deal a southern party with a northern annex. Meanwhile, the Republican party became a northern party with no pretense of even an annex in the South. Frémont in 1856 and Lincoln in 1860 were not even on the ticket in most of the southern states and received few popular votes from that part of the Union. The Republicans went for decades with almost no strength in the South and did not win an electoral plurality there until Richard Nixon did so in 1968. After Kansas-Nebraska the major political parties were no longer a significant cohesive force with strong bisectional strength. It was only Buchanan's success in carrying five northern states which kept up the illusion that there was a national party, and that illusion evaporated in 1860.

The Dred Scott Case: Constitutional Polarization

The Popular Sovereignty Doctrine. By the end of 1856, the Missouri Compromise had been repealed, the strife in Kansas had set a pattern of armed conflict, and the two major political parties were heavily sectionalized. Moreover such events as the publication in 1852 of *Uncle Tom's Cabin,* the classic fictional indictment of slavery by Harriet Beecher Stowe; the assault upon Senator Sumner; and the activities of abolitionists in aiding fugitives and nullifying the Fugitive Slave Act all added to the hostile feelings between the sections. At this stage of acute sectional friction, much of the moderate ground had been eroded away, and perhaps the only remaining hope of sectional harmony was the "popular sovereignty" doctrine of Stephen A. Douglas. Popular sovereignty had failed in Kansas, but perhaps that was largely because one faction had been permitted to steal a territorial election. If popular sovereignty were honestly administered, Douglas contended, it would localize the slavery question, leave it to a democratic solution by those immediately involved, and get it out of Congress. As late as the inauguration of James Buchanan, this still seemed possible, though not likely.

Harriet Beecher Stowe's novel became an instant best seller. The Fugitive Slave Law inspired the thirty-nine-year-old mother of six in Maine. Though she had little experience of slaves or slavery, the melodramatic passion she conveyed further polarized the emotions of North and South. *Bella C. Landauer Collection, Courtesy of The New-York Historical Society*

Two days after Buchanan became President, however, the Supreme Court handed down a decision in the case of a slave, Dred Scott, which effectively killed the possibility of applying popular sovereignty in the territories, and thus eroded away almost all that was left of the ground on which moderates might make a stand.

Popular sovereignty, as Douglas interpreted it, meant the right of a territorial legislature to admit slavery to or exclude it from a territory. But, as previously mentioned, from the time when popular sovereignty was first proposed, southern leaders had denied that Congress possessed power under the Constitution, either to exclude slavery from a territory (as in the Missouri Compromise north of 36°30′) or to give to a territorial legislature, which was created by Act of Congress, power which Congress itself did not have. According to the southern argument, the territories belonged not to the United States as one sole owner but to all the states as joint owners, so a citizen of any state had the right to carry property which was legal within his own state (meaning slaves legally held as chattels in the slave states) into a territory. Any act which denied this right, so the southern argument ran, was unconstitutional. This argument is, to say the least, questionable, for the Constitution clearly states: "The Congress shall have power to dispose of and make all needful Rules and Regulations respecting the Territory or other Property belonging to the United States." This clause certainly lends itself to the interpretation that Congress might itself exercise power over slavery or might delegate such power to a territorial legislature. But since many Southerners denied this power, political leaders had been hoping ever since 1848 for a judicial decision to settle the question. Congress had even passed legislation which would make it easier to get a case before the courts, but this proved unexpectedly difficult. The courts could not decide until a concrete case arose, and no case came to them from among the few dozens of slaves who had been carried to New Mexico or Utah or Kansas.

The Supreme Court Ruling The case which finally enabled the Supreme Court to deal with the question concerned a slave, Dred Scott, who had been taken from the slave state of Missouri into the free territory of Minnesota more than twenty years earlier and then about two years later had been taken back to Missouri. Some eight years after his return to Missouri he brought a suit in the Missouri courts, claiming his freedom on the ground that his residence in Minnesota Territory had made him a free man, since the territory was part of the Louisiana Purchase north of 36°30′, from which Congress had barred slavery by the Missouri Compromise. The case moved through a contradictory series of rulings in the lower courts and was at last appealed to the Supreme Court, where it was argued twice. Finally, in March 1857, the Court handed down a ruling. All nine justices wrote opinions, and several points were left in confusion by this multiplicity of judgments.

One thing was clear: a majority of justices held that Scott was still a slave, but the ruling was badly confused by the curious relationship between two questions which the Court had before it: first, did the federal courts have jurisdiction—was this a case which properly came before the Supreme Court? And second, if they did have jurisdiction, how valid was Scott's claim that the Act of 1820 had made him a free man by making Minnesota a free territory? Superficially it would appear that the Court had no reason to consider the second question unless it decided affirmatively on the first. On the first question, Scott's lawyers argued that the case came before the federal courts because cases involving citizens of different states may be heard in the federal courts. Scott was from Missouri, and his owner at the time of the litigation lived in New York. Here was certainly a diversity of states, but it was not diversity of citizenship unless Scott was a citizen. Well, was Scott a citizen? The justices said he was not, *partly* (a) because a person could not acquire citizenship except by birth or by naturalization, and Scott, born a slave, had not acquired it in either way; and *partly* (b) because he was not even free—Congress had no constitutional power to exclude slavery from a territory. Minnesota Territory was therefore not a free territory, and no slave could acquire freedom by living there; if Scott was not free, he was certainly not a citizen and not in a position to claim diverse citizenship.

The Questions Before the Court. Now having decided that Scott was not a citizen and that jurisdiction was therefore lacking, the Court had no reason to rule on Scott's suit against the man who claimed to own him. But Chief Justice Roger B. Taney (pronounced Tawney) nevertheless went on to say that, even if Scott could bring his case, he still could not win his freedom because the Act of 1820, on which he relied for his freedom, was unconstitutional. In saying that his plea was not valid, the Court was answering a question which it had ruled that Scott had no standing to ask—a question which really did not arise. Such comments by courts on questions not legally before them are not law but are just comments made in passing (*obiter dicta* in the terminology of lawyers). Antislavery men, obsessively eager to avoid recognizing that the Supreme Court had voided the power of Congress to exclude slavery from the territories, hastened to proclaim that this part of the ruling was *dicta*—mere gossip from the bench. Ironically, they flared up with denunciations of the Court for deciding a question which, during the previous decade, they had denounced it for failing to decide. Very little attention was directed to the much stronger contention that the Court had interpreted the Constitution incorrectly and that Congress *did* have power over slavery in the territories. But critics were more eager to make a case that the decision was not legally binding than that it was wrong. Hence their focus on a denunciation of the decision as *obiter dicta.*

Many historians have accepted the angry claim that the decision was *dicta*, but the case was extremely intricate, and when all angles are taken into consideration, it appears that the decision was not *dicta*. After deciding that the Court lacked jurisdiction, it is true that the justices did not have to decide whether the Missouri Compromise had made Scott *free,* but in the process of deciding whether the Court had jurisdiction, the justices did have to decide whether the Missouri Compromise might have made him a *citizen* which was, of course, linked with the question whether it had made him free. Paradoxically, the decision that the law had not made him a citizen for purposes of jurisdiction obviated the necessity of saying whether the law had made him free for purposes of his suit. But the Court had answered the question to which the suit sought a reply in the very process by which it decided that Scott could not bring the suit which asked the question.

Effects of the Decision. If all of this seems—and indeed is—a form of incredible hairsplitting, the point historically is that the intricacies of the decision lent themselves to the accusation that the judges were guilty of what, in a later generation, has been called "judicial usurpation"—of going against legislative enactments and deciding a question that did not have to be decided. Republicans attacked the decision savagely on this ground and also with accusations that the Court was overloaded with slave-state justices (five to four), that there had been an improper understanding about the decision between President Buchanan and some of the majority justices (many years later this accusation was proved to be true), and that the decision was part of a wicked conspiracy to spread slavery nationwide. In any circumstances, no doubt, a decision which deprived Congress of power over slavery in the territories would have caused a great increase in sectional antagonisms, but in this case the antagonism was made much worse by the widespread belief that the Court had gone entirely outside the judicial orbit to make a proslavery decision.

Also, apart from these special circumstances which accentuated the disruptive effect, the decision vastly sharpened sectional divisions for it weakened center positions. It did not especially matter that the Missouri Compromise was declared unconstitutional, because it had already been repealed by the Kansas-Nebraska Act. But it mattered a great deal that Congress could not regulate, nor authorize a territorial legislature to regulate, slavery in the territories. This destroyed the basis for popular sovereignty, and once that basis was destroyed, the opposing parties took completely polarized positions—that slavery should extend into all territories, or that the Court's decision should be ignored and slavery should be kept out of all the territories. The Dred Scott decision polarized the American people constitutionally, just as the party transformations of 1854-1856 had polarized them in terms of political parties. They were soon to be polarized emotionally as well. This emotional polarization was produced largely by the attempt of John Brown to lead a slave insurrection and by his subsequent hanging.

John Brown's Role: Emotional Polarization

After the killings at Pottawattomie, John Brown remained in Kansas for four months as a minor guerilla leader in the antislavery forces, but he never received a post of any responsibility, partly because the antislavery people did not like what he had done, and they distrusted him as a trigger-happy, lone wolf who would get them all into trouble. As peace was restored in Kansas, Brown saw with increasing clarity that there was really no longer a place for him here. Having organized a small volunteer company of about two dozen young men, he conceived the idea of keeping this force together and using it as the nucleus for a small army that would march into Virginia and start a slave uprising, which might then spread throughout the entire South. To raise and equip such an army would require secrecy and also the raising of money, but these two were hard to reconcile, since no public appeals for funds could be made.

Northern Supporters. Brown's plan evolved gradually, and underwent some changes during its evolution, but by 1859 he had enlisted some support from a wealthy antislavery man, Gerrit Smith, in New York, and from six well-to-do and intellectually very prominent Bostonians, including Theodore Parker, one of the most outstanding clergymen and intellectuals in the United States, and Samuel Gridley Howe, famous for his work with the blind and other philanthropies. Various other prominent people, including Henry D. Thoreau, Bronson Alcott, and Ralph W. Emerson, had met Brown, who understood instinctively how to play the role of a romantic hero of the Border War in Kansas. They admired him immensely and understood vaguely that he was up to something, but they did not know exactly what and probably preferred not to know.

Despite the help of Gerrit Smith and the "Secret Six," Brown's organizational efforts really must be regarded as a failure, though not through any fault of his own. He never raised more than $30,000 at the most, which is nothing in terms of financing an army, and he also failed in his efforts to recruit Negro followers. In April 1858 he went to Chatham, Ontario, where there was a large colony of Negroes—almost all fugitive slaves—and there, with reckless lack of secrecy, he revealed his plan for an "army of the North" and for a provisional government with a president (Brown), a congress, and a supreme court. But the Negroes of Chatham, more realistic than the intelligentsia of Boston, perceived that there was something peculiar about this man, and they would not follow him. He had really already failed before he moved to his base, a farm in Maryland, with twenty-two followers—seventeen whites and five blacks. Frederick Douglass, the most prominent and ablest Negro in the country, had refused to join him.

Harper's Ferry. After waiting in vain for three and a half months on the Maryland farm, hoping for money and recruits, Brown at last moved with his tiny force, on the night of October 16, 1859, to occupy the town of Harper's Ferry, Virginia. In many respects the operation was fantastically badly planned: Brown's men took no food with them, and they were hungry by the next morning; their objective, Harper's Ferry, was located at the convergence of the Shenandoah and the Potomac rivers, with high hills back of the town, and it formed a natural trap from which escape was almost impossible; Brown planned to seize a federal arsenal, which would bring the United States Army instantly into the picture; the area had a low proportion of slaves in its population; and because Brown feared betrayal, not one of the slaves had been informed that they were expected to join in an uprising. The whole idea of conquering the state of Virginia was so bizarre that it has led to the subsequent belief that Brown was insane. Yet it must be observed that his belief that the slaves were ready for instant revolt—that, as he expressed it, the "bees would swarm" as soon as he struck—was commonly believed in the North and commonly feared in the South. It is true that Brown was a strange sort of man—a loner, grim, rigid, preoccupied, obsessed with one idea, and given to alternations of inactivity and bursts of energy. It is also true that he combined rigorously high personal ideals with a record of financial irresponsibility which raises some questions, as does the sadism of the killings at Pottawattomie. Still, his "maddest" idea was one which he shared with countless antislavery men, including the best minds in Boston. The only difference was that he acted on the idea.

The complete surprise with which Brown struck enabled him easily to occupy Harper's Ferry and to seize the federal armory, with enough guns to equip a whole army of slaves. But no slaves came in—the bees did not swarm. Instead, local militia and federal troops converged on Harper's Ferry the next day and drove Brown's small force, with heavy losses, into an engine house which was part of the armory. On the second morning an assault party stormed the engine house and captured what was left of Brown's force. Brown himself was wounded in the final assault. Of his entire force, five had escaped the previous day, ten, including two of Brown's sons, were dead or dying, and seven were captured and later hanged by the state of Virginia.

The Aftermath. If Brown himself had been killed, the whole affair might have been dismissed by the public as the crazy act of a mere desperado. But in his hour of failure—wounded, imprisoned, and on trial for his life—Brown surpassed himself, behaving with a dignity, composure, bravery, and faith in the rightness of his deed which won the admiration even of the Virginians. Gerrit Smith might seek refuge in an insane asylum and Samuel Gridley Howe might flee to Canada, but Brown himself did not flinch. He had failed many of the tests of life, and he knew he was about to face the grimmest test of all. But he also knew that this was one which he could successfully pass. He was stating a plan of action when he said "I am worth now infinitely more to die than to live."

Brown was put on trial while still suffering from his wounds. The trial lasted a week, and he was sentenced to death. During the trial he conducted himself with complete calmness and self-possession, and when sentenced he delivered a brief statement which stands as a classic. Expressing satisfaction with the fairness of his trial, he also said, "I feel no consciousness of guilt. . . . Now if it is deemed necessary that I should forfeit my life for the furtherance of the ends of justice and mingle my blood . . . with the blood of millions in this slave country whose rights are disregarded by wicked, cruel, and unjust enactments, I say let it be done."

It was done, after a delay mercifully much briefer than the delays which have awaited condemned men in the late twentieth century. On December 2, 1859, John Brown was hanged in the presence of a large force of troops at Charlestown, Virginia (now West Virginia). Outwardly, and perhaps inwardly, he was the calmest man at the hanging.

Elsewhere there was not much calm. Brown's raid had touched the slave South on the exposed nerve of its fear of slave insurrection. Worse still, the activities of the "Secret Six," and the unrestrained expressions of sympathy for Brown throughout the North (church bells tolling, Emerson writing that Brown had "made the gallows glorious like the cross") convinced many Southerners that they were in a Union with fellow citizens who would rejoice to see them slain in a bloody insurrection of slaves. They knew of a good many statements by Northerners like Congressman Joshua Giddings of Ohio who said that he looked forward to the day "when the torch of the incendiary shall light up the towns and cities of the South and blot out the last vestiges of slavery," and they did not usually pause to ask how typical Giddings might be. In the North, on the other hand, the hanging of Brown seemed an unspeakable atrocity. He had been put to death because he alone was willing to do more than just talk about the oppression of slaves. The society which could take his life was a brutal blot on American civilization. In short, Brown was a martyr. To the extent that these feelings prevailed in the South and in the North, respectively, the emotional polarization of the sections was complete.

On the day John Brown was hanged, the first of the nominating conventions for the presidential election of 1860 was little more than four months away.

The 1860 Election

Party Alignments. As the 1860 campaign for the presidency opened, party alignments remained about as they had been in 1856. The old Whigs still had substantial strength in the border states and hoped to become a moderate center against the southern sectionalism of the Democratic party and the northern sectionalism of the Republican party. One of their leaders, Senator John J. Crittenden of Kentucky, had sought to revitalize them in a new organization, to be called the Constitutional Union party, where Whigs, Know Nothings, and, hopefully, moderate Republicans and moderate Democrats could meet on neutral ground. In December 1859, Crittenden and fifty other prominent men, mostly former Whigs, called for a convention of this party to meet in the following May.

The Republicans in 1860 had spent four years consolidating the organization which had been so new and so seriously jeopardized by its involvement with Know Nothingism in 1856; they were buoyed by the awareness that if they could hold the states which they had won in 1856 and carry three of the five free states previously won by Buchanan, they could win the election.

The Democrats held one great potential advantage: they were the only remaining party which could claim to be a national, bisectional party, and with fears of disunion becoming very widespread, this claim might have become a major asset. But they could not capitalize on it, because their Democratic party was itself profoundly divided. The bitter conflict over the Lecompton Constitution, in which Douglas and Buchanan fought each other with every weapon, was the foremost cause of this division, but Buchanan's whole policy as President had antagonized northern Democrats. Personally susceptible to southern influence, Buchanan had vetoed a tariff bill, a land grant college bill, and a homestead bill, all supported by northern Democrats and opposed by the southern elements in the party. The effect was to further weaken the Democratic party in the North and leave northern Democrats acutely conscious that they must throw off southern domination if they were to keep the party alive in their own states.

The Democratic Party Convention. Against this background, the Democratic convention met (as if planned by a spiteful fate) in the stronghold of nullification, Charleston, South Carolina, in late April. In the party convention the northern states still held a majority, which they no longer had in the party's Congressional representation; in the convention, if nowhere else, the Democratic party was still a national party. Douglas, once the darling of the South because of Kansas-Nebraska, was now hated there both because of his fight against the Lecompton Constitution and because he refused freely to accept the Dred Scott decision and insisted that a territorial legislature could still keep slavery out of a territory simply by abstaining from the passage of any laws to enforce a slave system. In this political reversal he had again become the champion of the northern Democrats and was clearly the most impressive figure in the Democratic party. With their convention majority, the northern Democrats confidently expected to nominate him. It was true that they did not have the two-thirds majority required by the Democratic party rules, but usually, when a candidate had a majority, his opponents conceded the nomination. Douglas had done so to Buchanan in 1856.

The Democratic Party Splits. In relying on this practice, the northern Democrats failed to recognize the depth of southern bitterness. As the convention proceeded, bitter sectional hostility was expressed in the speeches. The northern delegates were reluctantly willing to leave out of a platform any disavowal of the Dred Scott decision, but they were immovably opposed to adopting a platform which explicitly accepted the Dred Scott ruling and sanctioned slavery in all territories. When they voted down such a platform, the delegations of seven states from the deep South (all except Georgia) walked out of the convention. This act may have been intended as a maneuver to put pressure on the party, and for months frantic efforts were made to heal the breach. Such efforts were in vain. Sectionalism had destroyed the only remaining national party and by doing so it threatened the national union.

This Currier and Ives lithograph satirizes the split of the Democratic Party in 1860. *The Harry T. Peters Collection, Museum of the City of New York*

The remaining delegates stayed in session, balloted, and secured for Douglas a majority of the total votes (including those who had withdrawn) but they could not attain two thirds of the total, so finally they adjourned to meet later at Baltimore. The delegations which had walked out called another convention to meet at Richmond. At these meetings, further desperate efforts were made to reunite the party, but they failed. In the end the Baltimore convention nominated Douglas and the Richmond convention nominated the Vice-President, John C. Breckenridge of Kentucky. The last national party was now divided.

The Constitutional Union Party Convention. One week after the Charleston convention voted to adjourn, the convention of the Constitutional Union party met in Baltimore, with delegates from only twelve of the fifteen slave states, and eleven of the eighteen free states, but with all large states represented. This convention nominated John Bell of Tennessee for President and Edward Everett for Vice-President. Instead of a platform it adopted with unanimity a statement pledging support to "the Constitution as it is, and the Union under it, now and forever. . . ."

The Republican Party Convention. Exactly one week after that, the Republican convention met in Chicago. Most of the delegates thought they were meeting to nominate Senator William H. Seward of New York who was clearly the leader of the party. But some elements had a grudge against Seward and the more sagacious party leaders recognized that he had certain liabilities: (1) the Know Nothings hated him because he had been friendly to state support for Catholic parochial schools in New York; (2) he was identified with a strong antislavery position, largely because of two phrases that he had coined—"a higher law than the Constitution" and "irrepressible conflict"; and (3) his major appeal would not be to conservative states like Pennsylvania and Indiana which the Democrats had won in 1856 and which were precisely the ones the Republicans needed to concentrate on in order to win in 1860. Also, Horace Greeley, the powerful editor of the New York *Tribune*, who was publicly allied with Seward but privately held a personal grudge against him, was busily circulating the opinion that Seward could not win the election if he were nominated.

With the Democrats divided, the Republican managers perceived that they could certainly win if they avoided mistakes, and they made none. Broadening the party's policies to get away from a strictly antislavery position, they put planks into the platform for a protective tariff, a homestead act (160 free acres for anyone who would build a cabin and live on them), and a transcontinental railroad. Then, in the balloting they stopped Seward short of a majority, gradually wore him down, and on the third ballot nominated Abraham Lincoln of Illinois. Since Lincoln was an ex-Whig, they nominated an ex-Democrat, Hannibal Hamlin of Maine, for Vice-President.

The Campaign and Election Results. Although there were four candidates running for President, it was not really a four-cornered race, but rather a contest between Lincoln and Douglas in the North, and between Bell and Breckenridge in the South. Lincoln's campaign stressed the issue of what would today be called the "containment" of slavery—it must not be extended beyond its existing limits—while Douglas stressed the danger of disunion and argued that the territorial issue was unrealistic because there was no economic basis for slavery to flourish in the territories in any case. In the South, Bell stressed the Union, as Douglas was doing in the North, while Breckenridge, although not yet a secessionist, stressed "southern rights" as defined by the Dred Scott decision.

PRESIDENTIAL ELECTION: 1860

		Electoral Vote	Popular Vote
REPUBLICAN	Abraham Lincoln	180	1,865,593
DEMOCRATIC, SOUTHERN	John C. Breckinridge	72	848,356
DEMOCRATIC, NORTHERN	Stephen A. Douglas	12	1,382,713
CONSTITUTIONAL UNION	John Bell	39	592,906

On November 6, the dualism of the races in the two sections showed up very clearly. In the slave states, Bell and Breckenridge between them received 85 percent of the vote; in the free states, Lincoln and Douglas between them received 86 percent of the vote. This vote divided at 511,000 for Breckenridge and 500,000 for Bell in the slave states, but Bell was unlucky in the distribution of the vote and he carried only Virginia, Kentucky, and Tennessee. Douglas concentrated one third of his entire slave state vote in Missouri, and carried the state—it was the only state which he won clearly. Breckenridge carried the remaining eleven slave states.

In the country as a whole, Lincoln received only 39 percent of the popular vote—the smallest percentage with which any man has ever been elected to the presidency. This fact has led to a widespread belief that Lincoln won only because his opponents were divided. But in a statistical sense, at least, this is not true. He won because his vote was distributed in such a way as to pay off in electoral votes. With barely more than 1 percent of his vote in the fifteen slave states, and almost 99 percent of it concentrated in the eighteen free states, he carried all of the free states except New Jersey. In fifteen states, with a majority of electoral votes, he won more than 50 percent of the vote, and only in Oregon and California did his opponents have a vote which, if combined, would have been greater than his. Thus, the nominee of a party which had not existed seven years previously became President-elect of the United States.

The South Reacts: Secession

It is one of the ironies of history that Lincoln's reputation as an antislavery leader has undergone great changes over the last hundred years, and militant Negro leaders in the 1960's frequently denounced him as a "honky" or a racist. The actual complexities of his position on slavery and the status of Negroes will be discussed in the next chapter, but here it is only necessary to realize that in the South in 1860, Lincoln was regarded as a flaming, incendiary abolitionist. He had actually made many cautionary and conservative statements about the constitutional obligation of the free states to respect the legal rights of the slave states and even to enforce the fugitive slave law. The evidence is overwhelming that he planned no direct assault on slavery. But in the South all this was disregarded. Instead it was noted that Lincoln was receiving enthusiastic abolitionist support, and also that he had said that in 1858 a house divided against itself cannot stand, that the Union must become all slave or all free, and that slavery must be placed "in the course of ultimate extinction." The President-elect had not even been on the ticket in ten of the slave states; the South still had freshly in mind the widespread northern approval of John Brown; and certain questions inevitably arose. Was the Union really a union in any way except legally? Did North and South share any fellow-feeling for one another? And, if they did not, why should the South stay in the Union? Indeed, was it safe for the South to stay in the Union?

Southerners had argued for more than a generation that the Union was originally an association of sovereign states, each of which had joined the association by ratifying the Constitution and each of which was entitled to withdraw from the association by repealing the act of ratification. The original Union, they contended, had been subverted and a "consolidated nation" was being put in its place. Logically their argument was not bad and their observation of what was happening to the American union was realistic—a consolidated nation was indeed replacing a federation of states. But they were unrealistic, it would seem, in failing to realize that nations are created not by written agreements and legal contracts but by organic growth. The railroad network, the communications network, the network of internal trade, the financial network—all undreamed of in 1787—had changed the nature of the cohesion of the Union, and no resolutions passed by legislative bodies could undo this fact.

The Outlook of the South in 1860. But the United States was still an extremely decentralized country compared with what it has become since then. Rural districts still perceived the federal power as a remote and relatively marginal feature in their political life, and this was true most of all in the South. Spokesmen for "southern rights" had been warning for more than ten years that the North was becoming abolitionized, that it threatened the system of slavery, which was not merely a labor system of concern to slaveholders but also a social system basic to the whole southern pattern of life, and therefore of concern to nonslaveholders also. The plantation society, the cotton-planting society, the rural life and bountiful hospitality, the "idyllic relation" between a master who bore the responsibility and his "people" who gave their loyalty, the absence of commercialization (which means impersonal relationships and exploitation of "wage slaves")—all these southern values were said to be threatened. The North had begun in 1846 by cheating Southerners of their rights in territories which the South had done more than its share to win. By 1857 the North was refusing to obey a Supreme Court decision; by 1859 it was applauding an attempted slave uprising; by 1860 it was electing a strictly sectional President who said that slavery would, after a while, be eliminated. The South must defend itself, said these political prophets, now or never.

These warnings fell on the ears of a people who were growing increasingly aware that the balance of power was tipping against them. In 1790 half the people of the United States had lived in the South, and the slave states had outnumbered the free states (including New York and New Jersey) eight to five. But by 1860 the North had nineteen million people to the South's twelve million, and almost nineteen million white people to the South's eight million. There were eighteen free states and fifteen slave states, with several territories about ready to be added to the free state list but not one to the slave states. In the House of Representatives, the North had 163 members and the South had 85, where the ratio had originally been 35 to 30. The weakness of the South in the electoral college had just been strikingly illustrated by the selection of a man who was not even on the ballot in most southern states. These discrepancies were reflected in comparable imbalances in financial capital, railroad mileage, economic productivity, and other measures of physical growth and strength.

This was the situation within the United States. On the world scene, Britain had abolished slavery in her colonies in 1833, France in 1848. The only remaining strongholds of chattel slavery in the western world (Asiatic slavery was not truly comparable) were Cuba, Brazil, and the southern states of the United States.

The sense of a need for defensive action was urgent, and it arose in a society where the tradition of chivalry and the code of honor predisposed people to impulsive and even violent action. Some Southerners, such as Edmund Ruffin of Virginia, Robert Barnwell Rhett of South Carolina, and William L. Yancey of Alabama had been hoping for secession and talking about it for a long time—so long that many Northerners had ceased to pay any attention to them. A few of these southern fire-eaters had even welcomed the split in the Democratic Party because it might bring on a crisis.

Secession Begins. In the winter preceding the presidential election, the Alabama legislature had authorized the governor to call an election for a state convention if a "black" Republican should be chosen President. Lincoln was elected on November 6. Within five weeks after his election, seven legislatures in the states of the lower South had passed acts calling for elections to be held and for conventions to meet to consider the question of secession. Within another eight weeks events moved with incredible rapidity: (1) five state legislatures in states of the upper South also passed acts providing for elections either to hold state conventions or to decide whether they should be held; (2) seven states, beginning with South Carolina, and followed in order by Mississippi, Florida, Alabama, Georgia, Louisiana, and Texas, had adopted ordinances declaring that they were independent, no longer members of the American Union; and (3) six of these states had assembled at Montgomery, Alabama, on February 4 to begin the work of forming a new southern republic, the Confederate States of America. By February 8, they had completed a provisional constitution, and by February 22, they had chosen Jefferson Davis of Mississippi as President of the Provisional Government and had inaugurated him. It was still ten days before Abraham Lincoln would be sworn in. But, while the Confederates had moved with extraordinary promptness to set up a government, they had failed to use this time, which was very precious, to ship cotton abroad and to take other steps to give strength to the government-on-paper over which they were laboring so fondly.

Northern Response: The Crittenden Compromise. Meanwhile, the Buchanan administration marked time and the North waited through an agonizing interregnum of four months between Lincoln's election and his inauguration.*

---

*The interval between election and inauguration was not reduced to its present length until 1933.

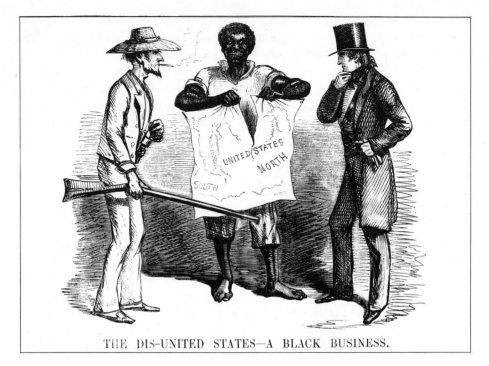

THE DIS-UNITED STATES—A BLACK BUSINESS.

Punch, November 8, 1856

Congress met early in December but it was the outgoing lame duck Congress. Without leadership from either Buchanan or Lincoln, it proved unable to take any positive steps. The northern public, which had grown accustomed to occasional threats of secession from the South, was slow to realize that the crisis had come at last. When they did realize, there was a hasty scramble by northern Democrats, border state Unionists, moderate Republicans, frightened Republicans, merchants and financiers with a stake in the cotton economy, and genuine devotees of the cause of Union, to work out some sort of compromise. The most important of these compromise efforts was a proposal by John J. Crittenden, the venerable Senator from Kentucky, trying to play in 1861 the role which Clay of Kentucky had played in 1850—a proposal for a constitutional amendment to revive the old Missouri Compromise line of 36°30′, extend it to the Pacific, and apply it to all future territory. This amendment should never be subject to future amendment; further, no future amendment should ever give Congress power to encroach upon slavery in the states.

Opinions differ about whether the compromise ought to have been adopted. Some historians believe that slavery could not have taken root in the southwest in any case, and that a restoration of the Missouri line would have been an inexpensive gesture if it could have prevented a war fearfully expensive in human lives. Others think Lincoln was right in fearing such an arrangement would open up the demand for new annexations south of 36°30′ as slave territories. Perhaps almost everyone will agree that the unrepealable guarantee on slavery for all future time was more serious. As it was drawn and stands today, the Constitution has only one clause which cannot be amended, namely the guarantee to the states of equal representation in the Senate. A guarantee to slavery in perpetuity would really have changed the course of history. Yet, although Lincoln never did accept the 36°30′ proposal, by March he had come around to accepting a permanent guarantee against federal interference with slavery in the states.

Many Republicans wanted to support the Crittenden Plan and there is strong evidence that a majority of the American people wanted to accept it or would have accepted it. But Lincoln quietly passed the word that it must be defeated. In December Republican members prevented its approval in committee, and in January an attempt to get it to the floor of the Senate was defeated 25 to 23, with all twenty-five of the negative votes cast by Republicans. It seems valid to believe that the South would have accepted the compromise if it had been offered. This would mean that the Republicans were responsible for the defeat of the compromise, and insofar as compromise was the alternative to war, Lincoln and his party might be charged with the responsibility for the war. On the other hand, no compromise could have healed the deep sectional disagreements about slavery; it could only have prevented an immediate collision, perhaps leaving another crisis to arise later, just as the crisis of 1861 had arisen a decade after the 1850 compromise. Also, as Lincoln thought, there was something self-defeating about making concessions to secessionists, for concessions strengthened them at the expense of the southern Unionists whom Lincoln really wanted to strengthen. Even with the perspective of more than a century, all we can say is that a compromise would have averted an immediate crisis, at the cost of very serious concessions on slavery, and would have left a deep disagreement about slavery and a strong likelihood of another crisis later on. Averting an immediate crisis is usually worth something, especially to the party which is gaining in relative strength, and the question was whether the rather precarious peace which would have been gained was worth the concessions of the Crittenden Compromise. Lincoln did not think so in December, but by March, after seven states had seceded and the Confederacy had been formed, he was ready to agree to what now seems a far more important concession—namely a constitutional amendment guaranteeing slavery against federal regulation, and not subject to alteration by any future amendment.

The Confederacy's Success Uncertain. For three months after Lincoln's election, with the prospects of compromise steadily diminishing, it appeared that the only alternatives left would be either a dissolution of the Union or war. During those months the secessionists enjoyed an unbroken series of successes, with secession adopted in seven states and rejected in none, and with acts passed in five more states and defeated in only one, calling for an election of a state convention to consider secession. But on February 4, the day when the Confederate Provisional Congress assembled at Montgomery, the tide turned and the movement for a united South ran into trouble. On that day, Virginia elected delegates to a state convention in which the opponents of secession won a clear majority. On February 9 Tennessee held an election to decide whether there should be a state convention, and voted against it. On February 18 Arkansas and Missouri both elected delegates to state conventions in both of which the nonsecessionists won by large majorities. Finally, on February 28, North Carolina elected delegates to a convention but voted that the convention should not meet. In little more than three weeks five slave states had rejected secession, confining the Confederacy to the lower South. A majority of the fifteen slave states refused to break with the Union. The South was divided as never before, and it appeared that the secession fever might have run its course when Lincoln was at last inaugurated on March 4, 1861. To the new President, who had never quite believed that the secessionists were in earnest, it now appeared possible that no choice would have to be made between coercion, separation, or compromise, but that Unionists in the lower South might gain the upper hand and bring their states voluntarily back into the Union once it became evident that the movement for a united South had failed. In his thinking on this situation, Lincoln probably failed to realize that most of the southern Unionists, unlike those of Illinois, were not unqualified Unionists, but were men who preferred to stay in the Union if they could receive assurances about southern rights.

A New President Takes Over

Lincoln faced a complicated situation on March 4. All during the preceding winter, as the states of the lower South seceded, federal judges, marshals, and postmasters in the seceding states had resigned; further, the secessionist governments had moved at once to take possession of federal property—courthouses, customs houses, post offices, and even forts and arsenals within their borders. The Buchanan administration did not resist this process so by March 4 federal authority had virtually disappeared throughout the lower South. Except for two forts far out beyond the Florida Keys, only two places from North Carolina to the Mexican border flew the American flag. Both were federal forts located offshore—Fort Sumter in Charleston Harbor and Fort Pickens in Pensacola Harbor. The evidence is clear that Lincoln thought that these fortifications were well supplied with food and that he could hold them as symbols of federal authority without taking any positive action which might precipitate a showdown. This would give him opportunity to affirm the indestructibility of the Union without inflaming the Southerners by resort to any act of force. With such a "cooling-off period," as it would now be called, the southern Unionists, who had already turned back the tide of secession throughout the upper South, might then rally in the lower South and bring all the states peaceably back to the Union.

Lincoln's Inaugural Address. Lincoln's inaugural address was framed in a way entirely consistent with such a policy. He declared clearly that no state could secede and that, "in view of the Constitution and the laws, the Union is unbroken." But instead of taking immediate issue with the secessionists he avoided any. Where federal officials had resigned and local appointees could not be found to replace them, he said, "There will be no attempt to force obnoxious strangers among the people"; the mails would continue to be delivered, "unless repelled"; as for the federal property which had been seized, Lincoln first wrote that he would "reclaim the public property," but he struck this out of the inaugural before delivering it. In addition to avoiding any direct issue, Lincoln made an eloquent and moving appeal to the Unionist sentiment of the South, announcing his willingness to accept a constitutional amendment, which the outgoing Congress had voted in its last hours to submit to the states for ratification. This amendment, which would not be subject to repeal, guaranteed slavery in the states where it existed against any future interference by the federal government. This was by far the greatest concession Lincoln ever made on slavery; he probably would not have made it if he had not felt extreme distress about the danger to the Union, and the South, no doubt, made its most serious tactical error in refusing to accept it. If the northern states had ratified, the South would have received a stupendous concession; if they had failed to ratify, the North would have been left divided.

The evidence is strong that Lincoln intended to try a policy of "masterly inactivity" to bring the seceding states back voluntarily, but on the day after his inauguration he was informed that Fort Sumter was being starved out and would have to surrender within four weeks if food was not received. This meant that the fort could not be held passively as a symbol of Union after all. It would have to be surrendered—a triumph for the secessionists—or the federal authority would have to take the initiative of sending supplies of food to save it.

Fort Sumter. Lincoln was desperately unwilling to follow either course. According to his own account, he tried to throw reinforcements into Fort Pickens, which could have been done without a military confrontation. If this had been done, perhaps he could have made Fort Pickens instead of Fort Sumter his symbol of Union and could have afforded to give up Fort Sumter. On March 11 Lincoln issued written orders to send troops into Fort Pickens, but the orders were sent by ship, which was not as fast as overland, and when they arrived a conflict between Army and Navy commands prevented their execution. After agonizing delay, Lincoln learned on April 6 that his orders had not been executed. It now seemed too late to be sure of saving Fort Pickens before the hour of decision at Fort Sumter, and on the same day Lincoln sent a message to the governor of South Carolina saying that food was being sent to Fort Sumter. If the delivery of this food was permitted, no attempt would be made to reinforce the fort. But the Confederate forces at Charleston felt that they could not tolerate an indefinite federal occupation of a fort located in what they regarded as Confederate territory, and on April 12, 1861, the Confederates began a bombardment which forced Fort Sumter to surrender about 34 hours later. The Civil War had begun.

Historians have disagreed both as to what Lincoln was trying to do and whether he ought to have been doing what they think he was trying to do in the final weeks before Fort Sumter. Some writers have held that he wanted to start a war, but craftily maneuvered to create a situation in which the Confederates would shoot first, and therefore be blamed for starting the war. Others have argued that he reluctantly began to recognize more and more clearly that war could not be prevented, if the Union were to be saved, and to believe that a situation must be created in which the inevitable war would be started by the Confederates and not by the Unionists. Still others, including the author of this chapter, believe that Lincoln did all that he could do to avoid a war, short of sacrificing the Union, and that whether he was optimistic or pessimistic about his chance of succeeding is beside the point. It is fair to ask what he could have done, more than he did, consistently with a policy of union, to avert war.

The Basic Issues Confounded. Like most wars, the American Civil War came about in a somewhat irrational fashion. For four decades North and South had been increasingly antagonized by the slavery question, and especially by the question of the extension of slavery. But on the slavery issue, the North itself was bitterly divided. While few Northerners really approved of slavery, even fewer apparently approved of Negro equality. If the North was antislavery, it was also to a great extent anti-Negro. If the South had held strictly to the slavery issue, the North would have been hopelessly divided in any confrontation with the South.

But the South inadvertently changed the issue from the question of slavery to the question of union. Abruptly, the southern acts of secession pushed the slavery question into the background and placed a focus upon the survival of the republic. To vast numbers of Northerners, the support of slavery was wrong, but the support of secession was treason. Therefore, a quarrel over slavery, on which the North was divided, suddenly became converted into a quarrel over the Union, on which the North was united—a war in which it was not even clear that slavery was an issue.

Thus, in 1861 the American people stood on the eve of paying a great price for the solution of a problem which they had never clearly defined and which they could hardly expect to solve without defining it, no matter how great a price they paid. The problem concerned the relations of blacks and whites in the United States. But first, people had seen it too restrictively in terms of chattel servitude rather than of racial subordination, which would perpetuate the problem after chattel servitude was gone. Then further, they had seen it restrictively in terms of constitutional questions about slaves in the territories, placing so much emphasis upon this aspect at the expense of slavery in the states that Lincoln was willing to guarantee the servitude of four million slaves in the states as late as March 1861, but was adamant on the question of slavery in the territories, where there were no slaves. Finally, at the moment when historical forces brought the country to a point where one great era in the relations of the races must end and another era must begin, the surface events diverted the attention of most Americans and caused them to think that the problem was one of union and not of the relations of the races at all.

Even the South agreed in attaching high value to the Union. This is shown by the readiness with which the South came back to the Union after the war. But to say this is to say that North and South were about to fight the world's deadliest war between the Napoleonic Wars and World War I, without perceiving that the ostensible issue over which they fought—the issue of union—was one on which they did not basically disagree. Yet the root cause of the conflict—the issue of race relations—was so poorly perceived that they did not recognize the extent of either their agreement or disagreement, or the relation of the issue to the war which it had precipitated.

SUGGESTED READING (Prepared by Carl N. Degler)

The literature on the coming of the Civil War is enormous. The most convenient entrance to the vast literature as well as being a good summary of that literature is James G. Randall and David Donald, *The Civil War and Reconstruction* (2nd ed., 1961). A more recent bibliography, but unannotated is Don E. Fehrenbacher, comp., *Manifest Destiny and the Coming of the Civil War** (1970). Thomas J. Pressly, *Americans Interpret Their Civil War** (1954) places the shifting historical interpretations of the coming of the war into perspective. Influential in seeing the war as a needless one is Avery Craven, *The Coming of the Civil War** (1942). The fullest narrative history of the prewar years as well as one that emphasizes the role of slavery in its causation is Allan Nevins, *Ordeal of the Union, 1847–1861* (4 vols., 1947–50). A striking interpretation of the meaning of the war by a sociologist and a quasi-Marxist is provided in chapter III of Barrington Moore, Jr., *Social Origins of Dictatorship and Democracy** (1966). Several essays in David M. Potter, *The South and the Sectional Conflict* (1968) offer incisive interpretations of events leading to the war as well as broad historiographical analyses. Arthur Bestor, "The American Civil War as a Constitutional Crisis," *American Historical Review*, XLIV (1964): 327–352 elucidates the meaning of the constitutional issues. Several knowing students of the coming of secession explore the issues in George H. Knoles, ed., *The Crisis of the Union, 1860–61* (1965). Comments at the time are conveniently collected and edited in Kenneth M. Stampp, ed., *The Causes of the Civil War** (1959).

Eric Foner, *Free Soil, Free Labor, Free Men* (1970) is an important new study of the ideology of the Republican party. Michael F. Holt, *Forging a Majority* (1969) is also new and important in delineating the forces creating the Republican party in Pittsburgh. W. Darrell Overdyke, *The Know-Nothing Party in the South* (1950) should be read in conjunction with Arthur Cole, *The Whig Party of the South* (1913). Reinhard H. Luthin, *The First Lincoln Campaign* (1944) is somewhat outdated, but still useful. It is the best general treatment. Except for Nevins' volumes, Roy F. Nichols, *The Disruption of American Democracy** (1948) is the fullest and most thorough analysis of the breakup of the Democratic party during the 1850's. More ideological and polemical is Harry V. Jaffa, *Crisis of the House Divided: An Interpretation of the Issues in the Lincoln-Douglas Debates* (1959). Don E. Fehrenbacher, *Prelude to Greatness: Lincoln in the 1850's** (1962) throws important new light on those same debates. The best study of the controversial John Brown and his curious raid at Harper's Ferry is Stephen Oates, *To Purge This Land with Blood* (1970).

The actual secession movement has been studied in great detail. An old but still useful general study is Dwight Dumond, *The Secession Movement, 1860–1861* (1931) though there is at least one book on the secession of each southern state. David M. Potter, *Lincoln and His Party in the Secession Crisis** (1942) is broader than the title suggests. Less interpretive, but filled with information not obtainable elsewhere is Ralph A. Wooster, *The Secession Conventions of the South* (1962), which examines the background of the men who took the southern states out of the Union. A fine interpretation of the role of Lincoln in precipitating war is Richard N. Current, *Lincoln and the First Shot** (1963).

Noteworthy among the biographies of the leading statesmen is Gerald M. Capers, *Stephen A. Douglas, Defender of the Union* (1959) and Benjamin Thomas, *Abraham Lincoln: A Biography* (1952), the best single-volume life of the President. David Donald, *Charles Sumner and the Coming of the Civil War* (1960) is certainly the best biography of that controversial leader. Hudson Strode, *Jefferson Davis, American Patriot, 1808–1861* (1965) lacks perspective and critical bite, but it is the most recent and fullest study of Davis.

*Available in a paperback edition.

Above: Landing From an Emigrant Ship. *Gleason's Pictorial Drawing Room Companion, Volume 1, June 14, 1851*
Right: Lure of America. *Museum of the City of New York*

Immigration / Pictorial Essay

by Carl Degler

During the decade of the 1850's, over two and a half million immigrants entered the United States, principally from Ireland—largely as a result of the famine of 1846 and its aftermath—and from Germany. More arrived in that ten-year period than in the preceding thirty years. Never again would the proportion of foreign born to native born be as high as it was in that decade before the Civil War. The picture of the landing of the emigrant ship shows something of the way in which that great migration took place. The ships were small, the vessels crowded, and the passengers generally poor and carrying what few possessions they owned. The man rushing to greet the woman in the left side of the picture epitomizes one pattern of migration: the husband would come first to find a job, earn some money, and then send for his wife or, as in the case of the old man and the smartly clad young man in the center, sometimes a son would come first and then send for his aged parent. The enthusiasm of some of the immigrants still on the ship represents what Americans liked to think was the attitude of all immigrants who came to America—their thankfulness. That is certainly the message given in more mundane terms by the cartoon in which the young woman is being held back by the grim and protesting European employer from taking advantage of the better wages in the United States. Castle Garden was the landing place in New York harbor where millions of immigrants entered the United States before the construction of Ellis Island in New York Bay, which became the immigrant depot of the twentieth century.

It is not accidental that the same decade which saw massive immigration into the country also witnessed the rise of political agitation directed against immigrants. Because many states permitted immigrants to vote before they became citizens—as an attraction to get them to settle there, if nothing else—the immigrant played a significant role in politics. This role was sometimes resented by native Americans. The Irish, who were almost invariably Catholics at a time when most Americans were Protestants, aroused suspicion and hostility for religious reasons, too. Many of the Germans who came during these years were also Catholics, but their interest in beer and "Bier Gartens" could arouse some native Americans to hostility for yet another reason. These objections to immigrants on the part of native Americans are depicted in the accompanying cartoon, in which whiskey-drinking Irish and beer-drinking Germans are running off with the ballot box during an urban election.

When immigrants settled in cities in this period, it was principally in big cities like New York, Boston, Philadelphia, and Baltimore. Their housing was often the tenement, a veritable rabbit warren of a dwelling, as this picture from New York in 1865 makes clear. The tenement house evil, with its overcrowded, cramped quarters, and its lack of light and air, became a principal object of reform in the years after the Civil War, but its beginnings were clear in the decade of the 1850's.

Above: The Irish and the Germans. *Courtesy of The New York Public Library, Astor, Lenox and Tilden Foundations*
Below: Tenement Houses. *Frank Leslie's Illustrated Newspaper, July 1, 1865*

Above: Know Nothing Party. *Maryland Historical Society*
Right: Germans in the Union Army. *Courtesy William B. Spinelli, Pittsburgh, Pennsylvania*

Native Americans like to think that violence, disease, and disorder were largely the product of massive immigration; violence against immigrants began as early as the 1830's and reached a climax in some cities in the 1850's. Certainly the most widespread political opposition to immigrants occurred in the latter decade with the formation of the American party, or Know Nothings. Basing its appeal on a program of keeping immigrants out of political life—by extending the period required for citizenship and confining office holding to the native born—the Know Nothings scored a number of electoral successes in the North in the mid-1850's. Nor were they above using terror or threats of violence, as this picture of a gang of toughs careening through the streets of Baltimore makes clear. Weapons, including firearms, were not licensed then and both immigrants and natives brandished them recklessly, and sometimes used them.

One of the reasons why opposition to immigrants died down during the Civil War was that large numbers of German and Irish immigrants volunteered for the Union Army. Sometimes whole regiments were made up of Germans or Irish, commanded by officers of the same background. Southerners, however, were not so grateful since they bore the brunt of the immigrants' fighting ability; their newspapers carried complaints that the Union's battles were being fought not by native Northerners, but by immigrants. In this sketch, Adalbert Johann Volck, a German immigrant dentist and artist living in Baltimore, who was devoted to the Confederate cause, shows the Germans in the Union army as foreign looters, even more heartless than native Northerners. Since relatively few immigrants entered the southern states, there were no large numbers of foreign born in the Confederate Army.

CHAPTER FOUR

ENGAGED
IN A GREAT
CIVIL WAR

O N THE DAY FOLLOWING the surrender of Fort Sumter, Abraham Lincoln issued a proclamation calling for 75,000 "militia of the several states of the Union" to serve for ninety days, for the purpose of suppressing "combinations" in seven states "too powerful to be suppressed by the ordinary course of judicial proceedings." This proclamation also called on Congress to meet in special session on July 4. Four days later Lincoln issued another proclamation declaring a naval blockade on the states of the Confederacy. On May 3 he issued a further call for recruits to the regular army, even though this would bring the army to a greater number than was authorized by law. On April 27 there was another proclamation by which he authorized the suspension of the writ of habeas corpus in certain areas. In pursuance of this proclamation persons who were believed to be secessionist sympathizers were soon being arrested in large numbers and held in prison without being charged with any violation of law and without recourse to trial. Ultimately at least 13,000—and probably well above 20,000—people were imprisoned for varying periods of time under this policy.

The Lines Are Drawn

These acts, at the very outset of the fighting, told a great deal about the nature of the conflict to follow and about the Union war leader who was to win it. First of all, the call for troops was the equivalent of a declaration of war in a contest where one belligerent did not recognize the other as a belligerent, and therefore could not formally declare war. To the Unionists, no states had legally seceded because no state could legally secede; the activities which, in the eyes of the South, constituted the governmental effort of a southern republic, the Confederate States of America, were, in the eyes of the North, simply the illegal doings of a vast number of individuals, too numerous to be dealt with in the usual way by federal marshals or police officers. Since these "illegal activities" included levying war against the United States, the Unionist theory, if followed to its logical conclusions, would have meant that all fighting Confederates were guilty of treason and therefore potentially subject to the death penalty. For a time it appeared that the Union would apply this theory, at least in part, by treating all sailors serving on Confederate privateers as pirates. But Lincoln soon recognized both that this was unrealistic and also that, if prisoners from the Confederate armed services were put to death, the Confederates would necessarily retaliate upon Union prisoners. Consequently the armed forces treated each other as belligerents and in fact extended a degree of humane consideration to one another which has not occurred in twentieth-century wars. But the government always took care to avoid any gesture, even in addressing a communication, which could be construed as a

Pickett's Charge, climax of the Battle of Gettysburg: the Confederate flanks were smashed, a tremendous clash of muskets followed, and then it was over. The Confederates withdrew, leaving half their men dead on the battlefield. *Gettysburg National Military Park, National Park Service, Department of the Interior* recognition of the Confederate organization. To Lincoln, theoretically, all the southern states were still in the Union, and after the war the South derived some advantage from this doctrine that each state was still intact, and that only individual citizens had been resisting the federal authority.

The Border States Take Sides. Lincoln's call for troops also had the effect of forcing a showdown in the eight border slave states of Delaware, Maryland, Virginia, North Carolina, Kentucky, Tennessee, Missouri, and Arkansas—all of which had refused to join the Confederacy as late as April 1861. These states had rejected with equal dislike both the Deep South's idea of secession and the North's idea of union imposed by military force. During the uneasy months before Lincoln's inauguration, they had bitterly denounced South Carolina and the fire-eaters for precipitating a confrontation which attempted to force them into a distressing choice between separating from the Union or separating from the South, of which they considered themselves a part. After the bombardment of Sumter, Lincoln's call for troops confronted them with an even more hateful choice: to fight against the South or to fight against the Union. Governor John Willis Ellis of North Carolina spoke for the entire border when he replied bitterly to Lincoln's call for militia: "I can be no party to this wicked violation of the laws of the country and to this war upon the liberties of a free people. You can get no troops from North Carolina."

In this dreaded predicament, when they could no longer avoid decision, Virginia, North Carolina, Tennessee, and Arkansas, realizing that they could never, in any case, fight against the South, followed the cotton states into the Confederacy between April 17 and May 20. Missouri and Kentucky were badly divided and Kentucky tried to maintain a position of neutrality, but this was, in fact, quite impossible; these two states, torn by dissension, experienced civil wars of their own, complete with rival organizations claiming to constitute the state government, and with representation in both the Confederate and the Union congresses. The entire Civil War witnessed no fighting more barbarous than the operations of such guerilla raiders as William C. Quantrill along the Missouri-Kansas border. The later careers of Jesse and Frank James, the most famous bandits in American history, grew directly out of their "service" under Quantrill. The only slave states that remained quite distinctly with the Union were Delaware, which did so by choice, and Maryland, which did so mostly because the governor was a Unionist and because the Lincoln administration moved swiftly and somewhat ruthlessly to arrest the potential secessionist leaders in Maryland.

Lincoln's call for only 75,000 militiamen, for a term of service of only ninety days, reflected the fact that very few Americans in April 1861 anticipated what an ordeal the nation faced. Lincoln apparently really was thinking in terms of "combinations" too powerful to be controlled by the ordinary processes of law enforcement, and was still not aware that the voluntary unionism of the border was a very different thing from the fiercely nationalistic unionism of the North, which recognized no middle ground between active loyalty and treason.

Abraham Lincoln, before the Civil War. *Reproduced from the collections of the Library of Congress*

Lincoln as a War Leader. Lincoln's proclamation of a blockade, coming as promptly as it did, suggested something of his decisiveness, and also his quick awareness, so lacking among Confederate leaders, of the close relationship between economic strength and military power. In the South, the romantic traditions of honor and chivalry predisposed the leaders to think of war too much as a test of valor on the field of combat, and not enough as a matter of the effective conversion, mobilization, and concentration of economic forces. But to Lincoln an interruption of the channels through which the Confederacy received supplies was comparable in importance to the recruitment of troops.

Finally, it is striking to note how little hesitation Lincoln showed in going beyond the law (increasing the size of the regular army beyond the statutory limit, ordering the suspension of habeas corpus, authorizing appropriations which had not been voted by Congress, etc.), and how ready he was to use the executive power without waiting for Congressional sanction. His call for volunteers to serve for ninety days was accompanied by a call for Congress to meet in special session on July 4, which would be about eighty days from the time of the proclamation. If the ninety-day men could do their work briskly, Congress would not meet until after all the problems were solved. The historians' image of Lincoln has so often stressed his humility and his patience that the legend has become misleading. Lincoln had no egotism whatever, and showed no more favor to those who flattered him than those who disparaged him. But this was not because of humility. It was because he valued results more than he valued flattery, and he wanted to work with men who could get results whether they were polite to him or not. He knew very well who was using whom, and it was a rare occasion when anyone deflected him from his own purposes. But while he had no egotism, he had strong self-assurance, which grew rapidly after he had taken the measure of the political leaders in Washington. Also, although he was matched only by Thomas Jefferson among American leaders as a master of words, he was conspicuously a man of action and a master of the timing of action. He could resist immense pressure to act when he considered action premature (a quality which is poorly described by the word "patient"), and he could act very swiftly when he thought the time was right.

The Union and the Confederacy

Comparative Resources. In April 1861, Lincoln was feeling his way into a situation of singular complexity. It oversimplifies this situation very badly to think in precise quantitative terms of numerical strength, as if one could measure the Union against the Confederacy by statistical inventories. Of course, the statistics cannot be disregarded altogether and it is useful to know that the states which supported the Union had a population of 20,700,000, while those which supported the Confederacy only 9,105,000. (This is leaving out Kentucky and Missouri; if their populations were divided, half Union, half Confederate, the figures would be 22,200,000 to 10,600,000.) It is also handy to know that the North had 1,300,000 industrial workers and the South only 110,000; that the North had 22,000 miles of railroad and the South only 9280

As the Civil War began, the North (the darker shade above) had more resources than the South (the lighter shade), and the North could also more easily replenish its supplies.

RESOURCES OF THE UNION AND THE CONFEDERACY

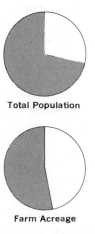

Total Population

White Population

Railroad Mileage

Farm Acreage

Workers in
Manufacturing

Annual Value of
Manufactured Goods

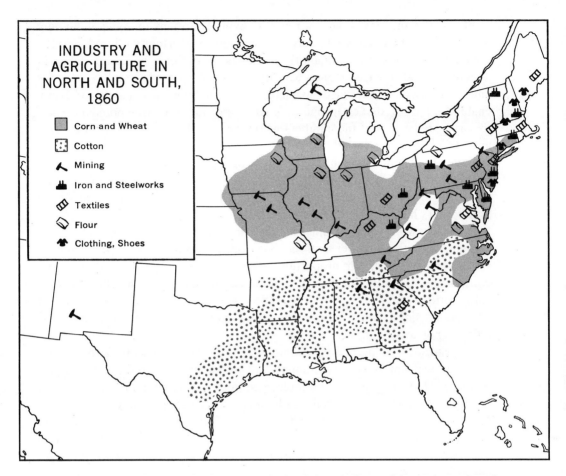

INDUSTRY AND
AGRICULTURE IN
NORTH AND SOUTH,
1860

Corn and Wheat

Cotton

Mining

Iron and Steelworks

Textiles

Flour

Clothing, Shoes

This map illustrates the North's advantage over the South in agriculture, mining, and manufacturing.

miles. It is vital to realize, as one historian states it, "At the outbreak of the war, the North produced annually, according to value, 17 times as much cotton and woolen goods as did the South, 30 times as many boots and shoes, 20 times as much pig iron, 13 times as much bar, sheet, and railroad iron, 24 times as many locomotive engines, more than 500 times as much general hardware, 17 times as much agricultural machinery, 32 times as many firearms, and 11 times as many ships and boats."*

But these precise-appearing data are not so simple as they look. Among the South's 9,105,000 population, for instance, there were 3,500,000 slaves. If these slaves had been as rebellious as John Brown believed and a number of historians have supposed, the South would have had its own internal civil war, and a large part of the white population of 5,600,000 would have been too busy fighting the slaves to give much of their energy to fighting the 20,700,000

*Charles P. Roland, *The Confederacy* (Chicago: University of Chicago Press, 1960), pp. 35–36.

Yankees. But the slaves did not revolt (leaving historians to argue about why they did not), though a great many fled, when the opportunity offered, into the Union lines. Thus the availability of slaves to perform necessary labor in agriculture and other economic activities probably provided replacement for labor which would otherwise have had to be done by whites, and this probably enabled the Confederacy to put a higher proportion of its free population into the army. Estimates of the numbers who served in the Union and Confederate armed forces are so varied and contain so many incalculable factors that one hesitates to accept any figure, but if the proportion of troops bore any relation to the proportion of survivors in 1890, the soldiers of the Union outnumbered those of the Confederacy about 5 to 2 though some estimates made by Southerners have run as high as 4 1/2 to 1.

Similarly with railroad mileage, the statistics are misleading unless one recognizes that, as another historian has said, "Of railroads they [the southern states] had a plenty, in proportion to population as much mileage as the North—only they did not connect." Most southern railroads had been built to carry cotton from interior districts to the various ports, and it is quite true that "A railroad simply ended at one point, and another began somewhere else. A union depot was unknown."*

Comparative Replacement Capacity. The crucial handicap of the South, however, was not that it was outnumbered both in manpower and equipment. It was rather that the North could replace equipment faster than it wore out. But the South's equipment—its rails, its locomotives, its supplies of critical metals, its stocks of textiles, its arms and munitions—had virtually all been brought into the South from the North or from Europe, and when they were used up there would be no way to replace them unless new equipment could be bought and shipped from Europe.

Ultimately they could not be shipped in from Europe and the Confederacy died of economic starvation. It is argued by some historians that the Confederacy collapsed because of the loss of civilian morale. What this means in fact is that a little more than a year after it became clear that they had been defeated, vast numbers of Southerners lost their will to keep on fighting. But it was losing the war which impaired southern morale rather than the impairment of morale which caused the southern loss of the war.

Why did the Confederacy not recognize at the outset that, in modern war, economic strength equals military strength, and that the South could not win its independence unless it could generate the military strength necessary for victory? There are, perhaps, three major reasons for this failure.

The First Major Southern Error: Romantic Concept of War

One of these was the cultural orientation of the South, with its heavy emphasis upon physical courage and its concept of war as a contest of physical

*Clifford Dowdey, *The Land They Fought For* (New York, Doubleday & Company, Inc., 1935), p. 92.

prowess. The romantic ideal of chivalry created a state of mind which caused Southerners to think of war somewhat as if it were an extension of the mediaeval tournament—a test of bravery upon the battlefield, and not a matter of firepower, transport, commissary, and logistics. After the war Southerners were prone to claim that they had not been "whipped," but had "worn themselves out whipping the Yanks." Translated into less partisan terms, this is a revealing indication that the Southerners believed that they had fought as hard as the Union troops, man for man, and they could not understand why an army that had fought as well as its opponent should lose. They had lost because outfighting the adversary, man for man, is only one of many factors in determining the results of a modern war.

They could not understand because, to the South (and to many rural districts in the North also), the military enterprise was still a kind of community project and not an organizational operation. Young men, scarcely more than boys, volunteered and were assembled in a regiment of neighbors who had known each other since childhood; their officers were other neighbors, a little older and more influential than they, but scarcely more aware of the meaning of war. The women sewed uniforms, made flags, and prepared knapsacks; and on a climactic day local orators, at a community festival of combined pride and fear, sped them off to war with speeches full of noble and unrealistic ideals. Later, when they reached the battlefields of Virginia or Kentucky or Tennessee, they gradually perceived that gallantry in combat was something that might occur for a few minutes during several months of slogging through the mud, surviving the measles and other unromantic and frequently fatal camp maladies, and getting used to the boredom, monotony, and deprivation of life in the field. They learned that a good officer might or might not be a valiant warrior; he might, indeed, be a prudent and unheroic fellow. What mattered was that he procured food for them—no matter how; made them keep themselves reasonably clean regardless of how much they complained; and marched them to death if a grueling march would enable them to save lives by getting to a strategic position and entrenching themselves before the enemy got there. Rail transportation, repeating arms, shoes, material of war—these were the things that counted.

By 1865 many soldiers had begun to get a glimmer of a new concept of war—of what is now called total war. The Civil War fascinated European observers partly because it was really the world's first major industrialized war. But it stood at the dividing line between the old and the new, and in some respects (for instance the use of cavalry) it was the last major war that was not industrialized. It is not surprising that the southern folk, who were completely preindustrial in their culture and largely preindustrial in their lives, were slow to understand what they were up against. Even the northern folk were just beginning to adapt themselves culturally to the industrial impact, and they too were hesitant and clumsy in seizing upon the potentialities of industrialized war. Much of the pathos of the Civil War, much of its appeal to the imagination of later generations lies in the fact that it was the last major war fought by men rather than by machines.

The Second Major Southern Error: Faith in King Cotton to Win British Support

A second feature which obstructed the Confederate view of reality was the "King Cotton" doctrine. It is always easy to laugh at any idea after it fails, and some historians have been very condescending about the parochialism of Southerners who imagined that the universe revolved around cotton. But in fact, the King Cotton doctrine was a rather logical idea. It ran somewhat as follows: First, Great Britain was mistress of the seas, and her navy could break any blockade she wanted to break. Second, Great Britain was also the world center of textile production, and the textile industry was the heart of the British economy. Out of a population of 21 million, not less than 4 million were dependent personally, or as family members, upon employment in the textile industry; two fifths of Britain's exports, which were vital to the island economy, were manufactured cotton goods. Third, Britain depended upon the South for her raw cotton. Needing over 900,000,000 pounds of cotton per year, she imported over 700,000,000 from the cotton states of the South. She knew that this was a dangerous degree of economic dependency, and had tried to increase her imports from India, but the quality of the Indian cotton was not as good, so these efforts had failed. All these points seemed the more convincing because they were not invented by boastful southern orators declaiming that "Cotton is King." They were originated instead by anxious British economists who were troubled that the most vital part of their country's economy was at the mercy of crops growing in such outlandish places as the river valleys of the Brazos, the Ouachita, the Tombigbee, the Chattahoochee, the Altamaha, the Savannah, and the Peedee.

As the South saw it, Lincoln's blockade of Confederate ports would also be a blockade of the British textile industry, and Britain need not, could not, and would not submit to this blockade. But breaking it would involve her in a naval war with the United States and such a war would force the Lincoln administration to recognize the independence of the Confederacy. The reasoning was as tight as the proof of a geometrical proposition: Q.E.D., Cotton is King.

The South was so confident of this reasoning that, during 1861 and early 1862, before the Union had enough naval vessels to make the blockade effective, the Confederates voluntarily stopped shipments of cotton which could have been sold in the British market to accumulate credits there or to purchase needed supplies. Some of the Confederate leaders argued vehemently against this policy, but President Davis and the southern majority overruled them.

King Cotton Countered. The South's cotton strategy, of course, failed. A major reason for the failure—perhaps the primary reason—was that in 1859 and 1860 the South had produced and sold too much cotton. With bumper crops available, British industry had stockpiled large surpluses. In June 1861 the stock of raw cotton on hand in Britain was 552,000,000 pounds, almost a normal year's supply and 225,000,000 more than had been on hand at the same time in the preceding year. This meant that, even if all supplies were cut off, Britain would not even begin to feel the shortage until the summer of 1862. But the South would feel very severely the effects of the disruption of the British trade long before that time.

By 1862 Britain did feel the pinch. Between June and September, unemployment in textiles drove the number of destitute up from 490,000 to 1,108,000 and by December, the number reached its maximum at 2,000,000. But by this time some unforeseen factors had come into the picture. While the textile industry languished, other British industries began to boom as a huge and lucrative market developed in America for war supplies for the Union armies. In fact the British economy was stimulated by the demands of the American war in 1861–1865 just as the American economy was stimulated by the demands of the European wars in 1914–1917 and 1939–1941. Further, the failure of British grain crops made Britain dependent on American wheat, which gave the Union a substitute for the cotton exports which it had previously relied upon to pay for imports, and which had been another aspect of the power of cotton. Still further, by the end of 1862 Union armies had penetrated the South at many points, where they usually captured some cotton supplies. Thus, raw cotton began again to trickle into Britain.

British Policy. The question of how close the British ever came to intervention is highly debatable. Certainly there were influential figures in England, even in the Cabinet, who wanted to intervene. These included William E. Gladstone who, in October 1862, declared that "Jefferson Davis and other leaders of the South . . . have made a nation. . . . We may anticipate with certainty the success of the Southern states so far as regards their separation from the North." There were constant tensions, especially because British shipyards were building vessels, under thinly disguised orders from the Confederacy, to serve as destroyers of American merchant ships. The British shipbuilders technically remained within the letter of the neutrality laws, though violating their spirit, by delivering the vessels unarmed, with artillery to be installed at sea. One of these vessels, the *Alabama,* became a famous marauder, captured sixty-two American merchant vessels, caused shipowners to sell or transfer their vessels to British registry, and thus inflicted upon the American merchant marine damage from which it never fully recovered. From this success, the Confederates moved on to order two powerful ironclad rams, which would have been easily capable of destroying any wooden naval vessel and thus of breaking the Union blockade and even terrorizing northern seaport cities. The delivery of the rams would have given the Confederacy its strongest weapon for winning independence, and very likely would also have embroiled the United States in war with Britain. But the building of the rams did not reach an advanced state until September 1863. By that time Lincoln's preliminary Emancipation Proclamation, which won many sympathizers in Britain, was a year old. Also, the Confederacy had lost Vicksburg and Gettysburg, so the handwriting was on the wall. British diplomatic policy was traditionally unsentimental in refusing aid to lost causes—even causes with which the British sympathized—and on September 3 the British Prime Minister, Lord John Russell, issued orders that the rams were not to be delivered. Two days later the American minister, Charles Francis Adams, who did not know of Russell's action, protested in the strongest possible terms—that is, he told Russell in writing that the release of the rams would mean war between Britain and the United States. This bold action was, in fact, unnecessary. Britain had survived the "cotton famine," and the British government had then waited to go with the winners. By September 1863, they knew who the winners were going to be. Britain remained neutral, selling war supplies to the Union at handsome profits; the blockade remained in force, and the Confederacy finally collapsed because of economic deficiencies.

It is sometimes suggested that the blockade was not really effective, for the Union did not have enough naval vessels until well along in the war to patrol southern ports. Also, British shippers sent cargoes to the Bahamas, where they were transferred to very small and swift vessels which could run into southern ports, sometimes almost under the noses of slower Union fighting ships. In fact blockade running became a kind of sport, psychologically gratifying to frustrated Confederates, and it continued until the end of the war. But because of the hazards and because of the kind of vessels used, the blockade runners could not afford to bring heavy cargo or cargo with low value in proportion to its bulk—iron, for instance. They brought important supplies of medicines, but too much of their cargo consisted of corsets, champagne, and similar necessities; the Confederate government could never control more than half of the cargo space.

The Third Major Southern Error: Defensive Policy

If the Confederacy miscalculated in supposing that wars were won mostly by valor, and in overestimating the immediacy of the British need for cotton, it made a third major error in supposing that northern sentiment was so badly divided that the northern public would not support a war of invasion against the South and that the wisest strategy for the Confederacy would be to pursue a defensive policy rather than to take any initiative against the North.

Strategic and Tactical Considerations. The situation in 1861 made a defensive policy seem extremely plausible; indeed some very able historians have continued to maintain that this was the soundest policy for a number of reasons. In strictly tactical terms, defensive welfare is less costly. An army loses fewer troops defending a position than it does in attacking one (especially if it is fighting primarily with rifles, as these armies were), and the outnumbered

Confederacy could not afford heavy losses. Also, an invading army has to maintain supply lines of wagon trains; the trains themselves, in the warfare of the 1860's, required immense numbers of draft animals and forage for the animals, as well as troops to prevent the lines from being cut by enemy raiders. Historically, no large army on the offensive had ever maintained supply lines as long as the Union would have to maintain in order to penetrate the lower South, and since railroads had never before played a major part in warfare, planners were slow to recognize that wagon trains might no longer be vital to the operations of an invading army. Thus, in a strictly strategic and tactical sense, there were strong reasons for remaining on the defensive, fighting close to one's own bases, in country whose terrain was well known.

Northern Sympathizers: Political Considerations. There were also political reasons. The Civil War was, indeed, a civil war, not only in the sense that two sections of the United States had clashed, but even more in the sense that neither section was united internally. Within the South, mountaineers in Tennessee, hill folk from the Ozarks to western Virginia, and isolated denizens of the swamps, the backwoods counties, or the piney woods, in some areas declared themselves openly as Unionists or, in other cases, sabotaged the war by taking to the woods when a conscription officer was in the neighborhood or by joining secret Unionist organizations such as the Peace Society or the Heroes of America. Within the North, there was great tension—to be discussed in Chapter V—between Unionists who had no use for an antislavery war, and antislavery men who had no use for saving a union in which slavery would still be legal. Many northern Democrats (who had continued to be very powerful in many of the free states, such as New York and Pennsylvania) were opposed to a war of subjugation against the South. Moreover, there were four slave states (Delaware, Maryland, Missouri, and Kentucky) still wholly or partly in the Union, and these states especially had strong proslavery and prosouthern sympathies. If these states were counted with the free states as Union states, then the Union states as a whole had given more votes to Lincoln's opponents than they gave to Lincoln when he was elected. Southern sympathizers were highly vocal and were not intimidated. They openly asserted that they would not support war measures such as conscription; they denounced Lincoln as a tyrant; and they formed secret societies. Lincoln, who anticipated all this, was forced publicly to reveal that he anticipated it when he authorized the suspension of the writ of habeas corpus. The Confederates, of course, knew all about this disaffection within the Union. They reasoned that a Confederate offensive into the North would tend to unite the North against them, whereas a defensive stance would make Lincoln appear an aggressor and would elicit the maximum degree of support from northern sympathizers.

The belief of the Confederates that they might get substantial benefit from support in the North was by no means a baseless illusion. The northern antiwar Democrats kept up a constant denunciation of the war. Probably they discouraged enlistments in some areas and even, in some instances, attempted to aid the Confederates directly. But most of the legend of a vast copperhead conspiracy to sabotage the war, or to form a separate federation of midwestern states, was devised by the Republicans to discredit Democratic opponents who were, for the most part, supporting the war. In 1864 Lincoln, a man not easily panicked, was genuinely apprehensive that the Democrats would defeat him for re-election and would then either give up the struggle for the Union or let the southern states come back on their own terms. But, in fact, Lincoln carried every state which he had won in 1860. This happened partly because the signs of a Union victory became unmistakable in the interval between Lincoln's nomination and his election. But no matter what the reason was, southern reliance on northern sympathizers turned out to be as futile as reliance on British intervention.

Despite the Confederacy's plausible military and political reasons for a defensive policy, these reasons have a prudent quality about them which does not seem appropriate to a revolutionary movement. Although it was a conservative revolution and therefore not very responsive to radically revolutionary ideas, the Confederacy was nevertheless a revolution and, as such, it could succeed only by bold strokes. Robert E. Lee, although not at all a reckless or impulsive man, understood this very clearly, but Jefferson Davis apparently never did. Davis, in fact, had such a strong preference for doing everything according to the rule book that it seems that the temperamental qualities of the commander in chief may have contributed as much as the strategic and military reasoning to commit the Confederacy to a defensive war.

Disadvantages of Defensive Policy. The defensive policy held certain ominous implications for the Confederacy. It meant that the Confederacy would forgo an effort to win; it would confine itself to preventing the Union from winning. In turn this meant that the war could continue until the northern government or the northern public got tired of fighting it. But a long war meant a war in which the South would steadily wear out equipment and use up munitions which could not be replaced, while the Union had ample facilities for replacing manpower and all kinds of supplies. The defensive policy also meant that southern crops, railroads, and productive facilities would be exposed to all the ravages of war, while those of the Union would not. Finally, it meant that the Confederacy would not attempt to seize the advantages offered by victories in the field, as for instance in attempting to take Washington and Baltimore. Of course there is no assurance whatever that such attempts would have succeeded, and some authorities believe that the Confederate armies were always badly disorganized by their victories. But there is assurance that victories were gained which were not followed up and from which no great advantage was derived. On a point as complex as this, one anecdote cannot tell very much, but after the overwhelming federal defeat at the first battle of Bull Run, a visitor to Washington from Pennsylvania reported a discussion between President Lincoln and General Winfield Scott, in command of the Union forces. Lincoln sat silent while Scott pontifically proclaimed more than once that the Confederate commander, Beauregard, could not take Washington even though he commanded a superior force. At last Lincoln, twisting his spectacles in his fingers, said, "It does seem to me, General, that if I were Beauregard, I could take Washington."

Jefferson Davis as a War Leader. Historians cannot be sure that Lincoln spoke these words nor, if he spoke them, that he was right. But they can be sure that a good many people on both sides believed what Lincoln is reported to have said. They can also be sure that Beauregard's Army did not even try to take Washington. The opportunity to take it was never put to the test, for which Jefferson Davis must be regarded as responsible. Davis was indiscriminately blamed during his Presidency for exercising too much power, and he has been indiscriminately praised since then for such irrelevant qualities as dignity and looking the part of a leader—something which was also said of Warren G. Harding. It has been asserted that he held the South together, against heavy odds, for four years; but the fact that the South did hold together does not necessarily prove that Davis held it. One historian even praises him for "holding his people together long after they had become too weak to continue the war effectively"—a dubious accolade, since it seems to mean that he prolonged the killing after further fighting was clearly hopeless, something it is quite certain that he did.

Another way to measure Davis is to try to imagine any distinguished war leader in history who, in Davis' position, would not have attempted to take Washington after First Bull Run. It is true that he faced many obstacles which even the most gifted leader could not have overcome except in part, but the question is whether he dealt with them as effectively as an able leader could. There is no evidence that he did.

Handicaps of the Confederacy

Lack of Economic Assets. The handicaps of the Confederacy were, indeed, severe. The newborn southern government was plunged into a full-scale war, with all the vast financial expenses involved in raising, equipping, and supplying armies, and it had neither a treasury nor any appreciable supply of capital in its economy. It could not have raised a formidable revenue even if its congress had been willing to vote heavy taxes, which it was distinctly unwilling to do. The largest economic asset in the Confederacy was the store of cotton, but the cotton policy forbade the sale of this commodity during the first months of the war, and later the Union blockade made a functional traffic in cotton impossible. Ultimately, almost the entire supply was seized by invading Union forces, or destroyed by Confederates to prevent its seizure, or smuggled out by private parties, so that in the end it was hardly an asset at all.

Without tangible economic assets, the Confederacy could only resort to printing-press money, with a promise that two years after Confederate independence, the printed notes could be redeemed in bullion. Such currency held up surprisingly well in value for more than a year. As late as early 1863, four such dollars would still buy a gold dollar, but thereafter their value declined rapidly. The Confederate dollar was worth less than five cents early in 1864 and continued to fall thereafter.

Inflation and Impressment Aggravate Supply Problems. Inflation confronted the government with an insoluble dilemma in procuring supplies. If the price of foodstuffs were left to find its own level on an open market, prices would rise so rapidly that the government's notes would become worthless. If, on the other hand, the government should attempt to control prices, production would be discouraged and the potential supply of goods would be further reduced. In a situation where there was no good solution, the government adopted perhaps the worst arrangement that could have been devised. It passed impressment laws, giving army agents the right to compel farmers to sell foodstuffs and supplies for army use at fixed prices far below the market price. This worked all kinds of hardships and inequalities: it made no provision for the civilian population, leaving civilians at the mercy of uncontrolled inflationary prices. Soldiers' families received little or no financial support from the government; in the face of exorbitant prices, this meant destitution and even starvation for many. For the farmers, impressment meant virtual confiscation of the commodities which the army "bought." Impressment operated most capriciously, for farmers far away from the scene of military action stood a good chance of being left undisturbed in possession of their crops, while those in the path of the armies were left without even their work animals. The policy also had serious disadvantages for the government, since it destroyed the incentive to produce, caused farmers to hide as much as they could from the impressment officers, and generated resentment destructive of morale.

Manpower Policy. No catalogue of the handicaps of the Confederacy can be complete without mention of two further items. One of these was the fact that the South did not make effective use of its manpower because of its curiously blind unwillingness to recognize that slaves were men. In April 1862, the Confederate congress passed the first conscription law in American history. This act made all able-bodied white men, between the ages of eighteen and thirty-five, liable to a three-year term of military service. At the time the act was passed, one third of the men in the South were Negro slaves. If the Confederacy was taking white husbands and fathers away from the support of their families on the theory that the war effort required their energies, there was no good reason why it should have left the energy potential of black slaves at the disposal of their masters. Slaves could hardly have been used as combat troops, for it would have been unrealistic and perhaps indecent to expect them to fight against their own liberation, but they could have been used as a labor force which was, in fact, badly needed. But the practice of slavery had inhibited the capacity of southern whites to see that manpower was manpower, whether slave or free, and that an important part of southern manpower was not being utilized in the war effort. Not only did this blindness prevent development of the full potential strength of the Confederate forces, but it also caused great unfairness between slaveholding and nonslaveholding farm families, for the slaveholding families still had black workers to cultivate the crops, and in addition the military exemption of one white man was allowed for every twenty slaves, in order that the labor of the slaves might be supervised. On farms where there were no slaveholders, the conscription of all able-bodied men left no one to "make a crop" and in many cases this situation produced acute suffering for women and children. This condition, more than any other, gave rise to the bitter complaint of many small farmers in the Confederacy that "this is a rich man's war and a poor man's fight."

States' Rights Doctrine. A second handicap developed, ironically, when the states' rights doctrine, on which the Confederacy had been founded, was turned against the Confederate government by state governors who were jealous of Confederate power. Especially Governors Joseph E. Brown of Georgia and Zebulon Vance of North Carolina showed a narrow, parochial jealousy of every exercise of Confederate power. These governors adopted their own revenue programs and tried to drive Confederate tax collectors out of their states. They secured the enactment of laws for recruiting state troops, after which they insisted on retaining control of these troops, refusing to make them part of the Confederate Army. Men who wished to escape Confederate military service could do so by volunteering for the Georgia militia. Once, although Sherman's invading army had penetrated deep into Georgia, Governor Brown sent the Georgia militia home on furloughs to prevent the Confederate Army from commandeering their services. In North Carolina Governor Vance never did anything as extreme as this, but he did interfere with the activities of Confederate conscription officers and he did stockpile, for North Carolina troops only, supplies which were desperately needed by the Confederacy. At the end of the War, when Lee's army in Virginia was suffering acutely for lack of adequate clothing, North Carolina was hoarding in its warehouses enough uniforms to have provided a new one for every man in Lee's army. As one historian has stated, the Confederacy was born of state's rights and died of state's rights. While this may not be the whole truth, it is an important part of it.

War-Dislocated Economy. A final hardship for the Confederacy lay in its economy which was severely dislocated by war, while the northern economy was stimulated by war. In the North, the demand for production of industrial war supplies made factories hum, caused wages to rise, and generated a widespread civilian prosperity. War was good for business and, as has ironically been the case in many American wars, only the soldiers and the civilians who were in the path of the armies suffered. In no American war since the Civil War have any civilians suffered directly, and in the Civil War itself, there were very few such civilians in the North. But in the South, war had a paralyzing effect on the normal economy. It destroyed the economic function not only of the cotton planters but of all those who furnished the plantations with supplies, those who were engaged in the transportation of the crop, and those who handled its financing. Plantations turned, perforce, to producing food but, since the facilities for transporting food were poor, and since there was no large public with buying power to provide a commercial market for food, the southern economy languished and lost its dynamism.

If history operated strictly in accordance with logic, one might demonstrate by logical reasoning that the Confederacy was hopelessly handicapped in a number of ways, that it was "fighting against the census returns," and that Confederate defeat was inevitable before the first shot was fired. The only difficulty with this is that the course of history frequently fails to conform to logic, and that, regardless of theory, the Confederacy more than once achieved military victories which brought it very close to a point where it might have gained its independence. The margin between Confederate success and Confederate failure on several occasions was far too narrow to support any belief that the result of the war was foreordained by deterministic forces.

Fielding the Forces

If the Confederacy almost escaped the penalty of all these handicaps, it was partly because the Union war effort was by no means a miracle of efficiency or of military skill. In fact, the war was a civilian's war, an amateur war, on both sides, though some of the amateurs finally became very proficient. The amateur character of the war was illustrated conspicuously by the way in which troops were recruited and military officers chosen. For the first twelve months of the war, the Confederacy relied entirely on voluntary enlistments; though the Union asserted the principle of universal service in 1862, it did not employ conscription until the war was more than half over.

Recruitment. In recruiting volunteer units, both the Union and the Confederacy relied primarily upon the states. The state governors, acting under Union or Confederate laws, accepted volunteers for enrollment, organized them in units, appointed their officers, arranged for equipping them, and then offered them to the army. The great majority of all troops entered the service in this way. But this practice was supplemented by allowing prominent individuals to take the initiative in raising companies, regiments, or even brigades, and rewarding them with captaincies, colonels' commissions, or brigadier rank. The activity of ambitious but not necessarily qualified men both created an injurious competition with regular recruitment, and saddled the armies with many fantastically incompetent officers. To make this picture complete, volunteer units on both sides were permitted to elect their officers up to the regimental level. In most such elections, military competence was not an important qualification and, even if it had been, few volunteers could recognize the qualities needed in a commander.

When conscription was at last adopted, it was intended primarily to stimulate volunteering, rather than actually to serve as a major means of raising troops. In fact, the term "conscript" carried a stigma, conscript soldiers being

Although lots are shown here being peacefully drawn for the draft, opposition to the draft led to riots in several northern cities. *Reproduced from the collections of the Library of Congress*

despised by the volunteers. The conscription law of the Union did not even apply in states which had met their given quota with volunteer troops. Therefore all states exerted themselves to recruit enough volunteers to avoid conscription. One way to encourage volunteers was to pay bounties of several hundred dollars to volunteers to enlist. This system of payment called into being a class of bounty-jumpers—men who enlisted, received their bounty, deserted at the first opportunity, and then enlisted again somewhere else, under another name, for another bounty. In states where conscription was applied, a potential conscript might secure permanent immunity from service by hiring a substitute to serve in his place, or by paying a fee of $300. Ultimately, only 46,000 of the 255,000 men who were called in the draft actually entered Union military service. The hiring of substitutes was regarded as so respectable that President Lincoln hired a substitute for his own son. Thus, although there were conscription laws, both armies were in effect armies of civilian volunteers, recruited and officered by other civilian volunteers.

Desertion. Desertion was a serious problem in both Union and Confederate armies, but this fact must be seen in the light of the fact that military pay was very low—never more than $16 a month in the Union Army, and never more than $18 in the Confederate army. Union pay in greenback dollars was worth $6.40 in gold, while Confederate pay in really worthless paper had a value only a fraction of that. There were no family allowances (except in a few localities) and many soldiers deserted in order to go to the support of their destitute families. Also, the Confederacy continued to fight for some seven months after defeat was clearly evident (i.e., after Sherman had taken Atlanta and Grant had trapped Lee in a state of siege at Petersburg), and Confederate desertions were especially heavy during these months.

Supplies. In view of the extreme amateurism of both sides, and their total unpreparedness for a conflict on the scale which developed, it seems astonishing that both sides gradually did get themselves organized, and even developed impressive combat efficiency. But it was a slow, painful, bungling, and frequently corrupt process. In the Union's offices of procurement, where contracts for war supplies were negotiated, corruption was rampant especially during 1861. Unscrupulous profiteers deceived incompetent purchasing agents or bribed corruptible ones to accept inferior supplies at high prices—especially inferior uniforms, made of a low-grade textile known as shoddy, which disintegrated as soon as they were exposed to a driving rain. But Edwin M. Stanton put a stop to the worst of this corruption when he became Secretary of War in 1862.

In sum, the Civil War involved armies ten times larger than the United States had ever seen, with no officers who had ever commanded more than a few brigades, with an acute shortage of men possessing any kind of military experience, with no officer-candidate schools to train officers in even the rudiments of warfare, and with no coordinating machinery to keep the operations of various armies in coherent relationship with one another. It seems remarkable that both sides ultimately took all the variously recruited, differently uniformed and equipped, randomly officered, totally untrained units, serving variously required periods of service—and shaped them into effective armies with a reasonably good level of company and platoon officers. (The election of officers by the troops was discontinued after August 1861, but it left many previously elected officers holding their commissions.) At the higher level of command, Lincoln quickly recognized that coordination was vital, but he had a succession of generals-in-chief because he experienced great difficulty in finding able men to appoint—Grant, Sherman, Thomas, and Sheridan all emerged as leaders relatively late in the war. The Confederacy had much better command leadership at the beginning, but it suffered from the fact that Jefferson Davis, with superior talent available to him than to Lincoln, was not willing to appoint a general-in-chief; further, the quality of Confederate generalship declined as commanders like Stonewall Jackson and J. E. B. Stuart were killed in combat and had to be replaced with men of less talent.

The Classic War in the East and the Decisive War in the West

The nature of any war depends upon the geography of the area where it is fought and the positions which have to be defended. In the American Civil War, the fighting quickly focused on an area in northern Virginia between the

Potomac and the James rivers. North to south, this region extends about a hundred miles; east to west, from the Atlantic Ocean to the Blue Ridge Mountains it ranges from about 100 to 150 miles. It was only a tiny fraction of the entire Confederacy, but it was vital to both sides because the capitals of the two governments were situated on the banks of the two rivers. Each government placed a great premium on defending its own capital and threatening that of its adversary. The Confederates, to be sure, did not have to place their capital in a war zone, as they did by moving it from Montgomery to Richmond in May 1861, and Jefferson Davis vetoed the act for removal but was overridden. But, even if Richmond had not been the political headquarters for the South, it was still the site of the only large ironworks of the Confederacy. Richmond, therefore, had to be defended desperately as a source of arms, and especially of artillery.

The Union government concentrated its first large force outside of Washington to defend the capital and threaten Richmond. The Confederacy responded by making a comparable concentration near a railroad junction, at Manassas, only about twenty-five miles southwest of Washington. In due course, these two forces became the classic armies of the Blue and the Gray—the Army of the Potomac for the Union, and the Army of Northern Virginia for the Confederacy. For three years these two armies engaged one another in a titanic battle, driving each other alternately north and south, and focusing the agonized gaze of Americans from Maine to Texas. To these armies, the opposing governments brought their best generals—Lee and Jackson for the Confederacy; Grant, belatedly, for the Union—and many of their best soldiers. The terrain was laid out in a way easy to understand, almost like a stage for the enactment of the drama. Because of all these features, the history of the Civil War has traditionally been told with heavy stress on the operations in Virginia.

But for anyone who cares more about the results than about the drama, it is important to recognize that the Civil War was not won or lost on the Virginia front. Armies marched, countermarched, and engaged each other in fiercely contested battles, inflicting immense losses of men. Great victories were won on both sides. But no army in this area ever captured or destroyed another—which is the supreme object of war—until what was left of Lee's once-great force surrendered at Appomattox. Union forces advanced more than once into sight of Richmond and Confederate forces into sight of Washington. But neither capital fell until a week before Lee's surrender.

Beyond the classic theatre of northern Virginia, west of the Blue Ridge and the Allegheny Mountains, the shifting and undefined border between the Union and the Confederacy stretched for another thousand miles, through western Virginia and Kentucky, all the way to the Mississippi River, and, beyond the Mississippi, across Missouri and even into Kansas. Around the coastal perimeter of the Confederacy, there were 3549 miles of coastline. There the Union Navy, only once really threatened by Confederate fighting ships, might strike at will, establishing federal positions deep within the South, from North Carolina to Texas. Through the heart of the Confederacy, separating Arkansas, Texas, and most of Louisiana from the other states, flowed the third-largest river in the world, with no bridge across it south of Wisconsin. Where the rivers of Virginia flow west to east, forming obstacles to armies moving north or south, the Mississippi forms an avenue for the quick movement of men and supplies. Furthermore, two other important rivers to the east of the Ohio—the Tennessee and the Cumberland—follow courses which are unusual in American geography. Both, arising from sources near the Cumberland Gap in southwestern Virginia, flow southwest—the Cumberland into the heart of the state of Tennessee, the Tennessee into northern Alabama—as if on their way to the Gulf of Mexico. Then both are deflected northward by the hills of northern Alabama and Mississippi and middle Tennessee, so they flow almost straight north, across western Kentucky into the Ohio. Thus the river courses of the Mississippi, the Tennessee, and the Cumberland pointed like pistols into the heart of the Confederacy. It was in this vast, cut-up, sprawling, confusing, poorly understood region that the Union won and the Confederacy lost the Civil War.

By the calendar, it was forty-eight months from Fort Sumter to Appomattox. In a sense, therefore, one can say the war lasted for exactly four years. But these years covered some periods of quick maneuver and frequent, fluid combat, other periods of preparation or even sheer inactivity, as well as some intervals of prolonged siege.

The War in the East 1861–1862

First Bull Run. The first heavy fighting took place in Virginia. By July 1861, Lincoln had elevated Major Irwin McDowell, who had never commanded more than a battalion, to a brevet Major-Generalcy. He had 35,000 soldiers, mostly ninety-day volunteers, under his leadership. McDowell knew that this force was still at least halfway civilian, not prepared to face any seasoned soldiers. But he also knew that the Confederates were probably not much better off, and his force outnumbered the Confederates if another Confederate force at Winchester, Virginia, could be prevented from joining the main Confederate force under P. G. T. Beauregard. Besides, the newspapers were screaming for action; the northern public was impatient; and worst of all, the ninety-day terms of Lincoln's first volunteers were about to run out before they had ever seen a gun fired with hostile intent. McDowell perceived his duty and moved south, engaging the Confederates at Bull Run (or Manassas Junction) on July 21. Before he did so, the Confederates at Winchester had slipped away from the army that was supposed to be shadowing them, and they joined Beauregard during the battle. Both McDowell's men and the Confederates fought like soldiers, green though they were, and for a time McDowell seemed close to victory. But by the end of the day, the reinforced Confederates were pushing the Union troops back. Soon they began to run, and when they ran, they ran like civilians. Some ran, with the aid of horses or wagons, all the way to Washington.

The Confederates did not run after them, which has caused disputes among military experts ever since. Both sides apparently recognized the need for more training, and Lincoln replaced McDowell with George B. McClellan, whose gift of rhetoric had secured him the credit for some Union successes gained in western Virginia while he was in command, but won more as a result of his subordinates' initiative than his own.

The Peninsular Campaign. McClellan was a remarkably good organizer, but more prudent than a banker, and deeply reluctant to expose any force which he had organized to the uncertainties of combat. He therefore kept on organizing and polishing the Army of the Potomac, and neither Abraham Lincoln nor anyone else could hurry him. Finally, when some kind of advance could be delayed no longer, he induced Lincoln to let him move his army on troop transports to the tip of the peninsula between the York and the James rivers. This would place him within about fifty miles of Richmond without having to fight his way, but it would also expose Washington to Confederate attack, since his army would no longer stand between the Confederates and Washington. In this operation, McClellan characteristically dragged his feet. He did not land on the tip of the Virginia peninsula until April, and he spent two months moving up the peninsula to the outskirts of Richmond, although he was opposed only by a very weak force which fooled him by painting large logs black and mounting them to resemble heavy cannon. At this point in time, the war was more than half way from Fort Sumter to Gettysburg, and the only real fighting which had occurred in the Virginia theatre was at First Bull Run.

The War at Sea. Meanwhile, however, a great deal had been happening in other places. The Union forces used their naval superiority to begin seizing island positions off the southern coast. In September 1861, they took Ship Island, off the coast of Mississippi. In November, Admiral Samuel F. Dupont, leading a combined army-navy operation, captured and occupied forts and islands on the South Carolina coast at Port Royal; his position became an important base for vessels engaged in the blockade all along the South Atlantic coast. In February 1862, another combined operation captured Roanoke Island off North Carolina. In March 1862, the Confederacy made an unexpected bid for naval supremacy by unleashing an ironclad vessel, the *Merrimack*, against the wooden-hulled fighting ships of the Union in Hampton Roads. It was not even a contest; the *Merrimack* withstood federal cannon with ease, destroyed two Union vessels, and left others to be destroyed the next day only because she was so slow. The Union Navy apparently faced disaster. But on the following day the Union put into action a new type of naval unit—a heavily ironclad vessel almost totally submerged, with only one gun turret well above the water line. The turret revolved, and in it were two powerful naval guns. This contraption, known as the *Monitor*, was exceedingly crude and faulty in

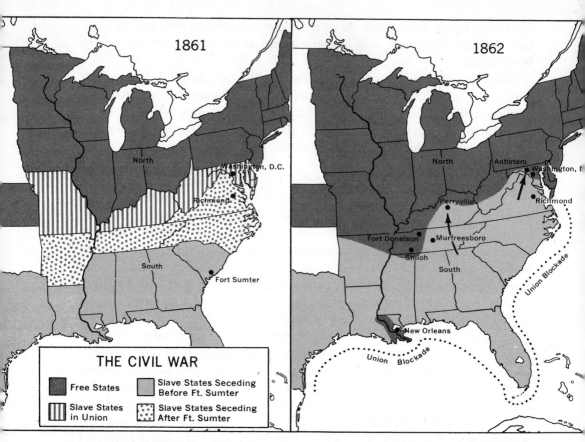

1861

1862

THE CIVIL WAR

■ Free States

▥ Slave States in Union

░ Slave States Seceding Before Ft. Sumter

⣿ Slave States Seceding After Ft. Sumter

The border slave states that remained in the union were the scene of much of the early fighting. West Virginia separated itself from Virginia. Lincoln thought holding these states to be essential to northern success.

Despite Confederate drives north, on both the eastern and western fronts, the Union consolidated its hold over much of the border area, established a naval blockade, and captured New Orleans at the mouth of the Mississippi.

many of its details, but it inaugurated the era during which armored warships with heavy firepower controlled the seas. With all its defects, it fought the *Merrimack* to a standoff, by which action the *Merrimack* was neutralized. The Confederacy enjoyed a period of definite naval supremacy, but ironically it lasted only twenty-four hours.

The War in the West 1861–1862

Missouri. While the Navy was gradually picking off islands on the South Atlantic and Gulf coasts, and before the Confederacy's single innovative bid for naval supremacy through the use of ironclads had been nullified by the Union's innovation in the use of naval armor and turret guns, the Confederacy was sustaining decisive losses in the West. To begin with, after extensive

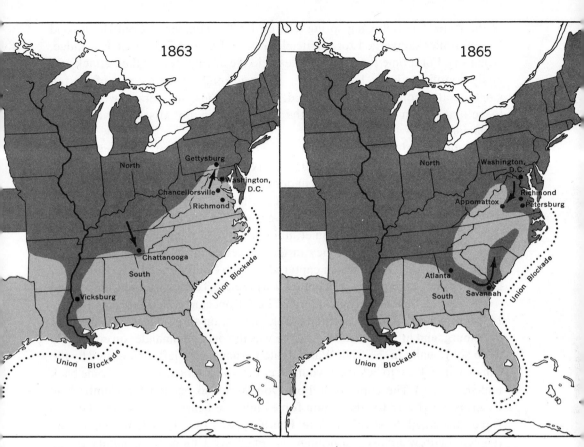

1863

1865

After Gettysburg, Lee never invaded the North again. The Confederates lost Vicksburg and the Mississippi Valley in the west. Sherman's army at Chattanooga prepared to march to the sea across Georgia, further splitting the Confederacy.

Sherman had moved across Georgia into the Carolinas. In a series of battles in Virginia, and then in the siege of Petersburg, Grant kept up unrelenting pressure on Lee's army. Abandoning Richmond, Lee surrendered at Appomattox on April 9.

fighting, it had lost Missouri. At the outset of the war, Missouri had seemed capable of going either way, but a fanatically zealous Union captain, Nathaniel Lyon, soon promoted to a generalship, drove the Confederates away from St. Louis in May 1861, and defeated them at Boonville in the northern part of the state along the Missouri River in June. The Confederates were forced to retreat to the southwestern corner of Missouri, leaving most of it under Union control. In August, Lyon, still pressing the Confederates relentlessly, engaged them at Wilson's Creek, where he was killed. The Confederates then once more surged back over most of the state, though not as far east as St. Louis. When they reached Lexington in the northwest corner of Missouri, the Confederate commander, General Sterling Price, was only able to hold his position for ten days. The Union's occupation was firm so when the Confederates appeared it was as invaders. Price retreated to Springfield, well down in the southern part of the state. The following spring (March 1862) a number of Confederate and Union armies converged for a crucial battle at Elkhorn Tavern or Pea Ridge, Arkansas. For a time the Confederates held the advantage, but their attack was badly coordinated, the Union forces received reinforcements, two of the top Confederate commanders were killed, and at last the Confederates were forced to retreat. From that time on, the Union's grip on Missouri was never threatened.

Kentucky and Tennessee. Even worse disasters overtook the Confederates in Kentucky and shortly thereafter in Tennessee. In January 1862 at Mill Springs, Kentucky, Union forces under General George H. Thomas defeated a Confederate force under General Felix Zollicoffer (who was killed) and made good the permanent Union control of eastern Kentucky. In February Major General Ulysses S. Grant, a quiet, unimpressive-looking man who had once been dismissed from a captaincy in the peacetime army because of frequent drunkenness, led a force which captured the two Confederate forts (Henry and Donelson) near the points in Kentucky where the Tennessee and Cumberland rivers entered the Ohio. The capture of Fort Donelson netted the Union Army 14,000 prisoners. (Grant captured whole armies on three occasions—here, at Vicksburg, and at Appomattox—and he was the only commander on either side to do so. Usually in the Civil War defeated armies were left unmolested by the exhausted victors, to lick their wounds, crawl away, reorganize, and come back to fight again.) The capture of Fort Donelson also opened the Cumberland River as a highway for the Union forces into the heart of Tennessee. Grant's forces occupied Nashville before February was out; President Lincoln appointed Andrew Johnson, a prominent Tennessee Unionist, as military governor, and most of Tennessee was back in the Union within nine months after secession. After that Grant began a campaign to drive the Confederates out of west Tennessee, and to use the Tennessee River as a water highway as he had used the Cumberland. However, the Confederates surprised him (to what exact extent is much debated) at Shiloh, and in one of the bloodiest battles of the war, almost destroyed his force. Nonetheless, the Confederate Commander, Albert Sydney Johnston, was killed; Union reinforcements arrived; and Grant rallied so strongly that Shiloh could be regarded as a Union victory. For some time thereafter, Grant could not accomplish much because the chief-of-staff in Washington distrusted him, partly perhaps because of his reputation as a heavy drinker and partly because of Grant's too brief and irregular reports to Washington. (But Lincoln, who was not a bureaucrat and who saw too much of generals filing their alibis both before and after military reverses, admired this quality and said, "General Grant is a very copious worker and fighter, but a very meager writer and telegrapher.")

Capture of New Orleans. In April 1862, the Confederates sustained one more great loss in the west when Admiral David Farragut brought a flotilla of vessels to attempt the capture of New Orleans. This appeared a desperate enterprise, for the Confederacy had two forts, with over a hundred heavy guns, on either side of the Mississippi about seventy miles below the city (shore batteries were normally far more deadly than floating batteries). The Confederates were also prepared to use naval vessels and fire rafts against invading ships. Farragut, in turn, prepared a special fleet of schooners to carry heavy mortars to bombard the forts, but in fact he did not expect to capture them or put them out of action. Instead he planned to injure them and then to run his fleet past them under cover of night. This he did at two in the morning of April 24, 1862. His ships did not get by undetected, but the darkness so hindered the accuracy of the Confederate fire that he successfully ran past the forts, encountered the Confederate fighting ships, fought fires caused by the Confederate fire rafts, and took New Orleans on April 25. A Union army of 18,000 was waiting on Ship Island, off the coast of Mississippi, to be brought in to occupy the city.

Thus, by the time McClellan started seriously engaging the Confederates outside of Richmond, the Union had already won most of Missouri, West Virginia, and much of Kentucky and Tennessee. It had occupied islands on the coasts of North Carolina, South Carolina, Georgia, and Mississippi; it had defeated the South's bid for naval supremacy through the use of ironclads; it had captured the largest city in the Confederacy; and it had gained control of the Mississippi River south as far as Memphis and north as far as Port Hudson, Louisiana. The links binding Texas, Arkansas, and Louisiana to the rest of the Confederacy were already precarious.

The War in the East 1862–1863

Robert E. Lee and the Virginia Campaigns. McClellan's first heavy engagement with the Confederates was at the inconclusive battle of Seven Pines. It was a discouraging encounter for the South, for the Confederates failed to drive McClellan back from the outskirts of Richmond, and the southern commander, Joseph E. Johnston, was wounded. This was unfortunate for McClellan, because on May 31, 1862, Jefferson Davis placed Robert E. Lee in command of the Confederate army.

Lee was a fifty-four-year-old Virginian, a graduate of West Point, and a professional soldier. A member of one of the South's most aristocratic families, he was personally characterized by a remarkable degree of self-control and a quite gentle quality—for instance, he did not display any personal aggressiveness either toward his enemies in the field or toward his most disappointing subordinates. Mild and rather prudent in his manner, he nevertheless had within him a terrifying boldness and decisiveness plus an awareness that the South's only chance for victory lay in taking daring chances against the steadily accumulating odds. For the next thirteen months, Lee constantly held the initiative, waged a whole series of campaigns against a succession of six opposing commanders, and made the Virginia campaigns forever the central

Robert E. Lee, after Appomattox, photographed by Matthew Brady. *Reproduced from
the collections of the Library of Congress*

focus in the history of the Civil War. But for all his brilliant generalship, the
war was neither won nor lost in Virginia.

Stonewall Jackson's Valley Campaign. At the very outset of his command,
Lee showed the nature of his generalship, in coordination with a subordinate,
Thomas J. ("Stonewall") Jackson, who was as daring and expert as Lee
himself. Although he was heavily outnumbered by McClellan and desperately
close to losing Richmond, Lee believed that McClellan was temperamentally
not an attacking general. Relying on this belief, he divided his already inferior
forces by detaching Jackson to move swiftly west, march through the mountain
passes of the Blue Ridge Mountains into the Shenandoah Valley which lay
beyond, and advance northward in the valley unobserved, to emerge again at a
point where he could threaten Washington. Lee sensed correctly the anxiety
that the Lincoln administration felt because McClellan, who constantly demanded more troops from Washington, was not protecting the capital. If
Washington were threatened, this would cause Lincoln to recall part of
McClellan's force to assure the safety of the capital, and this in turn would
inflame McClellan's chronic fear that he was outnumbered.

Jackson carried off the Valley Campaign with such *éclat* that it stands as a
classic in the history of warfare. After threatening Washington, he returned to
Richmond with phenomenal speed. Lee's reunited forces then struck McClellan's forces which, as Lee had anticipated, were now deprived of part of their
expected support. In a series of engagements known as the Seven Days' battles

(June 26-July 1) Lee attacked repeatedly. McClellan fought hard and was not decisively defeated, but he lost his nerve, bombarded Washington with hysterical messages accusing the government of deserting him, and fell back to a base on the James River. His army was still strong and still dangerously close to Richmond, with excellent supply lines.

Second Bull Run. At this point, Lincoln made one correct decision—to transfer most of McClellan's troops to another commander—and two incorrect ones—to abandon the strong and menacing base on the James and to place the major force under the command of John Pope. A remarkably self-assertive general, Pope had won successes in the West, particularly in capturing a strategically important fortified island (Island Number Ten) in the Mississippi, at the southern tip of the state of Missouri. While McClellan sailed north to turn over his command, Lee moved north overland almost as rapidly. After various preliminary encounters, Lee again resorted to the device of dividing his force, sending Jackson around Pope's army to raid his supplies at the earlier battleground of Manassas Junction. In an intricate series of maneuvers, Pope exposed his flank, which the Confederates instantly assailed, so he was badly beaten. Pope, who had taken command with a grandiose proclamation from "Headquarters in the Saddle" (where his hindquarters ought to have been, as Lincoln is said to have commented), lasted seven weeks before he was removed and the troops returned to the command of McClellan.

Antietam. This time McClellan lasted for less than ten weeks. After the defeat of Pope, Lee lost no time in proceeding north. Four days after the second battle of Bull Run he crossed the Potomac and advanced into Maryland. Again he detached Jackson, for a separate raid on the important federal armory at Harper's Ferry. But a copy of Lee's campaign plans was lost by a careless major general and fell into the hands of McClellan. Even then McClellan, who was truly not an attacking general, did not move swiftly, but he did bring Lee to a major engagement at Antietam Creek on September 17. The last-moment arrival of Jackson's forces saved Lee from a disaster and he was not driven from the field. But both sides sustained heavy losses, and Lee's were irreplaceable. In terms of Confederate expectations it was a terrible defeat. Lee withdrew into Virginia unpursued by McClellan, and in November Lincoln, weary of McClellan's varied excuses for avoiding combat, placed Ambrose E. Burnside in command.

Fredericksburg. Burnside lasted more than eleven weeks. In December he attempted a frontal assault across pontoon bridges over the Rappahannock River, against prepared entrenchments which the Confederates had thrown up on the heights back of Fredericksburg, Virginia (December 13). The attack was hopeless before it began and the fatalities incurred by the Union amounted to a slaughter. It took Lincoln a while to decide on another commander, but in January Joseph Hooker—"Fighting Joe"—was appointed.

Chancellorsville. Men and animals could not march and countermarch in the mud of a wet Virginia winter, so it was not until spring that Hooker

Thousands of Negroes were eventually used as troops by the Union. Two sons of Frederick Douglass served with this group, the 54th Massachusetts Colored Regiment, shown charging Fort Wagner, South Carolina, on July 18, 1863. *Reproduced from the collections of the Library of Congress*

attempted an offensive. In May he tried to cross the Rappahannock at Chancellorsville. Lee and Jackson caught him with his army straddled across the river. The Confederates won another victory, punishing the Union forces very severely. But Hooker saved his army and the South paid a fearful price: Jackson was accidentally shot by a Confederate and died of his wound a few days later.

Hooker was left in command, and Lee launched a second offensive against the North. Lee moved very skillfully, leaving a small force on the Rappahannock to deceive Hooker, and crossing the Potomac west of the Blue Ridge Mountains before Hooker realized what was happening. Hooker then set out northward, paralleling Lee's march on a more easterly line, but he never recovered his self-confidence after Chancellorsville. He made every excuse to avoid engaging Lee's forces, even by threatening Lee's line of communications, and on June 28 Lincoln replaced him with George Gordon Meade. Meade had less than a week to prepare before fighting the greatest battle ever waged in the Western Hemisphere.

Gettysburg. Though neither side had planned on this as a place of battle, a part of Meade's force collided accidentally with a part of Lee's on July 1 at

Gettysburg, Pennsylvania. Both commanders rushed up reinforcements to support the first units which became engaged. South of the town a valley runs north and south between two formidable ridges. The Confederates occupied the western ridge and tried to seize strategic positions on the eastern ridge as well, but the Union forces beat them to it. Thus the two armies confronted one another across the valley. With good communications, Meade could afford to wait. Lee, whose supplies were precarious, had either to withdraw, which would have been hazardous in the presence of Meade's well-positioned army, or to attack. He chose to attack, and on July 2 and 3 the Confederacy made its supreme effort, as Lee threw his troops against the Union positions in a series of bold and gallant assaults, the most famous of which was Pickett's charge. But Meade was too strong to be dislodged. Lee's forces, which had been fearfully punished, waited for more than a day to receive a counterattack which never came, and then marched south. To Lincoln's intense disappointment, Meade did not pursue until too late, ten days after Lee crossed unmolested to the south side of the Potomac.

In thirteen months Lee had fought against six commanders and had worsted all but one of them. Consistently outnumbered, he had fought six major battles or series of battles, and he had never been driven from the field. His strategic and tactical virtuosity had caused despair to his enemies and has dazzled military historians. The epic combat between the Army of the Potomac and the Army of Northern Virginia during these thirteen months has become one of the great legends of American history, and properly so in view of the deeds of the soldiers in these armies. But on balance, despite all the heroic action, the results were inconclusive. Inconclusive results, as Lee knew very well, spelled defeat for the Confederacy. No matter how many battles he had won, Lee had never succeeded in capturing or destroying an army. The Army of Northern Virginia had never been decisively defeated, but its great offensive power was forever broken.

The War in the West 1862–1863

Grant's Campaign for Vicksburg. While Lee fought his great campaigns in the east, military developments in the west seemed slow, confused, and unfocused. Grant's narrow escape from defeat at Shiloh led to a change in command giving Henry W. Halleck overall command of the Union forces in the west. He operated at a snail's pace for three months and was then called to Washington, theoretically though not in actual function, to be general-in-chief. When he left the West, the unified command went with him, and Grant received command of troops along the Mississippi, while less effective generals were placed in charge of an army that operated in central Tennessee. Though forced onto the defensive for several months, by the end of 1862 Grant was beginning a careful, patient, and immensely difficult campaign to get through the amphibious country that surrounded Vicksburg, Mississippi, and to capture that town, the last Confederate stronghold on the Mississippi. A stronghold it was indeed, for Vicksburg towered like a Gibraltar above the river, protected in the rear by concentric rings of steep hills extending back for many miles. By land, Grant met with acute frustrations from the raiding tactics of Earl Van Dorn and of Nathan Bedford Forrest—the latter perhaps unsurpassed in history for his bold and effective cavalry raids. By water, Grant was repeatedly foiled by the treachery of a great river bordered by swamps too liquid for any land vehicle but too solid for any water vehicle. One stratagem after another failed, but Grant kept on trying. Finally he got an army onto dry land on the west side of the river below Vicksburg. He prepared to cross over from there, abandon his line of communications, as he had seen General Scott do in Mexico, and stake everything on a victory before his army could be starved into surrender.

Kentucky and Tennessee. All of this dragged on for more than a year after Shiloh. While the armies in Virginia were making history, Grant was building dikes or digging canals that did not work. Meanwhile, in central Tennessee the Confederate command had devolved upon Braxton Bragg, who ultimately proved to be the chief military liability of the Confederacy. Bragg was not without talent, and he conducted at least three campaigns which began with skillful execution and which brought him to a point where major victory seemed assured. Yet on each of these occasions, he lost his initiative at the crucial moment and let victory slip through his paralyzed fingers. The first occasion was in the autumn of 1862. Making a bold raid into Kentucky, planned to coordinate with Lee's advance into Maryland, Bragg advanced all the way to the Ohio River. Soon after he came to a confrontation with the Union forces at Perryville, Kentucky. Instead of following up his initial advantage, Bragg abruptly turned south, retreating into Tennessee. In January, at Murfreesboro, Tennessee, in one of the war's deadliest battles with more than 20,000 casualties, Bragg fought another Union force to a deadlock, but then retreated from the field. Only the torpor of his adversary, General William S. Rosecrans, saved him from being driven out of Tennessee. As it was, Rosecrans did not pursue him until June, when he fell back to Chattanooga on the Georgia border. In the inconclusive, slow-motion engagements of second-rate commanders, the South had lost virtually all of Kentucky and Tennessee while Lee was engaged in his brilliant but unsuccessful series of efforts to score a knockout victory in Virginia.

Fall of Vicksburg. At last the fatal blow for the Confederacy fell in the west simultaneously with the one in the east. At the end of April, Grant crossed the Mississippi below Vicksburg; on May 2, the day Stonewall Jackson was shot, he established a secure bridgehead in Mississippi; within two weeks he had driven one Confederate force east and another into the town of Vicksburg, which he instantly besieged. For forty-seven days a relentless siege was pressed, and on July 4, the day after Lee's attack at Gettysburg failed, the

Vicksburg fortress surrendered, yielding more than 30,000 troops who became prisoners.

The war had continued for twenty-seven months up to the decisive events of July 1863, and it was to continue for another twenty-one months afterward, but in effect the result had been registered. The Confederate forces were hopelessly overpowered, and only once again did they come close to a major victory. That was at Chickamauga, south of Chattanooga, in September of 1863, when Braxton Bragg succeeded in trapping the entire army of General Rosecrans and almost destroying it. But George H. Thomas, the "Rock of Chickamauga," made a heroic stand, and this time more conspicuously than ever before, Bragg forfeited a victory that was already won. A few days later, the Union forces turned the tables completely at the Battle of Missionary Ridge.

The War 1864–1865

Grant in Virginia; Sherman in Georgia. In March 1864, Lincoln brought Grant east to become general-in-chief; Grant chose to make his headquarters with the Army of the Potomac, without technically superseding Meade in command. During May and June, using his superior forces relentlessly, Grant drove Lee back into a defensive position at Petersburg, where Lee remained virtually in a state of siege until the last week of the war. Simultaneously with Grant's offensive, William T. Sherman began an advance from Tennessee into Georgia. He met with skillful delaying tactics from his adversary, Joseph E. Johnston, and did not succeed in taking Atlanta until September. From there he marched unopposed to the sea, allowing his men to burn and loot as they went. The world received its first preview of total war as Sherman terrorized the defenseless civilians of Georgia.

Lincoln's Reelection and Appomattox. During these final campaigns, the Confederacy could have no hope of winning. The only reason for continuing to resist was the hope that the North might grow weary of the heavy losses and therefore choose not to finish the war that it had won. Grant's losses between the battles of the Wilderness and Petersburg were about as heavy as any that the Union ever experienced; he sustained 55,000 casualties, nearly as large a number as Lee's whole force. Lincoln himself feared the psychological reaction of the northern public to this slaughter, and during the summer he made plans to cover the contingency of his defeat in the election of November 1864. The Democrats had nominated McClellan to run against him, and he also encountered sharp opposition within his own party. However Grant's heavy casualties dropped off sharply after June, and the capture of Atlanta caused the morale of the northern public to soar. In November Lincoln was reelected with 55 percent of the vote; if realism had prevailed in Richmond, the Confederacy would have surrendered then. But Jefferson Davis seemed determined that the Confederacy must fight until its armies had been destroyed. They were virtually destroyed by April 1865. With Richmond captured and burned, and Jefferson Davis and his cabinet in flight, Lee surrendered the remnants of the Army of Northern Virginia on April 9, at Appomattox Court House.

Other Confederate units surrendered within a few days. The war had cost the lives of 618,000 soldiers, including 360,000 Union deaths and 258,000 Confederate.

A Nation and the War. The effect of the war upon the American people was a curious one. The northern states had begun the war claiming that the United States was a nation, when it was, in fact, too decentralized and too loosely integrated economically to be a nation in the full sense. But the task of fighting the war had created a national economy, a national government, and a national spirit. The war had, in a sense, created the nation that it was waged to preserve.

For the South, too, the effect of the war was paradoxical. The South also began by claiming to be a nation, when it fell considerably shorter than the North of being one, for it was hopelessly divided in April 1861. The war thwarted the South's effort to achieve political nationhood. Yet by the shared struggle and the shared sufferings which the war brought to the South, it created powerful bonds of psychological unity among a people whose political unity it destroyed. It created a fiercely nationalistic loyalty to the nation which it prevented from existing. This nationalism of the South in defeat added a great deal to the tensions of a reunion in which the very first order of business was the task of determining the new economic, political, and social status of the

AMERICAN WAR DEATHS

Vietnam War 45,661** — Revolutionary War 4,000*
Korean War 54,000 — War of 1812 2,000*
Mexican War 13,000

World War II 405,000

Civil War 618,000

World War I 117,000

Spanish-American War 2,000

*battle deaths only
**battle deaths only as of March 9, 1972

four million American Negroes who, until late in the war, had almost all been slaves. After April 1865 secession was dead and the Union had been preserved, but for the years that lay ahead, the Union seemed even more deeply divided than during the slavery controversy when the idea of secession had been alive.

SUGGESTED READING (Prepared by Carl N. Degler)

Writings on the Civil War are exceeded in volume only by those on the coming of the war. Again, the best entry into the literature as well as a convenient summary is in James G. Randall and David Donald, *The Civil War and Reconstruction* (2nd ed., 1961). An excellent, handy, but unannotated bibliography is David Donald, comp., *The Nation in Crisis (1861–1877)** (1969). A short and provocative discussion by knowing experts of four major reasons for the North's victory is in David Donald, ed., *Why the North Won the Civil War* (1960). Allan Nevins' four-volume study *The War for the Union* (1959–1971) is the most recent and fullest study of the period. Most readable even for those who do not like military history is Bruce Catton's trilogy on the Army of the Potomac, *Mr. Lincoln's Army** (1951), *Glory Road** (1952), and *A Stillness at Appomattox** (1953). An excellent single volume on the same subject by Catton is *This Hallowed Ground** (1956). He deals with the South as well as the North in his three-volume *Centennial History of the Civil War** (1961–1965), probably the best history of the war now extant. Engrossing and informative is John J. Pullen, *The Twentieth Maine* (1957). Kenneth P. Williams, *Lincoln Finds a General* (5 vols., 1949–59) was incomplete at the author's death, but it is the fullest military history of the northern army. Douglass Southall Freeman, *R. E. Lee* (4 vols., 1934–35), a masterpiece, and his *Lee's Lieutenants* (3 vols., 1942–44) cover in detail the war from the southern side. J. F. C. Fuller, *Grant and Lee* (1957) is a lively comparison of the two military giants by a knowing British general.

The role of the Negro is handled with authority in Dudley T. Cornish, *The Sable Arm** (1956), which deals with Negroes in the U.S. Army and in Benjamin Quarles, *Negro in the Civil War** (1953), a more general study. Two books by Bell I. Wiley treat the personal lives of soldiers of both sides: *The Life of Johnny Reb* (1943) and *The Life of Billy Yank* (1952).

Internal problems in the North are set forth in detail in James G. Randall, *Constitutional Problems Under Lincoln** (rev. ed., 1951) and in Frank L. Klement, *The Copperheads in the Middlewest* (1960). T. Harry Williams, *Lincoln and the Radicals** (1941) argued for a division between them, but David Donald in an essay in his readable *Lincoln Reconsidered* (1956), as well as in his biography of Sumner, already mentioned, shows the inaccuracy of that view.

Excellent studies of the intellectual and social impact of the war are George M. Fredrickson, *The Inner Civil War* (1965) which discusses the effect upon northern intellectuals and Edmund Wilson, *Patriotic Gore** (1962), which learnedly analyzes the imaginative literature that grew out of the war. Mary E. Massey, *Bonnet Brigades: American Women and the Civil War* (1966) treats both sides from a wide range of sources. A collection of important articles is Ralph Andreano, ed., *The Economic Impact of the American Civil War** (1962). In that collection is the important Thomas D. Cochran, "Did the Civil War Retard Industrialization?" which originally appeared in the *Mississippi Valley Historical Review* in 1961.

The fullest general history of the Confederacy is E. Merton Coulter, *The Confederate States of America* (1950). Briefer, but knowing is Clement Eaton, *History of the*

*Southern Confederacy** (1954). Rembert W. Patrick, *Jefferson Davis and His Cabinet* (1944) is important for understanding Confederate policy. One of the inherited weaknesses of the Confederacy is emphasized in Frank L. Owsley, *State Rights in the Confederacy* (1925); another is delineated in Georgia L. Tatum, *Disloyalty in the Confederacy* (1934). Internal problems of the Confederacy are well set forth in Charles W. Ramsdell, *Behind the Lines in the Southern Confederacy* (1944) and in Bell I. Wiley, *The Plain People of the Confederacy* (1943). Wilfred B. Yearns, *The Confederate Congress* (1960) points to other sources and signs of discontent. Charles Wesley, *The Collapse of the Confederacy* (1922) sums up many explanations offered for the fall of the Confederacy.

Ephraim D. Adams, *Great Britain and the American Civil War* (2 vols., 1925) though old is still authoritative on foreign affairs during these years. Broader in scope though shorter in length is Donaldson Jordan and Edwin J. Pratt, *Europe and the American Civil War* (1931). The fullest and most provocative treatment of southern diplomacy is Frank L. Owsley, *King Cotton Diplomacy* (1931).

*Available in a paperback edition

The Modernity of the Civil War / Pictorial Essay

by Carl Degler

A close scrutiny of the accompanying pictures shows that, in a number of ways, the Civil War was the first modern war. It introduced trench warfare, the repeating rifle, and the dependence upon large quantities and varieties of munitions and ordnance, as the picture of supply headquarters at City Point, Virginia, makes evident. It was also the first war of any size to be fought after the invention and development of the telegraph and the railroad. Movement and communication in the Civil War were considerably faster than in any earlier war, though most soldiers still marched into battle, Indeed, "Stonewall" Jackson's ability to move his men by foot over long distances at great speed earned his men the title "Jackson's Foot Cavalry." The railroad was particularly important in moving supplies to maintain the large armies in the field. It was because of the importance of railroads that during Sherman's march to the sea across Georgia, his men took care to destroy the southern railroads on which continuance of the war by the Confederacy would depend. The practice was to heat up the rails until they were bendable and wrap them around trees to discourage their reuse.

Left: War Equipment. *U. S. Army*
Top: Telegraph. *Harper's Weekly, January 24, 1863*
Bottom: Railroad Ties Twisted Around Trees. *Harper's Weekly, December 31, 1864*

After the historic battle between the *Merrimack* (C.S.S. Virginia) and *Monitor* in 1862, the ironclad vessel was increasingly used, both on the ocean front and on the inland waters. In the accompanying picture, the ironclads in the foreground have their paddle wheels in the interior of their structures, in contrast to the wooden ships along the docks of Memphis, Tennessee, on the Mississippi River. The first ironclads were simply that—wooden vessels covered with iron plates to deflect the enemy's cannon balls. In time, of course, ships' hulls constructed entirely out of iron would be built. After the Civil War the principal navies of Europe also began to add iron war vessels to their fleets.

In view of the use of the observation balloon, shown in the accompanying picture, a case of sorts can be made that warfare in the Civil War also introduced the modern aerial dimension. These balloons, however, were extremely vulnerable to enemy fire; hence they never ventured over enemy territory. They simply provided greater height for observation purposes. They were not fighting instruments.

Like all wars, the Civil War also used information obtained from spies, but the Civil War was perhaps modern in the sense that at least one woman spy was active. Belle Boyd's exploits as a Confederate spy depended partly on the refusal of the northern authorities to take her seriously—for she was detected and captured twice, but merely reprimanded. Yet she did pass on valuable information to Confederate General "Stonewall" Jackson at least once, the sources of which were northern officers who refused to think that a southern woman could be a spy. Later in the war she was jailed for a time, and then banished to Canada, upon pain of death if she were captured again.

Far Left: Ironclads. *Illustrated London News, July 19, 1862*
Top: Balloons. *Frank Leslie's Illustrated Newspaper, August 31, 1861*
Left: Belle Boyd. *Courtesy Chicago Historical Society*

If Belle Boyd, the railroad, and the telegraph were novelties, a good part of the war consisted of doing very familiar things many times over. The dreariness, monotony, and boredom of life in the army is well suggested in the photograph of the soldiers waiting outside their tents at a U.S. military railroad field hospital, while a couple of military trains move in the background. (The attempt to care for the Civil War wounded inspired Clara Barton to establish the American Red Cross.) The tedious and hard work that an army also required is suggested by the picture of Negroes digging trenches and canals along the Mississippi River during the siege of Vicksburg. In order to get their troops close enough to the town to assault it, Sherman and Grant experimented, though unsuccessfully, with draining some of the tributaries and swamps that prevented the movement of troops. Later, in the Virginia theater of the war, the ordinary soldier, not only slaves or free blacks, had to dig trenches for themselves in the war of position that characterized the Virginia theater in late 1864 and 1865.

Left: Military Railroad Field Hospital. *Association of American Railroads*
Above: Trenches. *Harper's Weekly, August 2, 1862*

CHAPTER FIVE

THE CONFLICTING GOALS OF RECONCILIATION AND FREEDOM

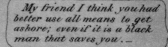

THE AMERICAN CIVIL WAR was caused by secession, but secession was caused by the slavery controversy. If these statements are accepted as axioms, it might be supposed that explanation would be simplified by leaving out the intermediate step and saying simply that the Civil War was caused by the slavery controversy, which is, in a sense, true. However, the elimination of the intermediate step makes it impossible really to understand the war, for the fact is that while the North was almost united against the secessionist South, it was seriously divided in its attitudes toward the slaveholding South and even more divided in its attitudes toward Negroes. As late as 1860 large numbers of northern Democrats condemned the "Black Republicans" for their agitation on slavery and resisted the extension of civil rights to Negroes in the free states. But secession transformed the issue from a question of slavery or race to a question of Union, on which most of the North could unite. Once antislavery men and Union men had joined hands against the Confederacy, it became easy to overlook the fact that northern support of the war was really based upon a coalition of Unionists who knew they could not defeat the secessionists without antislavery support and antislavery men who knew they could not abolish slavery without the unionist support, nor without defeating the Confederacy. Of necessity, therefore, Unionists and antislavery men stood together during the war, though only with a great deal of squabbling and reciprocal distrust. Ironically, of course, the victory of the coalition put an end to its reason for existence, for the two allies ceased to need one another. The Confederate surrender did just what secession had done, but in a reverse direction: it transformed the issue back again from a question of union to a question of the status of the Negroes, and on this question the Negroes had far fewer supporters in the North as freedmen than they had ever had as slaves. Whenever a successful coalition breaks up after a war because of dissension among the victors, the vanquished find an opportunity to assert themselves. This is what happened in the defeated South in 1865.

Lincoln and the Negro Question

One of the great ironies of the period of the Civil War is that for fifteen years before the war, there had been ceaseless discussion of what was spoken of as "the everlasting Negro question"—especially so called by those who wanted to keep it out of politics. Yet actually there had been no discussion of the Negro question in broad terms at all. The discussion had, in fact, not even dealt comprehensively with the slavery question, which was only one dimension of the Negro question; instead it had dealt with the issue of slavery in the territories, which was only one aspect of one dimension of the Negro question. This meant that when the Union won the war, it was unprepared to deal with

Reconstruction in the South: the Currier and Ives cartoon suggests the lost opportunity for working together toward a larger freedom. *Reproduced from the collections of the Library of Congress* the consequences of victory, which has been the tragic fate of America at war ever since the War of 1812—when there was no victory to bungle.

Why was the North so totally unprepared to deal effectively with the Negroes as members of American society after they ceased to be slaves? To this question, the most popular answer in the 1950's and 1960's—an answer often given by militant spokesmen of Negro rights—has been that the whole nation was "racist": i.e., it regarded Negroes as inferior and was antagonistic to treating them as anything except inferiors. Exponents of this view have reacted especially against an oversimplified, late-nineteenth-century view of Abraham Lincoln as a "Great Emancipator," born to a destiny of striking the shackles from the abjectly grateful slaves. They discovered that, as we shall see, Lincoln harbored racial prejudices at least in part of his mind; from this discovery they proceeded to a new oversimplification that Lincoln was a "white supremacist" or a "honky," as he was called after the pendulum had swung completely the other way. Neither of these oversimplified views will give anyone much insight into the realities—the complex realities—which caused American society to take some important but tentative steps toward Negro equality during the war and for nearly a decade after, and which then caused the country to draw back from the policy on which it seemed to be embarking.

The Ambiguity in Lincoln's Mind. Since all these questions lend themselves to being interpreted in more than one way, it is important to see just how far Lincoln had gone in expressing racist ideas, and just how far he had repudiated them. The strongest evidence of the racist strain in his thinking appeared in one of his debates with Stephen A. Douglas in 1858. At Charleston, Illinois, speaking with a precision which could hardly be more explicit, he stated:

> I will say then, that I am not, nor ever have been in favor of bringing about in any way the social and political equality of the white and black races; that I am not, nor ever have been in favor of making voters or jurors of Negroes, nor of qualifying them to hold office, nor to intermarry with white people; and I will say, in addition to this, that there is a physical difference between the white and black races which I believe will forever forbid the two races living together on terms of social and political equality. And inasmuch as they cannot so live, while they do remain together there must be the position of superior and inferior, and I as much as any other man am in favor of having the superior position assigned to the white man.

While Lincoln made this statement, however, he also recognized, at least privately, that color prejudice was totally irrational as a basis for determining race relations. Historians have found among his papers a statement which he wrote in 1854:

> If A can prove conclusively that he may of right enslave B—why may not B snatch the same argument, and prove equally, that he may enslave A?

You say A is white and B is black. It is *color* then; the lighter having the right to enslave the darker? Take care. By this rule, you are to be the slave to the first man you meet with a fairer skin than your own.

You do not mean *color,* exactly? You mean the whites are *intellectually* the superiors of the blacks, and therefore you have the right to enslave them? Take care again. By this rule, you are to be slave to the first man you meet with an intellect superior to your own.

But you say, it is a question of *interest;* and if you can make it your interest, you have the right to enslave others. Very well. And if he can make it his interest, he has a right to enslave you.

This lean and muscular bit of reasoning was never announced publicly as his view. But in the Lincoln-Douglas debates Lincoln did state publicly that he and the Republicans looked upon slavery as "a wrong . . . a moral, social, and political wrong." He also said, "let us discard all this quibbling about this man and the other man—this race and that race and the other race being inferior and therefore they must be placed in an inferior position. . . . Let us discard all these things and unite as one people throughout this land, until we shall once more stand up declaring that all men are created equal."

This statement clearly cannot be reconciled with the statements made at Charleston, and if our purpose were only to ascertain the consistency of Lincoln's logic, we could simply observe that on at least one occasion, he was totally inconsistent. But our purpose should be to understand Lincoln's thinking, including his doubts and confusions. To that purpose, one must say there was an ambiguity in his mind. It was like a photographic film that has been exposed twice. One exposure accepted racial discrimination; the other exposure rejected it—in one mind. This was not peculiar to Lincoln, but is rather a very widespread human phenomenon, especially when one attitude is at an abstract level and the other at a concrete level.

Lincoln's Value Priorities. This characteristic of ambiguity is an important one, and when a person's thought is examined from a purely philosophical standpoint, it is perhaps the most important characteristic. But when thought is examined as an aspect of policy—of the question "what to do," another consideration also comes into play. For purposes of action, it is not only important to know what a man believes on a given question, but how important that belief is to him in relation to his beliefs on other questions. Lincoln and great numbers of other Americans of his generation had a belief about slavery—that it was wrong. But they also had a belief about the Union—that its preservation was vital, and that nothing must be done which would endanger it. Lincoln spelled out this question of the priority of values in his usual explicit way in August 1862, when he wrote to Horace Greeley:

My paramount object in this struggle is to save the Union, and is not either to save or destroy slavery. [Lincoln was not saying that he had no object to destroy slavery; in fact the Emancipation Proclamation, though unannounced, was already in his desk. He was saying that his object to destroy slavery was not paramount.] If I could save the Union without freeing any slave, I would do it; and if I could save it by freeing all the slaves, I would do it; and if I could save it by freeing some and leaving others alone, I would also do that. What I do about slavery and the colored race, I do because I believe it helps to save this Union, and what I forbear [meaning that he does not do what he would like to do], I forbear because I do not believe it would help to save the Union.

In short, for Lincoln one belief—about the value of the Union—was more important than another belief—about the moral wrong of slavery.

Lincoln and the Art of Politics. In addition to the problem of the priority of values, there is still another important complicating factor which causes disjunctures between ideological beliefs and programs of action. This is the fact that while man may believe in the ideal, man never attains it; one of the greatest problems in philosophy is to decide whether men will come nearer to the fulfillment of their purposes by aiming without compromise at the unattainable, absolute ideal, or by calculating what is the optimum attainable goal and aiming for that. Revolutionaries usually lean toward the former alternative; political leaders toward the latter. Politics at its best is in fact a very sensitive process for ascertaining what is the optimum attainable, and aiming for it. This attitude has been summarized in the axiom that "politics is the art of the possible." Lincoln was thoroughly political in all his impulses, and his course of conduct constantly reflected his rejection of absolute goals and his concern for the contingent features that had to be weighed in calculating what was attainable. Thus, although both his racist statements and his equalitarian statements already quoted are very striking, they may be less revealing about his policies than his qualifying statements. For instance, he said that while the Republicans regarded slavery as wrong, "they nevertheless have due regard for its actual existence among us, and the difficulties of getting rid of it in any satisfactory way and to all the constitutional obligations thrown about it." Or, even more pointedly, on the question of freeing the slaves and making them "politically and socially our equals" he said that "my own feelings will not admit of this, and if mine would, we well know that those of the great mass of the white people will not. Whether this feeling accords with justice and sound judgment is not the sole question, if indeed it is any part of it. A universal feeling, whether well- or ill-founded cannot be safely disregarded."

The War Sets Lincoln's Policy. Thus, even before the war, Lincoln expressed his conviction that policy concerning American Negroes should be determined not only by considerations of abstract justice, but also by considerations of existing circumstances. When the war came, two sets of circumstances, of what seemed to him absolutely controlling force, shaped his policy and made him extremely reluctant to call attention to the question which the war itself inevitably raised—the question of the future status of the Negroes. One of these circumstances was that, whether other people recognized it or not, Lincoln *never* lost sight of the fact that he was fighting a war supported by an unstable coalition of conservative Unionists and radical antislavery men, and that if the coalition ever broke down, he would lose the war. If the Negro question were introduced in such a way as to make the war appear primarily as an antislavery crusade, the coalition would break down, and then neither the Unionists nor the antislavery men would get what they were fighting for. The other crucial circumstance was that the border slave states were on hair-trigger, and the slightest false step would send them into the Confederacy. Maryland was vital, but even more crucial were Kentucky and Missouri. Lincoln had seen Virginia, North Carolina, Tennessee, and Arkansas follow the lower South into the Confederacy when he called for volunteers. He was convinced that if Kentucky and Missouri followed also, the North would certainly lose the war. In this conviction he was probably correct, and all his policy was directed toward retaining the support of these two states. It was said that antislavery men urged him to free the slaves, saying that if he did so, God would be on the side of the Union, and that he had replied that "we would like to have God on our side, but we must have Kentucky."

Steps to Emancipation

Partly because of these circumstances, and partly because of Lincoln's own constitutional scruples and uncertainty about what either could be or should be done toward a new order of race relations in America, he refused for quite a long period to make emancipation an objective of the war, or to let anyone else make it an objective. This policy showed up repeatedly. At his inauguration, he offered to accept a constitutional amendment which would have given permanent protection to slavery in the slave states, and he reaffirmed his acceptance of the Fugitive Slave Act. Further, when Congress met in July after the war had begun, two border state members, John J. Crittenden of Kentucky and Andrew Johnson of Tennessee secured the passage, by an overwhelming vote in both houses, of a resolution which declared that "this war is not waged . . . for any purpose . . . of overthrowing or interfering with the rights or established institutions of those states [which had seceded], but to defend and maintain the supremacy of the Constitution and to preserve the Union, with all the dignity, equality, and rights of the several states unimpaired, and . . . as soon as these objects are accomplished, the war ought to cease." In short, victory in this war should not be used to deal with the underlying issue which had caused the war to break out. Lincoln accepted this position.

Early Efforts to Avoid the Issue. "After the commencement of hostilities," Lincoln wrote later, "I struggled for nearly a year and a half to get along without touching the institution." This statement was true in virtually every sense. When others tried to seize the initiative in freeing slaves or using

Negroes as soldiers, Lincoln stopped them. In August 1861, when General John C. Fremont, in military command in Missouri, proclaimed the freedom of the slaves of all persons resisting federal authority in his military district, Lincoln publicly ordered him to revoke the proclamation; in May 1862, when General David Hunter attempted a similar gambit on the South Atlantic coast, Lincoln overruled him also; in December, when Secretary of War Cameron proposed in his annual report that slaves should be armed and used as troops, Lincoln required him to delete this proposal from the final report, although Cameron had already farsightedly leaked it to the press. When free Negroes volunteered for service in the Union Army, Lincoln repeatedly refused to accept them, and no black soldiers were enlisted until after the Emancipation Proclamation at the beginning of 1863. When Congress acted, however, Lincoln could not arrest the action so decisively, so he felt compelled to accept a congressional measure in April 1862, emancipating the slaves in the District of Columbia, and another measure, the Confiscation Act of July 1862, which provided that the slaves of all persons supporting the rebellion should be freed. But he showed reluctance about both measures: he wanted the border states rather than the District of Columbia to be the first area of emancipation, and he wanted state rather than federal action to lead the way. He ignored the Confiscation Act so effectively that popular history has almost lost sight of the fact that Congress proclaimed an emancipation which was both earlier and more extensive in its coverage than Lincoln's own famous proclamation.

The Emancipation Proclamation. By the summer of 1862 the dynamics of the war now fifteen months old created a situation where Lincoln could no longer realistically expect to return to the old order. He recognized this, and recognized further that if he did not make a major move toward emancipation, Congress would wrest the control of the situation away from him. In the summer of 1862, therefore, he decided to take the initiative. With his usual mastery of timing, he waited for some kind of Union victory, so that when he acted it would not appear to be in desperation. General McClellan's limited success at Antietam gave him the opportunity he was waiting for, and on September 22 he issued the Preliminary Emancipation Proclamation.

This document and the later Thirteenth Amendment were the two fundamental measures in the overthrow of slavery, and the importance of the Proclamation should not be minimized. But its remarkable and significant limitations should be clearly understood. Basically, it stated that in the areas still in rebellion against the United States on the first of January, 1863, all slaves should be emancipated. This was indeed potentially sweeping, but if it could be read as a promise of freedom soon to come, it could also be read as a bid to the seceding states to cease their resistance before January 1, and thus to save their slaves. It had the further ironic feature that it would not physically free anyone, even after three months, because it applied only to areas over which the Union government had no control, and did not apply to areas over which it did have control. The London *Spectator* commented bitterly: "The principle is not that a human being cannot justly own another, but that he cannot own him unless he is loyal to the United States."

The Progress of Abolition. On January 1, 1863, six months before Gettysburg and the surrender of Vicksburg, most of the South was still "in rebellion against the United States." Lincoln issued the proclamation declaring "forever free" the slaves in all of North Carolina, South Carolina, Georgia, Florida, Alabama, Mississippi, Arkansas, Texas, and parts of Louisiana (excepting 13 parishes) and Virginia (excepting seven counties and the part of the state which had become West Virginia). Tennessee, having been brought completely under Union control, was not included at all. With the four border slave states also untouched, the result was that slavery still existed legally in five states and parts of two other states. It was abolished in West Virginia under the constitution by which that state was admitted to statehood in 1863. In April 1864, a reconstruction government sponsored by Lincoln abolished it in Louisiana and in November, the voters of Maryland, by an extremely narrow margin, adopted a new constitution, which ended it there. The following year, 1865, Missouri abolished it in January and Tennessee in February.

The Thirteenth Amendment. But slavery was legal in Kentucky and Delaware until eight months after the war, when the ratification of the Thirteenth Amendment brought it to an end. The amendment itself came very late in the war. Not formally proposed in Congress until December 1863 (five months after Vicksburg), it failed in June 1864 to get the necessary two-thirds vote in the House. It was revived in the next session, and with Lincoln exerting powerful administration influence, it passed on January 31, 1865, only ten weeks before Lincoln's death, and was not ratified until the December following the war.*

Lincoln's Colonization Program

As the man who issued the Emancipation Proclamation and as the key leader in securing Congressional adoption of the Thirteenth Amendment, Lincoln was certainly the Emancipator. Whether he can be called a reluctant one depends on how one looks at it, but it is perfectly clear that emancipation was not effected in the way that he hoped for. Lincoln preferred the states themselves to abolish slavery by a gradual process lasting until 1900. He wanted the federal government to encourage this process by paying compensation for the slaves and he did not want the slaves to remain in the United States as freedmen, but rather to be colonized outside the country—in Haiti, in Panama, or elsewhere. He first laid this plan for gradual compensated emancipation and colonization before Congress in a special message in March 1862, which was, in fact, the first time he had permitted anyone in the government to

*To obtain the required three fourths of the states, it was necessary to have the ratification of some of the former Confederate states. One of the many irregularities of the period was that ratifications were accepted from seven southern states whose governments were later rejected by Congress as invalid. Logically, if these governments were not valid, the amendment which abolished slavery had not been duly ratified.

discuss programs for freeing the slaves. Congress responded fairly promptly by agreeing in principle that the United States ought to give financial aid to any state that would adopt gradual emancipation and by voting $600,000 to start a program of colonization. Lincoln threw himself into this plan with great enthusiasm, but he met with frustrations at every step. First, although he assisted in drawing up emancipation plans for adoption by Delaware and Missouri, these states both hesitated at the crucial point. Then further, American Negroes proved reluctant to leave the land of their birth just at the moment when they saw a hope of freedom.

In August 1862, the month preceding the Preliminary Emancipation Proclamation, Lincoln invited a group of Negroes, some of whom had long been interested in colonization, to come to the White House to confer with him. Usually a man with very sensitive awareness of others' feelings, Lincoln on this occasion seemed callous and obtuse. Observing that whites and Negroes were of different races, he said further, "Your race suffers greatly and we of the white race suffer from your presence." Even "when you cease to be slaves, you are yet far removed from being . . . on an equality with the white race. On this broad continent, not a single man of your race is made the equal of a single man of ours . . . I cannot alter it if I would. It is a fact. It is better for us both to be separated." He then proceeded to describe to them the attractions of an area in Panama which had been made available and to urge them to emigrate thither.

Impossibility of Colonization. Entirely apart from the harshness of telling native Americans that they must seek equality in some place other than the land of their birth, Lincoln's plan was completely unrealistic because the United States had neither the facilities to colonize four million people nor a place to which it could send them. At the existing birth rate, no less than five hundred Negroes were being born in the United States every day, and there was no prospect whatever of colonizing the Negro population as rapidly as it was increasing.

Yet Lincoln actually got a colonization experiment into operation in April 1863, when a group of 453 Negroes, who had been induced to accept passage, embarked on a chartered steamer which took them to Cow Island (Ile à Vache), off Haiti. There they suffered the trials of smallpox, malaria, poisonous insects, infertile soil, and even insecure land titles, until in March of the following year, a Navy transport brought back 368 survivors to the United States. Even then, however, Lincoln continued to hope and plan that colonization might succeed.

The Real Question of Race Relations. What is the significance of this story, so full of episodes that came to naught? It is that the United States was fighting its greatest war over a quarrel basically about the existing system of race relations in the United States (that is, the relations embodied in the system of slavery), but it was not preparing to face the question of alternatives. Logically, to justify the sacrifices and losses of such a war, America should have confronted the question of what new system of race relations should replace the one that was so clearly on the way out. But historical circumstances had consistently repressed any realistic analysis of what social conditions the government should encourage if victory gave it a chance. Before the war, instead of recognizing that the intrinsic issue was the racial subordination of Negroes, whether slave or free, North or South, men had visualized the issue restrictively in terms of slavery, or even more artificially in terms of slavery in the territories. When the war came, the delicate and imperative necessities of holding together a coalition of Unionists and antislavery men had caused the government to avoid the potentially disruptive effort to define what social system should follow the war. Thus the war was virtually over before Congress even settled the question of emancipation which was merely preliminary to the real question. The decision that all slaves should be free was not formally disposed of until after the war. Meanwhile, the dream of colonization had prevented any significant amount of public discussion about the hard question of the position of the former slaves in American society.

Problems of Developing a New System of Race Relations

Economic Status of Negroes. This question involved some very concrete and difficult problems. For instance, if Negroes no longer had the economic status which slavery had assigned to them as involuntary agricultural laborers, forced to work because they were chattels, what was their economic status to be? Unless they acquired control of land of their own, they were likely to remain involuntary agricultural laborers, forced to work because their former masters held the land whose cultivation was the only occupation that the Negroes knew. On the islands off the South Carolina coast, Negroes had gained possession (not ownership) of some land when the Confederate plantation owners fled at the time of Admiral Dupont's occupation in November 1861 (above, page 131). They had adapted well to this opportunity and were operating fairly successfully as small independent farmers during the latter part of the war. But should land owned by Confederates throughout the South be confiscated, and should the title be given to former slaves? Aside from the extremely strong moral sanction which nineteenth-century Americans accorded to property rights, there were pragmatic questions about whether a population of former slaves, unaccustomed to the responsibilities of freedom and operating with small tracts of land, could maintain southern cotton production, which was essential to the prosperity not only of the South, but of a great deal of American business outside the South. (The performance of emancipated sugar plantation workers in the British West Indies had not been encouraging.) Also would hostility between blacks and whites be intensified to the level of racial war by confiscating the property of the whites to give it to the blacks?

Political Status of Negroes. Another problem was the political position of the freedmen. If they were not given any political rights, the whites who held political power could easily subordinate and exploit them and violate their interests. But giving them the ballot involved a number of tricky questions. The great majority of slaves were illiterate; therefore to enfranchise the slaves meant to enfranchise a great body of people who were illiterate, and what was worse, almost devoid of civic experience. If they used the ballot badly, it would be held against them, not as inexperienced persons, but as Negroes. But if only literate Negroes were enfranchised, they were too few to have much influence. That would be what was later called tokenism. Further, as the Constitution was then understood, the conferral of the ballot was controlled by the states, not by the federal government, and in the Union states Negroes were not accorded equal suffrage rights anywhere outside of New England.* In these circumstances, giving the ballot to Negroes would seem more a punishment of the white South than a recognition of the rights of Negroes as citizens. (Whether free Negroes were even citizens was still not entirely clear: the Dred Scott decision, which still stood, said they were not, but Attorney General Edward Bates, in an important ruling in 1862, said that they were.)

Both the questions of land title and of voting rights were complicated by the fact that, as Lincoln recognized, emancipation itself had come about in the worst possible way. At best a social transformation whereby former slaves might be put into positions of authority over their former masters was bound to generate tensions which would make harmony between the races extremely difficult to attain. If this was accomplished without the voluntary acquiescence of the southern states, but as a coercive penalty against the South in retribution for losing a war, then the constructive possibilities in the situation were greatly diminished. In Lincoln's view, the potential value of any step to improve the status of the Negroes had to be judged partly by its likely contribution to a harmonious reunion, or to a possible increase of racial strife in the South.

States' Rights. All of these difficulties were enhanced by the genuine and legitimate doubts which existed as to how far the federal government ought to expand its functions in the process of trying to solve them. It has been said that states' rights were shot to death at the battle of the Wilderness, and in the perspective of time, one can see that this is true. But it was not so evident in 1864. Before the war the Union had been a federal association of states which, as separate states, retained extensive political powers, and that was the Union Lincoln said he was fighting to maintain. The South had seceded with the complaint that the federal association was being subverted by a consolidated system with centralized powers. Lincoln was understandably reluctant to give justification to this complaint by creating centralized power to deal with questions previously left to the states. More directly, Lincoln had denied that the southern states were out of the Union, and had insisted that he was engaged only in suppressing "combinations too powerful" to be controlled by ordinary legal processes. He must have found it awkward as the war approached an end to see that the southern states, whose intact identity he had insisted upon,

*In New York, Negroes could vote if they were property holders; in other northern states outside of New England they could not vote at all.

might now obstruct plans for a peace settlement—and do so in a way which might compel him to deny their identity once they were defeated, after having declared his respect for it as long as they were putting up a fight. To state this in another way, it seemed impossible to transform (or revolutionize) the social structure of the South without first transforming (or revolutionizing) the political system of the United States. There were many people in the country who were willing for the states to transform themselves, but not willing to use federal authority to transform them.

Value Conflict: Reconciliation vs. Social Reorganization. Along with all the other difficulties, there was the overriding problem that the end of the war would not bring an end to the dilemma of deciding which value was more important—the restoration of a voluntary Union, or the reorganization by federal authority of southern society. The fact that the southern whites were defeated by superior force, and compelled to submit to the authority of the government in Washington, would not mean that the Union as Americans understood it was being restored. The American Union was and is based on consent, and Americans have been conspicuously unwilling to base social control upon the overt use of force. Because this society is a voluntaristic one, Unionists could justify to themselves the coercion of the South in the Civil War only by assuring themselves that secession had been accomplished by a kind of *coup d'état,* and did not represent the settled purpose of the South, not even the white South. To such Unionists, of whom Lincoln was apparently one, it was almost a psychological compulsion to win back the voluntary loyalty of the white South by formulating peace terms which it would accept. A defeated South would accept the abandonment of secession and of slavery, but it would still fiercely resist land confiscation, Negro suffrage, and the transformation of the social system. Insofar as Unionists felt that a generous peace avoided coercion, they were overlooking the fact that coercion could not be avoided in any case: either the white South must be coerced to create a new status for the Negroes, or the Negroes must be coerced into continuing to submit to a propertyless and inferior status. But the coercion of Negroes did not have the same psychological meaning to northern whites, partly because Negroes had scarcely been regarded as members of American society in the full sense, and partly because the coercion of Negroes was less readily apparent as coercion, since nearly all Negroes had long since recognized what was inevitable for them and had submitted to subordination without overtly resisting it.

Lincoln's Policies for White Reconciliation and Negro Freedom

As the leader of a wartime coalition of Unionists and antislavery men, and as one who personally cherished the values of both Union and freedom, Lincoln keenly felt the dilemma of reconciling policies for the welfare of the blacks with policies for the reconciliation of the southern whites. It was probably the insolubility of this dilemma, coupled with the old strain of racism in one part of his mind, that caused him to cling so longingly to the dream of colonization. But even before the hope of colonization began to fade (and apparently it never did fade entirely from his mind), Lincoln had begun to face the dilemma.

Lincoln's Plan for Reconciliation. Clearly, his first priority was upon reconciling the white South. This he revealed on December 8, 1863, in a proclamation which laid down conditions on which he would bring the southern states back into the Union. His basic plan can be stated in one sentence: Whenever, in any state, a body of citizens eligible to vote under the laws of the states, and numbering as much as one tenth of the number who had voted in the 1860 election (excepting specified classes of war criminals or high civil and military officials of the Confederacy), should take an oath to support the Constitution, the Union, and the wartime measures emancipating slaves, they might organize a republican form of government for the state, which would be recognized as the true government of the state, and they might receive a full pardon for any service to the Confederacy "with restoration of all rights of property, except as to slaves."

But though the terms were simple, the implications were sweeping. First of all, Lincoln wanted swift restoration of the states as soon as he could get a nucleus of loyal citizens—he planned no probationary period before the states might return. Second, he clearly anticipated that this process would be managed by former Confederates—he did not try to find a group of unwavering Unionists, and the oath was one that pledged future loyalty, not one that affirmed a record of past loyalty. Third, he did not anticipate Negro participation in the forming of these governments, for the participants were to be those qualified to vote under the existing laws of the state. Fourth, the proclamation contained no guarantees of rights for Negroes, beyond the recognition of their emancipation, and "any provision which may be adopted by such state government in relation to the freed people of such state which shall recognize and declare their permanent freedom, provide for their education, and which yet may be consistent as a temporary arrangement, with their present condition as a laboring, landless, and homeless class, will not be objected to by the National Executive." Finally (to mention a point much neglected by historians), he evidently did not contemplate any extensive distribution of land to former slaves, for he promised to give all their property back to those who were pardoned, though the Confiscation Act of 1862 had, at least theoretically, expropriated most of the land in the Confederacy by declaring forfeit, after sixty days' notice, all the property of persons who supported the rebellion.

The Wade-Davis Bill. The Republicans in Congress challenged Lincoln's plan, and in July 1864, adopted a measure known as the Wade-Davis Bill, providing for quite a different mode of restoration than Lincoln's. Instead of requiring 10 percent of the electorate, they required 50 percent; instead of accepting a pledge of future loyalty, they excluded all ex-Confederates by requiring an oath of continuous past loyalty (the ironclad oath); implicitly, they did not encourage a speedy restoration, for it was not likely that any former Confederate state could quickly meet these demands. The one point where they concurred with Lincoln was in excluding Negroes from participation.

The Wade-Davis Bill, which Lincoln vetoed, drew the issue not only as to what the policy of restoration should be, but also as to where the authority for deciding the policy lay. The Senate and House clearly regarded it as a Congressional function; Lincoln, as a Presidential function.

Lincoln's Efforts for Restoration with Negro Rights. During 1864, Lincoln pushed forward with his own project for restoring the southern states. He initiated steps toward the establishment of loyal governments in Arkansas, Virginia, Tennessee, and Louisiana. Ultimately none of these was accepted by Congress, but the one which came nearest to fulfillment was in the federally occupied part of Louisiana. Louisiana was a state where the merit of Negro suffrage seemed especially strong, for the state's Negro population had a remarkably high proportion of educated and civically competent members. Moreover, by this time Negroes had enrolled very heavily in the armed services of the Union and, though they were used disproportionately as labor battalions and were denied the opportunity to earn commissions as officers, many units had been engaged in combat, where they fought bravely. Altogether about 178,000 Negro troops—approximately one tenth of the manpower of the Union Army—was Negro, and Lincoln expressed more than once the value which he attached to the Negro contribution in waging the war. In March 1864, therefore, when Louisiana's state convention was about to draw up a constitution, Lincoln wrote to the governor who had just been elected. He was still not prepared, apparently, to advocate Negro suffrage publicly or to "interfere" with a function of the state, but he said, "I barely suggest for your private consideration whether some of the colored people may not be let in—as, for instance, the very intelligent and especially those who have fought gallantly in our ranks." The governor followed this cue from the President and tried to induce the convention to adopt an enfranchisement clause, but all he could get was a provision which left the control of suffrage to the legislature, and that body refused to give the ballot to Negroes. On April 11, 1865, Lincoln stated publicly that he wished that the suffrage had been extended to some of the Negroes of Louisiana.

In his attempts to reconcile the objectives of reconciliation and of Negro rights, Lincoln had by no means ignored the second objective. Although he would have preferred emancipation by state action, he had freed the slaves in the Confederacy by the Emancipation Proclamation, and had applied strong pressure on Congress to free the slaves throughout the Union by submitting the Thirteenth Amendment to the states. His position, moreover, showed some indications of changing. On March 3, 1865, the last day of his last Congress, Lincoln had signed a bill establishing a bureau to aid the freedmen in their transition from slavery to freedom (the Freedmen's Bureau), and this measure contained a highly important provision that, from the abandoned and confiscated lands of the South, forty acres should be assigned to every male citizen, whether refugee or freedman, to be rented for three years at not more than 6 percent of their appraised value in 1860, and then to be purchased from the United States government at their appraised value "with such title as it [the government] could convey." This measure clearly contemplated a postwar situation in which the Negro population would not be colonized or deported, but would remain as an independent, land-owning black yeomanry in the southern states. Then finally, three days before his assassination, Lincoln stated in a public address that "I would myself prefer that it [the elective franchise] were now conferred on the very intelligent [Negroes] and on those who serve our cause as soldiers." At the end of his speech, he added the cryptic statement that "In the present 'situation,' as the phrase goes, it may be my duty to make some new announcement to the people of the South. I am considering, and shall not fail to act, when satisfied that action will be proper."

These events during the last weeks of Lincoln's life have led some historians to emphasize that his career was one of constant development, and to suppose that he may have been on the eve of announcing a broader program for bringing the freedmen into membership in American society. There may be an element of truth in these speculations, but they are partly inspired by the desire to reconcile admiration for Lincoln with a commitment to Negro rights.

The fact is that the evidence is scant. Even the promise of land for the freedmen was by no means as solid as it looked. The land was to be *sold*, not *given*, at the appraised value of 1860, which was more than the market price would be in the shattered economy of the defeated Confederacy. Good land would be available only insofar as it was taken from Confederate owners under the Confiscation Act of 1862, but Lincoln was already engaged in freely granting pardons to former Confederates who took the loyalty oath, and thus restoring their property rights. When the Confiscation Act was adopted, he had expressed his doubts about the legality of expropriating property without judicial process, which is the reason for the disturbing phrase, "with such title as it [the expropriating government] could convey." Lincoln was prepared to assign available land to the freedmen but this did not mean very much in view of the fact that he was not prepared to make a supply of land available.

Land could not be confiscated without judicial proceedings to give the former owners opportunity to prove their loyalty and thus save their title. Very few such condemnation proceedings had been initiated, though the land of every supporter of the Confederacy was, under the Act, subject to forfeiture. The only lands actually in the hands of the government were those which had been abandoned by refugee owners: these were only held for safekeeping until judicial proceedings could be instituted. The delays of the administration in implementing the Confiscation Act had left most of the land in the South in an ambiguous status. It might be confiscated by judicial condemnation, or it might be regained by the original owners if they received a pardon under the Amnesty

Proclamation before judicial condemnation took place. The simple and immensely significant reality was that the rate of pardons had vastly outrun the rate of land condemnations. This disproportion was, of course, not a mere happenstance. It reflected the fact that Lincoln continued to give his first priority to reconciliation, which he regarded as incompatible with the wholesale confiscation of land. He wanted, as he said in his second inaugural, "to bind up the nation's wounds," and to restore a Union of men as well as a Union of laws. He wanted a swift restoration of the southern states and deplored all arguments about the legal status of defeated rebels. The situation as he saw it on April 11 was simply that "the seceded states so called . . . are out of their proper practical relation with the Union. . . . The sole object of the government . . . is to again get them into that proper practical relation. I believe it is not only possible, but in fact easier, to do this, without deciding or even considering whether these states have ever been out of the Union, than with it. Finding themselves safely at home, it would be utterly immaterial whether they had ever been abroad." Lincoln had dreaded that the war would become what he called "a violent and remorseless revolutionary struggle," and he did not contemplate a program to raze the social structure of the South and build a new one.

President Johnson's Reconstruction

Lincoln showed some awareness of the fact that the collapse of the Confederacy in April 1865 presented the country with a crisis comparable to the crisis precipitated by the bombardment of four years earlier. The new crisis was as difficult as the Sumter crisis, and considerably more complex. Sumter had presented the immense but straightforward task of subduing the Confederacy. The surrender of the Confederate armies presented the immense and delicate task of restoring the bonds of union which had existed before the war, without also restoring the servile status of Negroes in the South. Whether Lincoln might have succeeded in this task is a matter for speculation: many Republicans had been opposed throughout his Presidency to his policy of conciliating the South, and they were prepared to make an issue, as they had shown at the time of the Wade-Davis Bill. All that one can believe with reasonable certainty is that if Lincoln had lived, the situation would never have gotten as badly out of control as it did for all parties concerned under Andrew Johnson.

Like most Vice-Presidents in American history, Johnson had been chosen without reference to the fact that he might become President. In 1864 the Republican Party, desiring to prove that it was a Union Party in the broadest sense, wanted an ex-Democrat and a southern Unionist on the ticket with its northern Republican Presidential candidate. Andrew Johnson fitted these specifications. A lifelong, fighting Democrat from Tennessee, and incidentally a man who had owned slaves until 1862, Johnson had spoken loud and clear for the Union at a time when it took real nerve for a southern senator to do so. He had courage, but he also had a kind of rigidity. He never understood the attitudes of the northern people, and he lacked judgment. He had a deep-seated anti-Negro prejudice which was quite unlike that of Lincoln, whose mild prejudice was qualified by his philosophical belief in equality and his profound sense of the shared humanity of all men. The Republicans made him Vice-President and in April 1865, John Wilkes Booth made him President for a term only forty days short of the full four years.

Johnson's Program for Restoration. Johnson apparently intended to do in every respect as Lincoln had done. Lincoln, coming to the presidency when Congress was not in session, had not called Congress to meet as soon as war began but had allowed himself ninety days to try to put down the resistance in the South without legislative interference; Johnson, coming to the presidency when Congress was not in session, did not call Congress at all, but allowed himself more than seven months to deal with Reconstruction before Congress met. This was a dangerous tactic for a man who had never been a member of the party which he now led by the accident of assassination. Lincoln had asserted Presidential rather than Congressional power in setting policy for the restoration of the southern states. Johnson, too, assumed Presidential authority in this area.

Lincoln had given priority to conciliation and quick restoration by his 10 percent policy for the southern states and by his program of amnesty and pardon, without forfeiture of property rights, for former Confederates. Johnson issued a new proclamation of Amnesty and Pardon on May 29, 1865, which was very similar to Lincoln's in offering pardon to most Confederates who would pledge future loyalty, but seemingly less generous in that it excluded all former Confederates with property worth more than $20,000. However, persons not included were still eligible for pardon on an individual basis. On the same day he also issued a proclamation appointing a provisional governor for North Carolina, with authority to hold an election for a constitutional convention to reorganize the government of the state. Eligibility to vote in this election—again following Lincoln's pattern—was restricted to those who had taken the loyalty pledge (which admitted ex-Confederates) and who were eligible under the laws prior to secession (which excluded Negroes). Within the succeeding two months, similar proclamations were issued for all of the remaining Confederate states for which Lincoln had not already initiated such action. Outside of these formal proclamations, Johnson made it clear that there were certain terms which he regarded as mandatory for the states before they could be, as he insisted upon saying, *restored* to the Union rather than *reconstructed:* they must nullify their ordinances of secession, they must show their acceptance of the abolition of slavery by ratifying the Thirteenth Amendment, and they must repudiate the debts which they had contracted as Confederate states.

Delicacy of North-South Relations. Just as many of the overt steps which

Johnson took bore a close resemblance to Lincoln's, so also his primary objective, to restore the southern states to the Union with a minimum of punishment, delay, and perpetuation of wartime hatreds, was in line with Lincoln's purpose. The task of restoration was a subtle one, which required a sensitive and flexible perception of the relations between North and South, and an acute feeling for timing, so that the restoration would be made as soon as both sides were prepared for it, but not before. Lincoln had recognized that an extraordinary combination of persuasion and force would be necessary in order to restore the voluntary union of North and South. The South must never, as he saw it, be coerced to an extremity of terms which would irreparably alienate it from the Union, but it must be brought to such a degree of distress and hopelessness that in its despair it would be ready to comply with terms which it would previously have scorned. When this time came, the terms must be laid down in such a way that Southerners could accept them, not as a matter of decision, which would involve the defeated Confederates in a psychological struggle as to whether they should abandon their own principles, but as an inevitable consequence of their defeat, which they could receive fatalistically without agonizing over whether they were betraying their own cause. Whatever these terms might be, they must be acceptable to the North—both operatively to a northern majority in Congress which would go along with them even if it did not really like them, and psychologically to the northern people, who had paid a great price in human life for their victory, and who needed to believe that the sectional conflict had been settled, and was not merely being moved from the battlefield back into the legislative arena after four years during which it had been moved from the legislative arena to the battlefield. Historians cannot be expected to agree, of course, on exactly what the North wanted, for northern attitudes toward Negroes were both varied and ambiguous, and there was much anti-Negro prejudice in the North. But clearly at least the North wanted assurance that slavery was really dead—not merely disguised in a new institutional dress—and perhaps even more, they wanted to believe that the "slave power" was no longer dominant. The war, with all its killing, its maiming, its bereavement, its sufferings for prisoners, whose lot is cruel under the best of circumstances, all its physical devastation and its psychological harrowing of those who experienced its remorseless process —the war had left an immense heritage of hatred. It was a real question whether more damage would be done by attempting to reconcile the hostile forces before this hatred had time to cool, or by a prolongation of uncertainty and military rule.

To deal with such questions would have required the utmost of tact, of flexibility, of realism, of sagacity, and of deep human understanding in which there was an awareness that the gentlest treatment is not always the kindest. If one recognizes the delicacy of the task, and also that this should have been the crucial transition from slavery to freedom for American Negroes, one may doubt that any leader could have devised a policy that would have been both constructive and practicable. But one may readily believe that other leaders might have come closer than Andrew Johnson.

Liabilities of Johnson's Plan. Johnson's demands concerning secession, slavery, and the Confederate debt were, in any case, the minimum possible demands. From a policy viewpoint, they were fatally flawed by their failure to face up to the long-range question of the status of the freedmen. But it is not at all clear that the American people wanted to face up to this question, and from a tactical standpoint, a settlement which left this question unsettled might quite readily have been adopted by North and South if it had met the conditions of being psychologically acceptable to both sides. But even this tactical require- ment was not met, for Andrew Johnson fell back on a position of literal-minded states'-rights constitutionalism, which did not even recognize that men have always disagreed in interpreting the Constitution. In fact, it scarcely recognized that there had been a war. Johnson's position was that the states had never been out of the Union (which was also Lincoln's position). Therefore they still had all the rights of states, including, for instance, complete autonomy in controlling their suffrage. They must accept the results of the war—no more secession, no more slavery.* Otherwise they were free to write their own constitutions, reorganize their own governments, and elect their own Congress- men and state officials. Furthermore, Congress was obligated to accept them on this basis. The President did them the fearful disservice of telling them all this without finding out whether Congress would, in fact, accept them. To crown all his other liabilities, Johnson had been a self-made man, unable to write until his wife taught him—a plebeian in the patrician South. Always an outsider, he both hated the southern aristocracy and yearned for its approval. Now, as President, he was flattered and sentimentally moved when his old enemies among the planter class assured him of their loyalty to the Union and their dependence upon him to save the South—his and theirs—and the Constitution.

Johnson's Restoration Moves Forward. On this precarious basis, events moved far more rapidly than the circumstances justified. During the summer and autumn of 1865, elections were held for constitutional conventions in all of the states for which Johnson had issued proclamations; these conventions met and drafted constitutions which were acceptable to Johnson. A second set of elections was held to choose state officials, members of state legislatures, and also congressmen; these legislatures met and passed various laws which were urgently needed in view of the economic prostration of the South—laws, for instance, protecting debtors by staying foreclosures upon mortgaged property. By the time Congress assembled in December, these processes had been completed in every state except Texas; Johnson's provisional governors had turned over control of the states to the newly elected officials; and the newly chosen senators and representatives were on hand to claim their seats.

*Johnson's logical position was faulty in that he assumed that it was perfectly proper for the President to insist that the defeated states ratify one constitutional amendment (the Thirteenth) but a rank violation of the rights of the states for Congress to insist that they ratify another amendment (the Fourteenth).

Meanwhile, the President had begun, around midsummer, to issue a flood of pardons for men who had not been included in his general amnesty because of their wealth or high rank in the Confederate government or army. By September 1865, pardons were being granted at the rate of more than one hundred daily, and by February 1866, about fourteen thousand pardons had been issued for persons in the excepted classes. Every one of these not only removed any risk of imprisonment or political disqualification, but also gave back to the pardoned person any claim by forfeiture which the government might have upon his lands. That was, in fact, the main reason why the pardons were sought.

It was a remarkably brisk and neatly packaged Reconstruction. Indeed, it was too neat and brisk, for once the process started, Johnson failed to control it. He had reconciled the South on terms which he might have anticipated would not be acceptable in the North.

The Southern States Challenge Johnson

In short, Johnson stated the terms which the southern state governments must meet, but he failed to enforce them. He made it perfectly clear that the states must ratify the Thirteenth Amendment either in their conventions or their legislatures, but he did not compel them to meet this requirement. Four times he sent messages to his provisional governor in Mississippi urging the point ("I hope" . . . "it is all important" . . . "I do hope"), but in the end Mississippi did not ratify and Johnson nevertheless recognized the reconstructed government. Alabama refused to ratify the part of the amendment which gave Congress powers of enforcement. Also in repudiating their ordinances of secession, the state conventions made difficulties and South Carolina refused to nullify her ordinance, since nullifying it would have meant that it had been void from the outset. Instead, the convention repealed it, which implied that a perfectly legal action had been subsequently reversed. South Carolina and Mississippi also refused to repudiate their Confederate debt.

The important aspect of these recalcitrant acts was less in their actual content, though that too was significant, than in the fact that the former Confederates were testing whether Johnson would maintain a firm line with them, and were discovering that he would not, even on points which he had stipulated in advance as essential. Once they learned this, they quickly moved to do other things which seem astonishing now, and which did astonish many sober Southerners in 1865.

Rejection of Negro Suffrage. For one thing, they refused to grant Negro suffrage. The first state convention to meet was that of Mississippi. Johnson wrote to his provisional governor: "If you could extend the elective franchise to all persons of color who can read . . . and write . . . and all persons of color who own real estate," of a value of not less than $250, "you would completely disarm the adversary" [by which he meant the Republicans who demanded

Negro suffrage]. Johnson's phrasing contained two fatal flaws. First he said, "if you could" which was essentially pleading; it gave the members of the convention a responsibility which they could not accept without being punished subsequently by their constituents. To have said "you must" would have seemed harsher, but would actually have made it easier for the delegates by relieving them of responsibility. Second, by alluding to the Republican advocates of Negro suffrage as "the adversary" he tacitly aligned himself with the former Confederates against the members of his own party. There were some influential whites in the Mississippi Convention who believed they ought to yield on this point: one reminded the delegates that all of them were a conquered people, another warned that the Northerners were a determined people not to be trifled with; still another said, "We have no choice." But it became increasingly clear that so far as Andrew Johnson was concerned, they did have a choice. Mistaking his voice for the voice of the North, they proceeded to exercise the choice by restricting the suffrage to white persons only. A number of prominent Southerners—James L. Alcorn of Mississippi, Alexander H. Stephens of Georgia, Wade Hampton of South Carolina—advocated a limited Negro suffrage, but once Mississippi had successfully defied Johnson, all the other states defied him also. Not one allowed any Negro to vote.

The southern rejection of Negro suffrage was a bold challenge to be made by people fresh from an overwhelming military defeat, but it was at least mitigated by the fact that most of the northern states still did not give the ballot to Negroes either. Only six states—five in New England, plus New York with a property qualification which applied to Negroes only—admitted Negro voters. In the autumn of 1865, at the very time when the southern conventions were rejecting Negro suffrage, three northern states rejected it also by vote: Connecticut by 33,000 to 27,000; Wisconsin by 55,000 to 46,000; and Minnesota by 14,000 to 12,000.

The Black Codes. Even more likely to arouse an explosive northern reaction were two other developments in the South. One of these was the enactment by Mississippi, South Carolina, and Alabama (to be followed by other states in 1866) of codes of laws defining the rights of Negroes in so restrictive a way as to leave doubt as to whether they would be, in any real sense, free. Most of these codes excluded Negroes from jury service and from testimony in court cases to which whites were a party; South Carolina forbade Negroes to take up any occupation except agriculture without special permission from a court; and other laws forbade Negroes to rent land, to possess firearms, to go about after curfew, and so forth. Most alarming of all were vagrancy laws which provided that Negroes without employment could be arrested and fined, and if unable to pay the fine, bound over to work for whoever would pay it. Whether or not such a worker could be called a slave, he could hardly be called free, and Senator Henry Wilson of Massachusetts spoke for a good many Northerners when he said, "This arbitrary and inhuman act makes the freedmen the slaves of society, and it is far better to be the slave of one man than the slave of arbitrary law." It may be argued, perhaps correctly, that the freedmen were in such a disorganized condition in the months immediately after the war that special legislation to regulate them was necessary. But the laws that were adopted, which quickly became known as the "Black Codes," were a travesty upon the idea of freedom, and they suggested the alarming thought that the South either had not accepted emancipation or did not know its meaning.

Congressional Elections in the South. Johnson permitted the Black Codes to be adopted without even warning against them. In fact, he seemed increasingly to abdicate entirely, giving "his" southern states free rein. As they sensed the absence of controls, they became more and more reckless in "daring" the North to interfere with them. This defiance took a final, rather startling form in the election of prospective congressmen. In the spring of 1865 former Confederates were trying not to be conspicuous, but during summer and fall they grew less reticent and began to run for political office even while they were still disqualified because they had rebelled against the United States. But when they were elected, Johnson, instead of barring them because they were disqualified, removed their disqualifications by pardoning them.

When the northern Congressmen went home at the end of the session in March 1865, Lincoln was still President; the war was still on; and the possibility of trials after the war, for treason, was not absent from their minds. When they reassembled in December, a lifelong Democrat and former slaveholder from Tennessee was President, and Congressmen-elect were present from the states with which they had been at war. These would-be colleagues included the vice-president of the Confederacy, four Confederate generals, five Confederate colonels, six Confederate cabinet officers, and fifty-eight members of the Confederate congress. It looked as though Richmond had moved to Washington. These claimants were not petitioning to be seated; they were demanding to be seated, on the ground that their states, as Lincoln himself had said, had never been out of the Union. Besides, their new governments had met all the requirements prescribed by the President, while they themselves had received a full pardon. The law did not require them to repent and they showed no sign of repentance. In some of the southern state legislatures, they were still wearing their Confederate uniforms, and perhaps not entirely because these were the only clothes they had left.

Congressional Reaction: The Joint Committee on Reconstruction

The Thirty-ninth Congress did not hesitate. It refused to seat them. Nor would it wait to hear the President's message before appointing a Joint Committee on Reconstruction. This itself had a special meaning, for the Senate and the House are usually too jealous of their separate powers to act in concert, but in this situation, the two chambers were creating a kind of legislative authority to counter the executive authority of the President.

After the Joint Committee was set up, events moved very slowly, for the Republicans did not want to break with the man whom they had made President, if a break could be avoided. Further, while they were agreed in disliking the Black Codes and the new Confederate invasion of Washington, they were far from agreement about what they wanted as an alternative. Nearly all were concerned, to some degree, both with questions of policy and questions of political power.

Republican Policy Questions. At the level of policy, there were a few members—a minority of the Republican membership—who believed that a complete revolution in the power structure of the South was needed to fulfill the emancipation of the slaves. Charles Sumner, in the Senate, thought of this revolution primarily as political. The freedmen should receive citizenship and all the rights pertaining to complete legal equality: Negroes should not be subjected to any discrimination or exclusion in the use of public facilities, nor should public education be segregated. Moreover, as citizens, Negroes should have full rights in the courts, as litigants, as witnesses, as jurors; they should vote and hold office. Above all, Sumner believed in the vote to give them the leverage to change the southern power structure and thus make good their claims to equality. In the House, Thaddeus Stevens thought of the revolution primarily as economic. The large plantations should be confiscated, broken up into small parcels of land, and distributed among the blacks to make them a landowning yeomanry. Only in this way, thought Stevens, could they be independent, and only through economic independence could they achieve equality. "Forty acres . . . and a hut," said Stevens, "would be more valuable . . . than the . . . right to vote." In fact, he was somewhat qualified in his enthusiasm for Negro suffrage.

Although Sumner and Stevens possessed personal qualities which carried them into positions of leadership, their views were not representative of the Republican majority in Congress, for the majority, like the northern public, was not committed to the idea of Negro equality. They objected to Johnson's program essentially because it left the freedmen without any protection against being thrust back into a servile condition, and the Black Codes gave a clear indication that they would be thrust back unless guarantees of some kind were devised. Thus, neither Senator John Sherman of Ohio nor Lyman Trumbull of Illinois believed in equality for Negroes, but both opposed Johnson's restored regimes, because, as Sherman said, "To have refused the Negroes the simplest rights granted to every other inhabitant, native, or foreigner, would be outrageous," and Trumbull expressed a fear that the freedman would "be tyrannized over, abused, and virtually reenslaved without some legislation by the nation for his protection."

Republican Power Concerns. All this was at the policy level. At the level of political power, the reappearance of the former Confederates, claiming seats in

Congress, suddenly threatened the Republicans with an immediate danger of being reduced to a political minority, before they could consolidate any of the results of the Union's military victory. One supremely ironical element in the political situation was the fact that the emancipation of the slaves had ended the constitutional arrangement by which slaves were counted at three fifths of their actual numbers for purposes of determining the representation in Congress of the slave states. Since slaves did not vote, this practice had given southern voters an overrepresentation as compared with northern voters, and before the war this had been a source of chronic northern complaint. The overthrow of slavery would change the ratio at which the Negro population was counted from three fifths to five fifths, regardless of whether Negroes were actually allowed to vote. Since they were *not* allowed to vote under the Johnson governments, the net effect would be to give the southern states an increase of about twenty seats in Congress as a bonus for losing the war. Republicans were acutely conscious that if the South came back into political participation on this basis, they would probably be left in a minority. They had won the election of 1864 with only 55 percent of the vote, and with the eleven Confederate states not participating. Once the South was restored, they perceived with indignation, a combination of copperheads and unrepentant rebels would be in position to seize control and undo everything for which 360,000 Union soldiers had died. Thaddeus Stevens spelled out this intolerable contingency with precision: "If [Negro] suffrage is excluded in the rebel states, then every one of them is sure to send a solid rebel . . . delegation to Congress. They, with their kindred copperheads of the North, would always elect the President and control Congress."

All Unionists, one must suppose, would object to a settlement which threw away a military victory gained by such heavy sacrifices. Their objection would be based upon a mixture of selfish partisan desire to maintain power for the sake of personal gains and of unselfish purpose to save an idealistic program. This mixture would vary from one congressman to another, with diverse proportions of hate, avarice, idealism, and civic virtue. The difficulty of distinguishing the two elements is suggested by another speech of Thaddeus Stevens, in which he declared his commitment to Negro suffrage, not entirely for its own sake, but as a means to preserve Republican political control. He recognized that this would lead to the accusation that he was motivated by partisan purposes but, he said, "I believe that on the continued ascendancy of that party depends the safety of this great nation."

In any case, regardless of motives, the President and the Republican majority in Congress were at odds, and the Republicans were divided between a moderate contingent which wanted guarantees of southern loyalty and protected minimal rights for the freedmen, and a radical contingent which wanted to keep the South politically helpless until southern society could be rebuilt on a new basis. Further, the moderates were predisposed to come to terms with the President, by finding a basis on which to admit or recognize the state governments which he had sponsored, rather than to overthrow these governments. But as events developed, the rigidity of Johnson's position made any alliance between him and the moderates increasingly difficult.

Congressional Reconstruction, the Moderates in Control

The Freedmen's Bureau. The moderates took and held the initiative throughout the Congressional session which began in December 1865. First, they sponsored two bills. One of these, the Freedmen's Bureau Bill, provided for an indefinite extension of the agency which had been established by the previous Congress to aid emancipated slaves in various ways. The Bureau was operated by the War Department, and was therefore managed by military officers who distributed food, supervised labor contracts between freedmen and their employers, sponsored schools for Negroes (which were privately financed since the Bureau had no funds for this purpose), and, in general, oversaw the welfare of a group of people as yet too inexperienced to protect their own interests. But the Bureau also exercised military jurisdiction; it could take a case involving a freedman out of the civil courts and deal with it by military law. Southern whites accused the Bureau of corruption, of recruiting for the Republican party, and of causing unnecessary friction between white employers and Negro employees. All of these accusations were probably true in some cases and false in others. In some cases, the Bureau was guilty of a fault for which it was never blamed: cooperating too closely with white planters at the expense of its Negro clients. But at bottom, the white South hated the Bureau because it represented an assertion of Negro rights, and because if Johnson's state governments were valid, there was no place for a military agency which could suspend the operation of laws adopted by the civil government, could set aside the decisions of civil courts, and could bring citizens to trial and impose sentences upon them. The existence of such an agency was a tacit denial of the legitimacy of the civil government. Yet the moderate Republicans hardly intended it as such. They intended only to give the freedmen some measure of federal protection.

The Civil Rights Act and the Freedmen's Bureau Bill. Johnson vetoed the bill, primarily on the grounds that the civil authority in the South was functioning adequately and that military law in peacetime was not warranted. The veto was upheld by a narrow margin. The fact that it was sustained probably helped to secure votes for the second Republican measure, the Civil Rights Act of 1866. This act sought to protect freedmen's rights by bringing such rights under federal jurisdiction. This was, of course, prior to the Fourteenth Amendment, which is the basic support for all federal action in defense of civil rights, and without such an amendment, the act was of doubtful constitutionality. It declared all persons born in the United States (except Indians not taxed) to be citizens; it specified certain rights for all persons, and

Despite fierce southern opposition, the Freedmen's Bureau, supported by federal troops, distributed food and medicine to Negroes and poor whites. Under its auspices, the first widespread free public school system was built up in the South, wit over 4000 schools and almost 250,000 students. Many Northerners, encouraged by various church organizations, went as teachers into the hostile southern communities. This picture shows a primary school for freedmen at Vicksburg, Mississippi. *Harper's Weekly, June 23, 1866*

added a generalized affirmation of the right "to full and equal benefit of all laws and proceedings for the security of person and property, as is enjoyed by white citizens"; and it extended exclusive jurisdiction to the federal courts in cases involving these rights. Johnson vetoed the Civil Rights Act on the grounds that it exceeded constitutional limits. This time, Congress passed the bill over the veto, but Republicans knew that the Supreme Court might throw it out as unconstitutional. Congress also adopted another Freedmen's Bureau Bill, and this time, when confronted with a veto, it overrode the President's opposition.

The Fourteenth Amendment. By the summer of 1866, the situation had reached a real impasse. The war had been over for more than a year. The President believed that the southern states had been restored to the Union and he doubted the legality of *any* acts of a Congress in which eleven states were not permitted to participate. Congress, on the other hand, believed that the President had unconstitutionally usurped a Congressional function by his process of restoration. Hatred was incredibly bitter, as is reflected in the fact that Johnson accused leading Republicans of conspiring to assassinate him, and some Republicans accused Johnson of involvement in the conspiracy that had led to Lincoln's assassination.

At this point the Republican moderates made their final and most strenuous effort to find a solution which would be accepted by the South and which would provide the desired minimal guarantees for the freedmen. They framed an elaborate Fourteenth Amendment to the Constitution. This amendment dealt with the civil rights of Negroes by declaring that persons born in the United States are citizens both of the nation "and of the state wherein they reside"; it forbade any state to adopt legislation which would "abridge the privileges or immunities of citizens" or to "deprive any person of life, liberty or property without due process of law" or to "deny to any person within its jurisdiction the equal protection of the laws." It disqualified for public office, federal or state, anyone who had held public office before the war, had taken an oath to uphold the Constitution, and had then supported the Confederacy. But it permitted removal of the disqualification by act of Congress passed by two-thirds majority. It affirmed the binding obligation of the public debt of the United States and the nullity of the Confederate debt. It dealt with the explosive question of Negro suffrage, not by conferring the ballot, but by creating a dilemma for the South which might induce southern states to confer it themselves. Any state which denied the ballot to any adult male citizens (except criminals or those who had participated in rebellion) should have its basis of representation in Congress reduced in proportion to the number of persons disfranchised.

In plain language, this protected the North but not the Negroes. It encouraged the southern states to adopt Negro suffrage by providing that a state could have full representation only when it allowed all its adult male citizens to vote, but if a state disliked Negro suffrage enough to give up seats in Congress, rather than adopt it, it might do so. In either contingency, the Republicans would be assured of a gain—by a reduction of the number of southern congressmen, or by the addition of Negro voters (potentially Republican voters) to the southern electorate.

Significance of the Fourteenth Amendment. By adopting this amendment and submitting it to the states, Congress accomplished several things. It affirmed the rights of the freedmen under the Constitution, and brought these rights (apparently) under federal jurisdiction; this would dispose of the Black Codes. It escaped the problem of Negro suffrage on a nationwide basis, which was especially difficult since the majority of northern states preferred Negro suffrage at a distance but not at home. It slammed the door on the "Confederate brigadiers" who were clamoring for seats in Congress, yet it did this without seriously encroaching upon the pardons issued by Johnson; it might well reduce the political influence of ex-Confederates in the southern states. Also, it avoided the drastic action that would have been involved in overthrowing the Johnson governments. Finally, it brought back into the process of reconstruction the factor of consent by both sides, which had been lost. The North was stating terms of reunion. The South was requested to accept these terms by ratifying the amendment. The North made no blind promises to readmit the southern states until it could see the spirit in which the South acted. But there was an implied promise, which many Republicans publicly stated that they regarded as binding. If the southern states ratified, the Johnson governments would be recognized by Congress, and Reconstruction would have been completed. And since all these provisions were incorporated in a constitutional amendment, they were not vulnerable to arguments against their constitutionality, as the Freedmen's Bureau Bill and the Civil Rights Act conspicuously had been.

The submission of the Fourteenth Amendment was the point at which the country came closest to arriving at a voluntary settlement—a settlement with some degree of consent—of the issues of the Civil War. The North had stated its terms. By accepting them, the South could have returned to the Union without adopting Negro suffrage or experiencing the slightest measure of Negro rule. In fact, the only parties at interest who had good reason to resist this settlement were the Negroes whose suffrage might be denied. If these terms had been laid down at the time of Confederate surrender in 1865, the South would probably have accepted them without hesitation. In the summer of 1866, if Andrew Johnson had warned the southern states that he could not protect them against the fury of the Republicans if they refused these terms, they might still have accepted. But Johnson was increasingly far gone in a kind of logic which takes no account of reality. Legally, in his opinion, the southern states were valid states, but the Congress, from which eleven states were missing, was hardly a valid Congress. Even if it were, the proposal that states should be *forced* to ratify an amendment in order to obtain their rights as states was a mockery. Whatever theoretical strength this argument may have had, it disregarded the controlling reality that the South had lost the Civil War and the North had made sacrifices so heavy that merely going back to the status of 1860 was not enough. But Johnson advised the southern states to reject the amendment, and to rely on the defeat of the Republicans in the 1866 elections.

The South Rejects the Amendment. In November, the Republicans won the Congressional elections by greater majorities than they had ever scored, even during the war. If Johnson's restored states had been watching for a sign, the election should have told them how far it was safe to be guided by Johnson, and what they should have done. They should have ratified the Fourteenth Amendment. But the war had been over for nineteen months, so the sense of urgency and the sharp shock of defeat had worn off. The southern states felt no assurance that Congress would recognize them if they ratified the amendment, and they had no perception of the harshness of the terms that might be imposed if they did not. Texas rejected it before the election; Georgia did so in November; six others in December; two more in January; and one in February. Tennessee ratified and was readmitted by Congress. But James A. Garfield of

Ohio declaimed in the House, "The last one of the sinful ten has flung back into our teeth the magnanimous offer of a generous nation."

Radical Reconstruction

The rejection of the Fourteenth Amendment marked the end of a phase in the history of Reconstruction. Up to that point, the Republican party had been divided, and the dominant moderates had steadily worked for an arrangement that would provide guarantees for the freedmen on a basis that Johnson's restored states would accept. The element of negotiation or consent had always been present, though sometimes in a very attenuated form. But the southern rejection of the amendment combined with other factors to draw the Radicals and the moderate Republicans together, at least temporarily. President Johnson had alienated them further by denouncing them in vituperative terms during the election campaign. Their worst suspicions concerning the attitude of the white South toward the Negro had been confirmed by violent anti-Negro riots in Memphis and New Orleans in May and July 1866. By the beginning of 1867, so far as Congress was concerned, the basic issue had changed. It was no longer a question of what terms Johnson's governments should be pressed to accept. It was rather a question of whether the southern states should be readmitted without a long period of probation, and what terms of readmission should be imposed.

Congress dealt with this question at the short session which ran from December 1866 to the following March. It was characteristic of the short session that measures were rushed through in great haste and confusion during the final days before adjournment. The reconstruction legislation, accordingly, went through very intricate and tangled parliamentary maneuvers, so no one attained exactly what he intended. But essentially, the Republicans agreed that the Johnson governments should be rejected entirely. Some of them now leaned toward what Abraham Lincoln had dreaded most—a long probationary period during which the South would be reduced to a territorial status, and would have no voice in the federal government. Others wanted to reconstruct the southern states swiftly but harshly, by starting over again on the basis of a suffrage including Negroes and excluding those white Southerners marked for disqualification by the proposed Fourteenth Amendment. But as events turned out, even those who disliked harsh terms still preferred them to an indefinite exclusion of the southern states. As a result the prolonged deadlock over Johnson's governments was at last broken, nearly two years after the end of the war, when Congress adopted on the final day of the session a military reconstruction bill. This, supplemented by three other bills at the succeeding session, laid down a new program of Reconstruction.

The Program of Military Reconstruction. Under this program, the South was divided into five military districts with a general of the army in charge of each. The military governors were to conduct a voter registration, for which

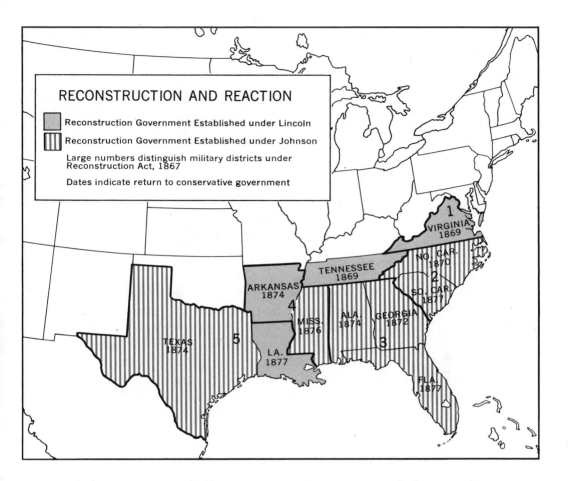

RECONSTRUCTION AND REACTION

▨ Reconstruction Government Established under Lincoln

▥ Reconstruction Government Established under Johnson

Large numbers distinguish military districts under Reconstruction Act, 1867

Dates indicate return to conservative government

VIRGINIA 1869
1

NO. CAR. 1870
2

SO. CAR. 1877

TENNESSEE 1869

ARKANSAS 1874
4

MISS. 1876

ALA. 1874

GEORGIA 1872

TEXAS 1874
5

LA. 1877

3

FLA. 1877

Negroes would be eligible, but whites who held public office before the Civil War and supported the Confederacy would not. When the registration was completed, the governors were to hold elections for new constitutional conventions for each state. These conventions were required to write Negro suffrage into the new state constitutions. When constitutions had been drafted by the conventions and ratified by the voters and when the Fourteenth Amendment had been ratified, the state's constitution might be submitted to Congress for approval. If it were approved, the state could be admitted to the Union and its senators and representatives could be seated in Congress.

Reaction of Johnson and the South. As Andrew Johnson saw it, all this was entirely outside the Constitution, and it involved Congress in the logical absurdity of applying the terms of an amendment which had not been ratified to a political unit which was denied identity as a state and yet was required to function as a state for purposes of ratifying the amendment, which was demanded as a prerequisite to statehood. If in the eyes of Congress Johnson's restored states were illegal, in the eyes of the President a Congress which excluded ten of the member states was illegal, and its measures would not have been valid even if they conformed with the Constitution, which they did not.

For the white South, it was a trauma. Two years after the war, after renouncing slavery and secession, after organizing new governments according to instructions from the President, they were back in chaos, with their traditional ruling class barred from public life, and with an electorate in which illiterate exslaves seemed likely to constitute a majority. They had no idea how long it might be before their states could return to the Union, but when the time came, they feared, exslaves rather than ex-Confederates were likely to represent them in Congress. To white Southerners, chronically haunted by dread of a slave insurrection resulting in Negro control, this looked like a nightmare come true. The century-long bitter resentment with which the South later remembered the "horrors" of Reconstruction was probably a product more of the anticipatory fear and dread than of the actual experiences of Military and so-called Black Reconstruction.

As the white South saw it, the whites of the North had delivered them mercilessly to the ordeal of rule by former slaves. It is true that when the registration had been completed in the ten former Confederate states, about 660,000 whites were enrolled and about 703,000 Negroes. No one knew accurately how many whites were disqualified and the estimates ranged wildly from 50,000 to more than a million. The white people of the South shrank from their impending fate and later remembered this moment in history as a kind of descent into the pit. If given a choice, they would probably have stayed out of Congress indefinitely rather than submit to the terms dictated by Congressional Military Reconstruction.

Significance of the Situation. If we examine the situation through our own eyes, however, and not through those of the participants, the situation of the former Confederates was by no means so desperate. It was true that there would be military governors and military law, but in fact the Freedmen's Bureau had been administering military law ever since the end of the war, and it had been using the army to do it. It was true also that they would have to submit to the humiliation of seeing exslaves vote while leading Confederates could not, but Negroes were a numerical minority in the South as a whole, and the South had already been subjected to the humiliation of exclusion from Congress. For months the battle over the status of the white South had been fought in Congress, while the Southerners were forced to look on as helpless spectators. Now the arena was being shifted to the southern states, where the ex-Confederates could at least enter the contest themselves and wrestle with the Republicans, both white and Negro, for domination. The Negroes were armed, to be sure, with the suffrage and with a measure of northern Republican support. But the former Confederates, though partially disfranchised, were armed with advantages which gave them the upper hand in the contest almost from the beginning. They had education and experience in leadership; the freedmen had neither. They could rely on the fact that the North shared the South's prejudice against Negroes. The North was not imposing Negro suffrage because of conviction on its merits, but because there seemed to be no other way to prevent the Confederates from reestablishing slavery in a new form, and then returning to Congress to join the copperheads in seizing control of the government. They could also rely on the fact that the North did not care nearly as deeply about the equality of the Negroes as they did about the subordination of the Negroes, and in a test to see who would hang on longest, they were sure to win. Finally, they had held on to their land, and land as a weapon of economic strength was far more potent than the ballot as a weapon of political strength.

The Question of Land for the Freedmen

Only a few white Republicans, apparently, perceived clearly the strategic importance of landownership. The Negroes, whom the white Southerners scorned and to whom the Northerners condescended, saw it very plainly. A delegation of them told William T. Sherman in 1865, "The way we can best take care of ourselves is to have land and turn it and till it by our own labor." But they could seldom get many Republicans to listen to them, perhaps because landownership would have helped only the blacks, whereas the ballot would help both them *and* the Republican party.

The South Carolina Settlement. Many antislavery men had wanted to provide land for the freedmen, and many had looked to the confiscation of Confederate plantations as a way to provide it. That had been the meaning of the Confiscation Act of 1862. But though the Act established a judicial process for forfeiture, the process was not used extensively during the Lincoln administration. Where it was used, shrewd Yankees on the make, who saw the advantage of buying up southern estates at distress prices, had a way of beating the freedmen to the acquisition. About the only place where the freedmen came into possession of land on a large scale was in coastal South Carolina, where the Navy established a bridgehead as early as 1862. On the Sea Islands, some land was legally forfeited and a portion of it was acquired by Negroes who were protected in their title after the war. Along the coast, a far greater quantity of land was opened to Negroes who settled on it and cultivated it while condemnation proceedings were pending. By the middle of 1865 there were forty thousand Negroes settled on the coastal lands. These black farmers were seemingly protected by a Special Field Order Number Fifteen (January 1865), issued by General William T. Sherman, which decreed that a coastal strip, including all islands and the mainland for a depth of thirty miles, should be set apart for exclusive Negro settlement and made available, with "possessory title" in tracts of no more than forty acres. This was as close as anyone during the Civil War ever came to providing a new life for the Negroes to move into when they moved out of slavery. It might have become a protected haven in which the Negroes could have established an independent yeoman society of their own, or it might have become a vast reservation, like the Indian reservations, in which the Negroes, segregated from the main body of society, would have sunk steadily deeper into wretchedness. No one will ever know, because they were not permitted to keep the land.

Failure of Confiscations and Homesteads. About seven weeks after Sherman's order, Congress passed the Freedmen's Bureau Bill, which seemed to reaffirm and extend more broadly the promise of land, though it now spoke of "sale," and used the innocent-looking but ominous phrase "with such title as it [the government] could convey." But none of these gestures meant anything until land was actually confiscated by regular judicial process, that is, by proving in court that the previous owner had forfeited his title by aiding the Confederacy. This process of forfeiture, which had moved very slowly under Lincoln, was halted entirely by Johnson. By the autumn of 1865 Johnson's flood of pardons was reversing the process by restoring all of the federally held acreage to its original owners unless forfeiture had already been completed. Even the land already occupied by freedmen had to be given back in cases where forfeiture was still pending, and one of the saddest of the many disillusionments of the freedmen came late in 1865 and early in 1866 when the military began putting most of the forty thousand settlers out of their homes on the coastal lands which were now being returned to their fully pardoned former owners. One of the freedmen, when informed that he must give up the land which he had occupied, could not believe it, and protested, "To turn us off from the land that the government has allowed us to occupy is nothing less than returning us to involuntary servitude. They will make freedom a curse to us."

Economic conditions for Negroes were not much changed by the Civil War, although the occupants of these quarters were no longer slaves. *Duke University*

It was easy to see that an injustice had been done to these Negroes, but many Northerners were willing to provide land for the freedmen if it could be done without the confiscation of property. The federal government still held public lands in the states of Alabama, Arkansas, Florida, Louisiana, and Mississippi—lands which had never been held by private individuals—and in July 1866, Congress passed a Southern Homestead Act to make these lands available at $1.25 an acre, with exclusive priorities until January 1, 1867, for freedmen and Unionist whites. But this measure also failed, because freedmen did not have even the small capital required, because farming requires equipment and money with which to get started, and because the available land was inferior. (The reason that the government still held it was, for the most part, because no one had thought it worth buying, even at cheap public land prices.)

A few people recognized the crucial importance of the land question. For instance, Elizur Wright of Massachusetts warned in 1867 that the southern landowners could afford to laugh at Negro education and Negro suffrage— "your schoolma'ams and ballot boxes"—so long as the Negroes had no access to employment except upon white men's land. "They who own the real estate of a country control its vote," he asserted.

The Proposals of Thaddeus Stevens. One person who never lost sight of the importance of the land question was Thaddeus Stevens. As early as September 1865, Stevens came forward with a grandiose plan which proposed to confiscate all the land of all the former slaveholders in the South. This would have amounted to more than three fourths of the cultivable land in the region. The land of nonslaveholders, who were more numerous, would remain untouched; the slaveholders had numbered about seventy thousand so that in terms of population only a limited number, he argued, would be affected. Stevens advocated giving forty acres to each adult male freedman, which would take about 40,000,000 acres and leave 350,000,000 to be sold. From the sales, he would pay pensions to Union soldiers, compensate southern loyalists, and apply $3 billion toward repayment of the national debt.

The details of his plan reveal a great deal. Although Stevens announced it as primarily for the freedmen, the former slaves would in fact receive scarcely one tenth of the land which he proposed to confiscate. One might ask, therefore, why he did not advocate taking one tenth of each former slaveholder's land instead of taking all of it. The answer must be in part that he was motivated as much by hatred of the slaveowners—"proud, bloated, and defiant rebels"—and by desire for vengeance on them as by his humane concern for the freedmen. Hate and humanitarianism were curiously blended in Thaddeus Stevens. Further, one may ask whether Stevens made the plan very broad in the hope of gaining support from potential beneficiaries who would never adopt such a drastic measure for the freedmen alone. In short, the grants to the Negroes would cost only a small fraction of what would be given to others to buy support for the grant.

Stevens quickly learned that very few, even of the radical Republicans, were prepared to go this far. The New York *Tribune* perhaps touched the vital point of the opposition when it denounced "any warfare against southern property." Respect for property rights, and a belief that no one should have anything that he had not earned were basic ideas in the ethos of nineteenth-century America, and Stevens was challenging these principles.

In February 1866, Stevens offered a measure in Congress to set aside three million acres of public land or forfeited land to be distributed to freedmen at a cost, after three years, of $2 per acre. In presenting his proposal, he pointed out that when serfs had been freed in Russia, their emancipation had included an opportunity to acquire land at a nominal price. But it is notable how far he had retreated from his plan of the previous September. Now he was talking of using public lands and lands already forfeited, rather than of a revolutionary forfeiture. He was down from forty million acres for freedmen to three million acres, and he was speaking in terms of a purchase rather than a gift of land. Despite these concessions and despite the fact that he was widely regarded as a kind of parliamentary dictator, cracking a whip which the Congress dared not defy, he was voted down by the humiliating majority of 126 to 37.

Stevens only raised the issue of land for the freedmen once again. Nine days after the adoption of the Military Reconstruction Act in 1867, he introduced a new bill which called for federal expropriation of public lands in the former Confederate states and for the implementation of the land forfeiture provisions of the Confiscation Act of 1862. From these lands, he would distribute to each adult male or head of a family among the freedmen forty acres (which could not be sold or alienated for ten years) plus fifty dollars for each homesteader. On March 19, he made a speech in support of his bill, but it was never even brought to a vote, though it was roundly criticized. Representative John W. Chanler of New York remarked that "All confiscation is robbery," and Henry Wilson of Massachusetts, alluding to the bitterness which confiscation would generate, said, "I don't want an Ireland or Poland in America."

Land and Reconstruction. In view of the wretched condition of southern Negro agricultural labor in the decades between 1865 and the New Deal—or even beyond—it is tempting to suppose that forty acres and a mule would have solved the seemingly insoluble problems of Reconstruction. Yet there are some problems for which there are no solutions—an ancient truth which Americans are peculiarly unwilling to recognize. If Negroes had received their forty acres, they would have had to choose essentially between using these acres as a family farm, raising their own food and avoiding commercial agriculture, or else farming a commercial crop, which would have meant cotton. Family farming had no future in America, which was rapidly converting to an exchange economy in which money income is essential. Without money income, over the long term the freedmen would have been little better off than serfs. Yet if they had taken to growing cotton, they would inevitably have run into all the evils of the cotton economy, with its chronic indebtedness, its overproduction, and its low prices. These evils caused hundreds of thousands of landowning farmers, both white and Negro, to lose their farms between 1880 and 1940 and to fall into a condition of tenancy or sharecropping. The trend was continuous throughout the South. There is no reason to suppose that the recipients of forty acres and a mule would have escaped this inexorable process.

But to return to 1867. The North was still torn by the dilemma that it wanted both a genuine reconciliation with the South and a genuine freedom for the former slaves. It did not really want equality of the races, so the northern public of the 1860's and 1870's was not torn by that problem as a later generation was to be. But it had proved difficult to harmonize even freedom and reconciliation. President Johnson's policy had sacrificed freedom to reconciliation, and now the Military Reconstruction Acts seemed likely to sacrifice reconciliation to a more genuine freedom. These acts, in effect, transferred the conflict from the halls of Congress to the southern states, and did so on terms which were bitterly resented by the white South. They might better have been resented by the freedmen. For, while the Military Reconstruction acts gave the black folks most of the ballots, the total indifference of Congress to the Stevens bill left the white folks owning virtually all of the land.

SUGGESTED READING (Prepared by Carl N. Degler)

The literature on Reconstruction is well canvassed and annotated in James G. Randall and David Donald, *The Civil War and Reconstruction* (2nd ed., 1961). A briefer, though more recent compilation, also by David Donald, is *The Nation in Crisis, 1861–1877** (1969), a Goldentree Bibliography. The early years of Reconstruction have been recently reexamined by historians. William B. Hesseltine, *Lincoln's Plan of Reconstruction** (1960) is favorable, while W. R. Brock, *An American Crisis: Congress and Reconstruction, 1865–1867** (1963) locates the problems that led to Radical Reconstruction in the nature of the American government. It has the virtue, too, of being written by an Englishman. Andrew Johnson's reputation has suffered in the new interpretations, as compared with the favorable view provided in the old and influential Howard K. Beale, *The Critical Year: A Study of Andrew Johnson and Reconstruction* (1930). The best study of Johnson and Reconstruction is now the critical and provocative Eric L. McKitrick, *Andrew Johnson and Reconstruction** (1960). LaWanda and John Cox, *Politics, Principle, and Prejudice, 1865–1866** (1963) emphasize Johnson's hostility toward blacks. Hans L. Trefousse, *The Radical Republicans* (1969) lauds the Radicals and traces their origins to the prewar years. David Donald, *The Politics of Reconstruction** (1965) seeks to explain the origins of Radical Republicanism through an examination of Congressional constituencies, without complete success.

An important ingredient in early Reconstruction, as well as later, was the continuance of antebellum political differences into the postwar years. Thomas B. Alexander, "Persistent Whiggery in the Confederate South, 1860–1877," *Journal of Southern History* XXVII (1961) traces the Whig influence through Reconstruction. The standard study of an important early Reconstruction institution is George R. Bentley, *A History of the Freedman's Bureau* (1955). Extremely well written and very helpful in understanding northern activities in the South, despite its narrow scope, is Willie Lee Rose, *Rehearsal for Reconstruction: The Port Royal Experiment** (1964). Joseph B. James, *The Framing of the Fourteenth Amendment** (1956) is the standard study on that important measure. It should be supplemented by Jacobus Ten Broek, *The Antislavery Origins of the Fourteenth Amendment* (1951). The Fourteenth Amendment as it applies to the twentieth-century issue of segregation in the schools is authoritatively discussed in Alfred H. Kelly, "The Fourteenth Amendment Reconsidered: The Segregation Question," *Michigan Law Review* LIV (1956): 1049–86.

The best biographies of the two leaders of Radical Reconstruction are Fawn M. Brodie, *Thaddeus Stevens: Scourge of the South** (1959) and David Donald, *Charles Sumner and the Rights of Man* (1971).

The weaknesses as well as the rationale of Johnson's policies in the early years of Reconstruction are exposed in Jonathan T. Dorris, *Pardon and Amnesty under Lincoln and Johnson* (1953), in Thomas B. Alexander, *Political Reconstruction in Tennessee* (1950), which emphasizes the rule of old Whigs, and in William C. Harris, *Presidential Reconstruction in Mississippi* (1967).

The issue of redistribution of land to the freedmen is canvassed in LaWanda Cox, "The Promise of Land for the Freedman," *Mississippi Valley Historical Review* XLV

(1958): 413–40 and explored in a single, but important state in Carol Bleser, *The Promised Land: The History of the South Carolina Land Commission, 1869–1890* (1969). James S. Allen, *Reconstruction: The Battle for Democracy** (1937), a frankly Marxian analysis, also emphasizes the failure to give the freed slaves an economic base in the South.

*Available in a paperback edition

CHAPTER SIX

THE
STRESSES
OF REUNION

HISTORICAL MOVEMENTS very often reach the peak of their dominance after they have passed the peak of their strength. This was true of the so-called movement for Radical Reconstruction. The period of Radical Reconstruction did not begin until the adoption of the Military Reconstruction Act on March 2, 1867, and it continued in three southern states for ten years, yet it lost ground steadily for the entire decade before it was completely overthrown.

Radical Reconstruction and Reunion

This assertion would have seemed baffling indeed to men toward the end of the 1860's, for it appeared that the Radicals were now sweeping all before them. No matter how reluctantly he did so, Andrew Johnson was forced to appoint the five military governors. As required by law, these five held new voter registrations in which Negroes were enrolled, while any whites who had ever "been disfranchised for participation in any rebellion" or who had taken an oath to uphold the Constitution and had subsequently supported the Confederacy were excluded. Since there was great, perhaps deliberate, uncertainty as to what categories of people had actually been "disfranchised for participation in any rebellion," estimates of the number of such disfranchised whites fluctuated wildly from less than 150,000 to more than 500,000. Under these registrations, Negroes were in a majority by a margin of 703,000 to 627,000. Breaking this down by states, Negroes held majorities in South Carolina and the four Gulf Coast states from Florida to Louisiana (but not Texas).

Before the end of 1867 these electorates chose state conventions which met and drew up new state constitutions. In early 1868 the electorates ratified these constitutions in seven states,* and in 1868 Congress seated the Congressmen from all seven of them. As we shall see further on, these new governments were not as drastic, either in their assertion of Negro rights or in their hostility to the former slaveowners, as many people expected them to be. But they were firmly Republican. In every case they started out with Republican governors and Republican majorities in the legislatures, and they sent Republican Congressmen to the Senate and the House. In 1868 five of them did their bit for the party by casting their electoral vote for Grant for President, but the Democrats were not completely overpowered, for Louisiana went Democratic.

Meanwhile, in Georgia the Democrats gained an ascendancy in the legislature and used their power for the purpose of expelling Negro members, whereupon Congress revoked its admission of Georgia. This left four states,

---

*Alabama was brought in by a separate act, for the first Reconstruction Act called for ratification by a majority of the voters. Opponents of the new government defeated it by abstaining from voting and thus preventing a majority. Congress thereupon repealed the majority requirement, making the repeal retroactive.

The end of Reconstruction: though the South Carolina House of Representatives was preponderantly Negro in 1876, white conservatives had recaptured it by 1877. *Culver Pictures*

Virginia, Mississippi, Texas, and Georgia, which for one reason or another had been slower to complete their reorganization; they were not admitted until 1870. When Georgia also came in, again, all these four except Virginia reentered with solid Republican regimes, and since the Fifteenth Amendment had been proposed by that time, they were required to ratify it as well as the Fourteenth. Virginia shared with the other southern states the experience of military reconstruction, but she uniquely escaped Radical rule as the Democrats successfully formed a coalition with the moderate Republicans against the Radicals, in the election of the first governor under the new regime. There was never a time when all of the former Confederate states were under Radical rule at once, but during part of the year 1870 all but two (Virginia and Tennessee) of them were.

Radical Republicans vs. Supreme Court and President

While the Radical wing of the Republican party was strengthening itself by taking control in the South, the large majorities that had driven many pieces of legislation to passage over President Johnson's veto were moving to destroy any opposition which they might encounter in the judicial and executive branches of the government.

The Question of Military Courts. The first clear indication to the Radicals that the federal courts might curb them in some of their more drastic policies came with the decision in April 1866, in the case of one L. P. Milligan. He had been sentenced in 1864 by a military court in Indianapolis to be hanged for conspiring in wartime to release rebel prisoners and to join with Confederate forces. The point at issue was that, at the time of the trial, civil courts were functioning in Indianapolis and there was no state of emergency. Could a military court try a civilian in a jurisdiction where civil courts were active and where there was no invasion or immediate threat of an invasion? In a decision subsequently much praised by liberals, the Supreme Court held that martial law could function only in an emergency in which civil courts were not operative, and it voided Milligan's conviction. This occurred at a time when the military courts of the Freedmen's Bureau were operating throughout the South, where civil courts were also functioning. The decision implicitly struck at the validity of any judicial process of a military nature anywhere in the South, and the Radicals recognized the threat very distinctly. Three months after the Milligan decision, when Congress was angry with both the Supreme Court and the President, it adopted a law to reduce the size of the court from nine justices to seven, by eliminating the first two seats which should fall vacant. This would effectively deprive Johnson of any opportunity of making court appointments.

The vulnerability of military rule was brought into focus again in 1868 by a case involving William H. McCardle, editor of a Vicksburg, Mississippi, newspaper, who had been very vigorous in denouncing the policies of military reconstruction. McCardle was arrested and put on trial before a military tribunal. Following the Milligan ruling, he challenged the jurisdiction of the military court, which amounted to a challenge of the Military Reconstruction Acts themselves. The Supreme Court agreed to hear his case on appeal, and appeal was pending when Congress passed a law in March 1868, over the President's veto, depriving the Court of appellate jurisdiction in this and similar cases. The Court thereupon felt constrained to cancel its hearing of the case. This is, perhaps, the most flagrant successful attack in American history upon the independence of the Supreme Court, and it showed that the Radical Republicans had reached a point where they were ready to destroy anything that stood as an obstacle to their program.

The Question of Presidential Appointees. By the time of the legislation to prevent the judiciary from administering justice in the McCardle case, Congress was also deeply involved in an attack on the executive branch of the government. On the same day that it passed the Military Reconstruction Act, it had also passed a Tenure of Office Act which forbade the President to remove officeholders who had been appointed by him and confirmed by the Senate. About five months later Johnson suspended Edwin M. Stanton as Secretary of War because he believed, correctly, that Stanton was serving as a spy for the Radicals in the inner councils of the administration. As for the Tenure of Office Act, he believed that it did not cover Stanton since he had not appointed Stanton, but had inherited him from the Lincoln administration. Further, he believed that Congress could not constitutionally interfere with the President's control over one of the executive departments—a belief which was confirmed by a Supreme Court decision in 1926, fifty-eight years too late to help Johnson.

Impeachment of Johnson. Johnson tried to initiate litigation by which he could get a Supreme Court ruling on the question of constitutionality, but the Radicals skillfully avoided this, and in March 1868, the House impeached the President for a number of somewhat nebulous offenses (such as delivering "inflammatory and scandalous harangues"), but especially for violating the Tenure of Office Act. For three months the Senate sat as a court of impeachment, though it frequently violated principles of judicial impartiality, such as when Senator Wade, who as president *pro tempore* of the Senate was next in line for the Presidency, voted for the conviction which would have made him President. During the trial, suspense mounted as it became clear that conviction would succeed or fail by a very narrow margin. On May 16 the Senate voted on one of the charges, and the result showed 35 for conviction, 19 for acquittal—one vote short of the required two thirds. For the next ten days immense pressure was exerted upon seven Republican senators who had voted for acquittal, but when the next vote was taken, every one of them held firm, and the vote of 35 to 19 was repeated. With this result the attempt to remove Andrew Johnson collapsed. What is more important, an act which would have permanently damaged the role of the President in the American political system was averted. In this sense the acquittal of Johnson was an event of great significance.

The Election of 1868

The Radicals had shown how ready they were to strike down all opposition although they had not succeeded as well with the President as they did with the Supreme Court. But Johnson's term was ending anyway, and during the last suspenseful days of the impeachment trial, the Republican Convention at Chicago nominated Ulysses S. Grant for the Presidency. His was the only name presented to the Convention. The Democrats, by contrast, had a difficult time agreeing on a rival candidate. The leading contender for the nomination at the outset was George Pendleton of Ohio, an advocate of a greater supply of greenback money, a popular view in the Middle West. However, it was not popular in the East, and the conservative Democrats from that region finally brought about the nomination of the governor of New York, Horatio Seymour.

Republicans Reappraise Their Strength. Although Seymour was defeated in the ensuing election, he made a strong enough showing to lead the Republicans to reappraise their position completely. They recognized that despite their victory they were in a highly vulnerable situation politically. In both Lincoln elections the Republicans had carried every northern state.* In 1866 they had won 143 seats in the House of Representatives to the Democrats' 49. When seven southern states were reorganized under Military Reconstruction in 1868, with Republican governments and large Negro constituencies in all seven to help maintain these governments, it might have seemed that the Republican control was completely secure. Yet in fact the state elections of 1867 shook the Republicans badly. They lost the governorships in Connecticut and California, both houses of the legislature in Ohio and New Jersey, and one house in New York. In the previous year they had won in ten out of nineteen Congressional districts in Ohio, but in 1867 they won only three districts. But if 1867 had shaken them, 1868 pointed to possible disaster. In the South the Democrats showed an unforeseen capacity to control the Negro vote; actually Seymour received a larger vote than Grant in the former slave states, though most of it was concentrated in Georgia and Louisiana. If the Democrats could extend this practice to other southern states, the Republicans would have to maintain their monolithic control in the North if they were to keep their political ascendancy. But the 1868 election showed that they could not rely on this either, for though Grant polled huge majorities in the Middle West and upper New England, Seymour carried New York—the richest prize of all—and New Jersey. He also gave Grant a close race in Pennsylvania, which he lost by less than 5 percent of the vote cast, and Connecticut and Indiana, by less than 3 percent.

As the Republicans must have viewed it, if the "party of treason and rebellion" could give the party of Union and freedom this kind of competition, less than four years after the Union's military victory, and with the immensely popular "Hero of Appomattox" at the head of the Republican ticket, the

*In 1860, Lincoln did not receive the entire electoral vote of New Jersey, but he did receive four electoral votes in that state to Douglas' three.

Republicans had something to worry about.

Renewed Interest in Negro Suffrage. The recognition of their vulnerability soon led Republican strategists to reappraise their position on the question of Negro suffrage in the North. Ever since 1865 they had been seeking to extend the ballot to Negroes in the free states, which could in most cases be accomplished only by popular referenda on amendments to the state constitutions. But only Iowa and Minnesota had joined the five New England states in voluntarily extending the franchise. Twelve northern states, including such major ones as New York, Pennsylvania, Ohio, and Illinois, had stoutly rejected Negro suffrage either by voting it down or by refusing to bring it to a vote. The Republicans had not dared to challenge this attitude very vigorously. Many of their own members felt that it was shameful to impose Negro suffrage on the South by the Military Reconstruction Act, while refusing to adopt it for themselves. But they had evaded the dilemma somewhat lamely by affirming in their platform in 1868 that "The guaranty by Congress of equal suffrage to all loyal men at the South [meaning especially Negroes] was demanded by every consideration of public safety, of gratitude, and of justice, and must be maintained; while the question of suffrage in all the loyal States properly belongs to the people of those States." In short, there was to be a double standard on Negro suffrage—one standard for the North and one for the South. By maintaining this double standard, they had supposed that they could avoid antagonizing the voters in crucial and closely divided northern states on the suffrage question.

Negro voters were registered in large numbers in the South before the Fifteenth Amendment extended suffrage equally to the North. *Courtesy of The New York Public Library, Astor, Lenox and Tilden Foundations*

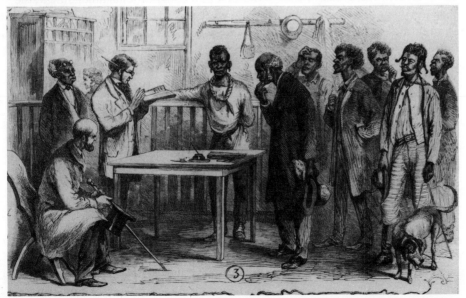

But in reappraising, they saw the situation in a different light: by raising the suffrage issue in the South, and previously in the northern states, they had already lost the votes of those who were anti-Negro, without getting any of the political benefit of potential Negro support; by fighting the battle state by state in popular referenda, they had made the suffrage question a focus of prolonged controversy, in a situation where they would have to conduct a whole series of battles. If they could outlaw disfranchisement of Negroes on a nationwide basis by a constitutional amendment, there would be several advantages: (1) they could avoid the angry disputation aroused by public referenda by dealing with the question through state legislatures, where considerations of party advantage would be better understood and would count for more; (2) they could fight one battle instead of a whole series; and (3) they stood a better chance of winning and thus gaining some Negro votes for the Republican Party as a partial offset to the anti-Negro votes which they had already antagonized. One Republican Congressman estimated that Negro enfranchisement would add roughly 146,000 voters, nearly all of whom would be Republican, in the North. Furthermore, they would be very strategically distributed in unusually close states—for instance, ten thousand in New York, five thousand in New Jersey, fourteen thousand in Pennsylvania. A Republican senator identified these potential votes as "the balance of power in many of the largest and most populous of Northern States."

The Fifteenth Amendment. Along with this change of mind went an awareness that if the action were to be taken it must be at once. The final Congress under Andrew Johnson still had one more December-to-March session—the lame duck session before Grant's inauguration. In this Congress, the Republicans still had a two-thirds majority, as they would not have in the newly elected Congress. If they were to seek a constitutional amendment, they must act without delay. In December they set about framing an amendment and as they did so, a division developed between those who favored universal suffrage—by a positive amendment guaranteeing the right to vote—or impartial suffrage—by a negative amendment which guaranteed against exclusion on grounds of race. In the debates it was clearly understood that, under impartial suffrage, literacy or other qualifications might still be adopted by a state, which would have the effect of disfranchising large numbers of Negro voters without literally disqualifying them as Negroes. The parliamentary twists and turns were intricate and confusing, but in the end, the advocates of impartial suffrage won. So at last, four working days before Grant's inauguration, Congress submitted to the states a proposed Fifteenth Amendment which provided that no state should deprive any person of the ballot because of "race, color, or previous condition of servitude."

With thirty-seven states in the Union, twenty-eight were required for ratification, and for a time it appeared that it would be impossible to get this many. The Republicans could count on the votes of the six southern states under Republican control, and also four still under military reconstruction, which could be required to ratify as the price of readmission. They could also count on the seven northern states which had adopted Negro suffrage voluntarily and on Wisconsin, which had arrived at it by a judicial decision, and Nebraska, for which Congress had prescribed it in the act granting statehood in 1867. But this left nine more still to be lined up, and a bitter struggle was required to secure them. During the contest, New York first ratified, then later rescinded her ratification. However, within a year the strategy of a single amendment instead of numerous referenda paid off, as Republican legislators in Nevada, West Virginia, Illinois, Michigan, Pennsylvania, Connecticut, Indiana, Missouri, Kansas, and Ohio proved more obedient in following the party line than Republican voters might have been. Ratification was completed in February 1870, and between January and July of the same year, the four southern states still under military reconstruction were readmitted to the Union.

Effects of Radical Success

It was at this point that the success of the Radicals seemed most complete. The Fourteenth Amendment had written Negro citizenship and civil rights ("equal protection of the laws," no deprivation of life, liberty, or property, no abridgement of privileges or immunities) into the Constitution. Negro suffrage had been written into southern state constitutions as a result of requirements in the Military Reconstruction Acts. Nine southern states seemed to be under secure control by the Republicans, though Tennessee and Virginia had already slipped away. The Republicans held good majorities in both branches of Congress, and the Hero of Appomattox had replaced the ex-slaveholder from Tennessee in the White House.

Radical Success Exhausted. Yet, in fact, the Radicals' program of Reconstruction, in its moment of triumph, had exhausted its capacity for further affirmative action. The program would still linger for seven years in three of the states, but in giving Negroes a legal claim to the ballot, northern voters had psychologically paid to be released from further responsibility for a problem which troubled them very seriously. Many good Unionists wanted to regard the ex-Confederates as their fellow-Americans, but they had never regarded the slaves as such and they did not really regard the freedmen as such. It disturbed them that this question of rights for the freedmen was complicating the reconciliation of the North and the South, and it made them feel a little bit guilty that the Confederates, whom they had respected as military adversaries, were apparently being placed under the dominance of former slaves as the price of defeat. Were not the devastation of defeat itself and the emancipation of the slaves, at a cost to the South of some $2 billion, enough? But circumstances had led them on to provide the guarantees laid down in drastic legislation and in additional amendments to the Constitution. Now, they felt, the freedman was legally in possession of a full set of rights; it was up to him to make the most of them. They had done as much as they were going to do.

Further, the election of Grant was not quite as much a victory for the Republicans, especially the Radical Republicans, as it appeared to be. Grant in 1868, like Eisenhower in 1952, was more a soldier than a party leader, a nonpartisan hero rather than a professional Republican. The Radicals supported his nomination, as Republicans supported the nomination of Eisenhower in 1952, because they knew they could win with him, but they would have far preferred to nominate Salmon P. Chase of Ohio, an antislavery leader well known in political circles for more than two decades, just as the Republicans of 1952 would really have preferred Robert Taft of Ohio. The Republicans of 1868, in a sense, sacrificed their Presidential candidate in order to avoid losing the Presidency.

The Country's Mood in 1870. There was a profound difference between their mood and the mood of Grant, and this difference showed in a striking phrase from his inaugural address. Grant said, "Let us have peace," which probably reflected accurately the mood of the country. On its face this was not a proposal with which anyone could disagree, but its tone was quite different from Lincoln's statement four years earlier, about binding up the nation's wounds. Grant's words had two implications: first, let us have reconciliation rather than more conflict-breeding reforms; second, it seemed to say, "Oh, give us a rest." A few years later he would express his distaste for further policing of the South in even plainer terms.

Any account of Reconstruction is likely to be deceptive simply by virtue of the fact that it holds a sharp focus on a single theme and almost inescapably gives the impression that public attention was similarly concentrated and alert to the ideological issues involved. But realistically most active politicians were more interested in winning elections than in implementing ideals. And most people were concerned with an immense variety of personal goals more important to them than the future status of Negroes in the United States. At that time 90 percent of the Negro population lived in the South and the border states; it was easy, therefore, to think of the problem of the status of Negroes as essentially a regional problem. Let the blacks and the whites in the South work this out, and if need be, stew a bit in their own juice. Meanwhile, there were many other things to do in a new economic world that was opening up and had begun to display some of its new features prominently with the coming of the Civil War. Such was probably the attitude of many people in the North. For the American public, Reconstruction became a secondary concern in 1870, though the economy and society of the South were both in an extremely disordered condition at that time.

Economic Transformation

There was also a great deal happening in the government during these years that had nothing to do with Confederacy, slaves, or freedmen, and a great deal happening in the country that had little to do with the government. In fact a case could be made that the most significant development in American history in the three decades between 1846 and 1877 was not the Civil War but economic transformation. To what extent this transformation was hastened by the war and the political changes that went with it, or to what extent it resulted simply from the working of economic forces entirely outside the orbit of politics is a matter on which historians do not agree.

The Pre–Civil War Clash of Interests. Whichever view they take about the direct and explicit effects of the war, most historians do agree that, prior to 1861, there was a political struggle between the northern Whigs, supported by a few of the southern Whigs, against the southern Democrats, supported by some of the northern Democrats, about what kind of economy the federal government should sponsor. The Democrats tended to identify themselves with agricultural interests; these interests wanted a generous policy in the distribution of public lands, and very often they also wanted governmental support for railroads or canals that would help them to get their crops to market. But otherwise they distrusted any centralized control of money or the adoption of tariffs. Most agricultural products were sold on the world market and could not benefit by tariffs. In short they were responsive to low taxes, restricted governmental functions, and political decentralization—a Jeffersonian position. The Whigs, by contrast, had an affinity for commercial and manufacturing interests; they believed in affirmative policies, such as protective tariffs to encourage industry, and the provision of a stable and uniform supply of currency with which the economy could operate. They believed in the active sponsorship of such semipublic enterprises as railroads. But though the Whigs had won two presidential elections (Harrison in 1840 and Taylor in 1848), they had never really controlled public policy, and from the time of Andrew Jackson until the Civil War, the Democratic philosophy prevailed. Tariffs were kept low; grants of public lands were made sparingly; and after Jackson's veto of the recharter of the Bank of the United States, the government made no attempt to provide a circulating medium. It did, to be sure, coin gold and silver, but this currency was entirely inadequate to the money needs of the economy. These needs were met by banks chartered by the states, with a power to issue notes, over which the federal government exercised no control. Different bank notes circulated at varying discounts from their face value. Some states regulated this note issue closely, but others did not, and there were always a certain number of loosely regulated "wildcat" banks, so that the supply of currency remained relatively abundant. This made for a condition of cheap money, was inflationary in its tendency, and broadly favorable to debtors, though it also contributed to cycles of prosperity and depression, in which debtors could be badly trapped. Because of its decentralized character, however, the banking system was not conducive to integration or to large-scale organization in the economy. Nor was the relatively low level of tariffs conducive to the growth of giant industrial enterprises. Even without government encouragement—at least encouragement by the federal government—the rate of industrial growth in the two decades before the war was very rapid, and it seems evident that technological change plus economic growth was moving the country rapidly toward industrialization, regardless of the Civil War.

Transformation of Conditions for Economic Growth. There is no doubt, however, that the war changed a number of the basic conditions of growth and perhaps diverted a greater proportion of the national income into the hands of capitalists who would use it for purposes of economic expansion. The election of Lincoln in 1860 was not only an antislavery victory; it was also a Whig victory, for Lincoln had been a Whig. It was likewise a northern victory, and the North was committed to economic diversification, to the economic mobility of a system of free wage labor, and to an exchange economy in which work was concentrated on the production of goods for sale, with the expectation that the worker or producer would receive his compensation in money income rather than by consuming the products of his own labor.

Transformation of Tariff Policy. As the Republican Party had approached the election of 1860, deliberately trying to alter its image as a one-idea antislavery party, it had included in its platform a pledge to support high tariffs, free land in the West for homesteaders, and the construction of a transcontinental railroad. Lincoln's victory and, even more, the withdrawal of the secessionist senators and representatives from Congress, made it possible for the Republicans to proceed rapidly with this program. During the winter of 1860-1861, even before Lincoln came to the Presidency, they enacted the Morrill tariff, which did not raise duties very high, but which did increase them. Many years were to pass before the country would see a tariff reduction again, and three additional increases were adopted during the Civil War.

Transformation of Public Land Policy—The Homestead Act. In 1862 Congress turned to a program of rapid economic development—not to say exploitation—through the use of public lands. First of all, on May 20, 1862, it adopted the Homestead Act, which offered 160 acres of public land free to any person who would build a dwelling, even a cabin, and reside on the property for five years. This measure undoubtedly contributed something to the settlement of the West, but romanticists have greatly exaggerated its impact; though it was adopted in good faith, it was later used to some extent as a cover to conceal what was really happening to the public domain. Altogether about 600,000 homesteads of 80,000,000 acres were patented by the end of the century, but these could have accomplished their real purpose only if homesteaders had received a priority of access to desirable land, and if the rest of the public domain had been conserved as a national resource. But in fact neither of these things was done. The best land continued to be offered at public sale, often in very large tracts which were bought up by speculators or by large-scale operators. Many a man who went west to acquire a homestead ended by buying land from a dealer or from one of the large owners such as the railroads.

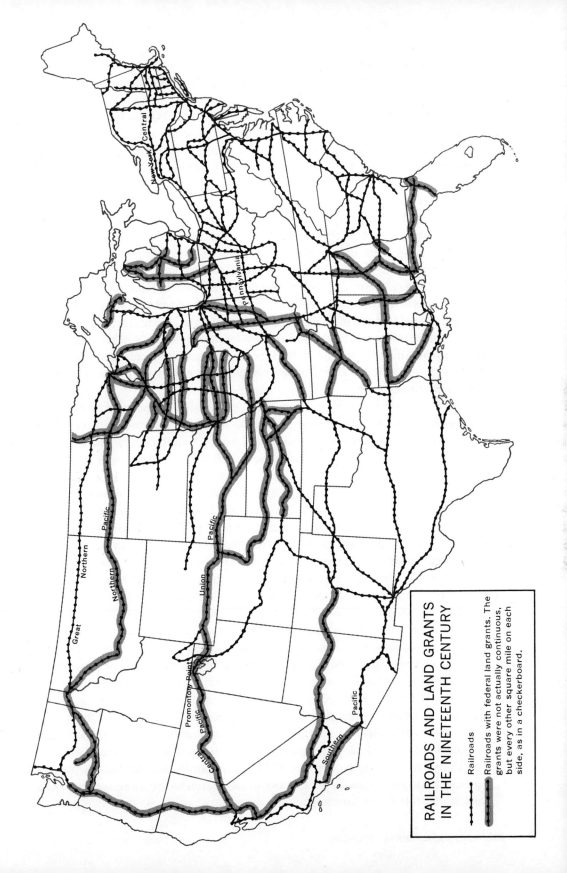

RAILROADS AND LAND GRANTS
IN THE NINETEENTH CENTURY

•—•—• Railroads

━━━ Railroads with federal land grants. The grants were not actually continuous, but every other square mile on each side, as in a checkerboard.

Great Northern

Northern Pacific

Union Pacific

Central Pacific

Promontory Point

Southern Pacific

New York Central

Pennsylvania

The Railroad Land Grants. Once the principle of free land was introduced, it was rapidly extended for other purposes varying greatly in their merit. For instance, only six weeks after the Homestead Act Congress went a long way toward gutting it by passing in two days the Morrill Land Grant College Act and the first Pacific Railroad Act. The former was designed to aid college education, especially in the field of agriculture. It gave to each state (later extended to the southern states) 30,000 acres of the public domain for each senator and representative for the establishment of colleges and especially of agricultural colleges. The latter was designed to secure a transcontinental railroad at last, by chartering the Union Pacific Railroad Company to build west from Omaha, and encouraging the California-based Central Pacific to build east from Sacramento. As an inducement to lay their lines through empty, non-revenue-producing country, the government would donate not only the right of way but also 6400 acres per mile of road built, and would lend them $60 million which represented sums of between $15 thousand and $48 thousand a mile. The land grant was doubled in 1864, to 12,800 acres per mile, and from then to 1871, similar grants were made to the Santa Fe in 1863 and the Northern Pacific in 1864 and the Southern Pacific in 1866 (both at the rate of 25,600 acres per mile, with no loans). After 1871 a reaction against such grants set in, and Congress voted no more of them.

The magnitude and folly of the railroad land grants has been, in many ways, exaggerated. Grants were made for 18,000 miles of road, which was only 8 percent of the railroads built in the United States, and the actual market value then of the vast acreage granted (about 130,000,000 acres) was so nearly negligible that relatively modest financial grants to the railroads would have been worth more. All the loans which they received were repaid with interest. Still it is ironical that between 1864 and 1871 Congress committed to five railroad companies three times as much acreage as Thaddeus Stevens had, in vain, proposed to give to one million freedmen. In immediate terms, however, the major significance of the railroad land grants was not in the extent of their acreage, but in the fact that they (as well as the college grants) undercut any idea of reserving the public domain for individual homesteaders. Not only did the large grantees get more land than the homesteaders, but they and the purchasers got first choice of the land. The country was embarking on a policy of rapid and somewhat predatory exploitation of the national domain, in the interests of large speculators and operators. This process has continued with diminishing recklessness for more than a century, but it has by no means halted even today. In the larger picture the Homestead Act was little more than a sentimental valentine denoting affection for the American dream of the family farm, with little relation to the realities of the national economy. It is the unrealism of this ideal, incidentally, which leads one to wonder whether Thaddeus Stevens may have avoided the naive fallacy that the ballot would be a panacea for American Negroes, only to fall victim to the more sophisticated fallacy that forty-acre farms would be a panacea.

Their culture threatened, Cheyenne Indians tore up the encroaching new railroad tracks. *The Kansas State Historical Society, Topeka*

Transformation of Monetary System. If the transformation of American land policy grew somewhat accidentally out of the feeling of urgent need for a Pacific railroad and the inconvenience of paying for it, the transformation of the American monetary system grew accidentally out of the difficulty which the Treasury Department found in borrowing funds to finance the Civil War. As always in wartime ordinary tax revenue was entirely inadequate to pay the costs of the war. New taxes, including an income tax (which survived from 1863 until 1872) as well as important new excise taxes such as the tax on whiskey (which came to stay), did not make much difference. By the beginning of 1862 Secretary of the Treasury Salmon P. Chase was finding that he could not sell government bonds except at ruinous discounts, and the financial institutions of the country as a whole were feeling the strain, as was indicated by the fact that on January 1, 1862, the banks suspended specie payment—that is, stopped redeeming their notes on demand in bullion. In response to this situation, Chase resorted to two highly significant devices.

Greenbacks. First, in February 1862, he secured the passage, in spite of constitutional objections, of an act authorizing the issue of $150 million in paper money—"greenbacks" as they were called—which were not redeemable in bullion though the government promised, in indefinite terms, to redeem them later. But they were lawful money which sellers were required to accept in payment for purchases. Later the amount was increased to $430 million.

Since greenbacks could not be exchanged for gold, but gold could always be exchanged for greenbacks, people inevitably preferred gold dollars to greenback dollars. This preference had a number of ramifications. First, it caused gold to disappear from circulation, since holders of both kinds of dollars always spent their greenback dollars first. Second, it caused the development of an exchange in which one gold dollar would buy more than one greenback. If the North lost the war, greenbacks would be in trouble, but gold would be unaffected; when the Confederacy appeared to have a good chance of winning, greenbacks declined to a point where it took 2 1/2 of them to buy one gold dollar. But—this was a tricky factor in the situation—one could still buy government bonds, payable in gold, with greenbacks, which means that investors could buy with depreciated dollars a promise of repayment in dollars worth more than those with which the promise was bought. This anomaly was to become an important public issue during the Grant administration.

National Bank Notes. Chase's second device was embodied in two acts —of February 1863 and June 1864—known as National Bank Acts. They were designed to create a market for the slow-selling government bonds by inducing the banks of the country to buy them. This legislation provided that existing banks, or those newly formed, if they possessed a stated minimum of paid-in capital (varying according to the size of their locality), might apply for and receive charters as national banks, if they would invest a minimum of one third of their capital in government bonds. Once they obtained such charters the government would permit them to issue notes, known as national bank notes, on the bonds which they had bought, up to 90 percent of the total value of bonds held. These notes would, of course, be lent to borrowers, and the feature which made the arrangement attractive to bankers was that the banks would receive interest both on the bonds (which would be deposited with the Treasury to protect the government) and on the bank notes which were lent.

Athough Chase was primarily interested in creating a good basis for government borrowing by making it worthwhile to the banks to buy government bonds, he was at the same time, almost without intending it, creating a quite new and rather peculiar system of money for the United States. National bank notes would become a major and uniform system of currency—the first the country had ever had. When first launched, they were expected to circulate along with, and in competition with, all the hundreds of different bank notes issued by banks chartered in various states. However in March 1865, Congress placed a tax on these miscellaneous notes, and bankers in general perceived that they must join the national system. By the end of 1865, there were 1600 national banks. These institutions found the practice of receiving interest both on their government bonds and on their national bank notes very attractive. But the peculiarity of their situation lay in the fact that these notes, which were becoming the national currency along with greenbacks, could be issued only against bonds, which is to say government debt. This meant that, ultimately, the volume of circulating currency would be rigidly controlled by the amount of the government debt, instead of being flexibly responsive to the needs and the assets of the economy. If the amount of debt was reduced while the needs of the economy were expanding—which is exactly what happened—the country would be faced with a shortage of dollars. Such a shortage would have a deflationary effect on the currency, and would work to the advantage of creditor interests, who stood to collect their loans in dollars worth more than those they had originally lent. Creditor interests, which frequently had a Whiggish or Republican orientation, would at last have the upper hand over Democratically inclined debtor interests. It was a change of prime importance, and one historian declares: "This tipping of the class [creditor *vs.* debtor or industrial *vs.* agricultural] and sectional [North *vs.* South or North *vs.* West, or city *vs.* country] balance of power was, in my opinion, the momentous change over the twenty-three-year period, 1850–1873."*

The Civil War Impact on Industrialization

From such a point of view, the importance of the Civil War as a great dividing point in American history has been exaggerated, except insofar as it is regarded as the cause of these economic changes. The extent to which it was a cause is, in turn, another topic of historical controversy. To an older generation of historians, who regarded the basic importance of the Civil War as axiomatic, it was customary to consider the war's economic significance as no less vital than its political meaning. To Charles A. Beard, for instance, the real revolution of 1861–65 was neither the overthrow of slavery nor the defeat of states' rights, but the victory of industrial society over agrarian society. Industrial capitalism, asserts Beard, "marched forward with seven-league boots." Projecting this idea to its logical conclusion, Beard and others proceeded to make, without substantiation, the claim that industrial production increased with unparalleled speed during the Civil War, and thus carried the country across the threshold from agrarianism to industrialism. This sweeping claim has led a number of economic historians to measure as carefully as they can the actual increase in industrial production during the Civil War, and to conclude that, by accurate measure, the rate of increase in the output of industrial goods was less between 1861 and 1865 than in the period immediately before and immediately after.

However, there are some features which such data do not measure or take into consideration. One is the fact that, with the diversion of a major part of the nation's manpower into nonproductive (i.e., military) activities, it is remarkable that the wartime increase in productivity could have kept pace as well as it did with the increase in peacetime, when there was a full labor force. During most wars in history, production has experienced an absolute decline. Another point to note is that as increases cumulate, it takes a much larger gross increase to maintain the rate of percentage increase: if, over two decades, production increases from 100 units to 200 to 300, the first increase is one of 100 percent but the second, though equally great, is only one of 50 percent. Professor Thomas Cochran seems not quite warranted in his terminology, which speaks of the Civil War "retarding" industrial production, when what he means is only

*Robert L. Sharkey, in David T. Gilchrist and W. David Lewis, eds., *Economic Change in the Civil War Era* (Greenville, Del., Eleutherian Mills-Hagley Foundation, 1965), p. 27.

that despite a steady increase in the volume of production, and indeed a gross increase greater than ever before, yet the percentage increases were not as steep as they had been in the past or were to be in the future.

There are other dimensions, too, to be considered. For instance the country as a whole made increases between 1860 and 1870, while southern production was declining in absolute terms, yet North and South are often combined in the data! The North's industrial increase, therefore, represents a net gain even after the South's decrease is deducted. Beyond these purely arithmetical points, one must also note that industrialization may gain in other ways besides increasing its annual product. For instance, it may gain by the accumulation of capital in the hands of industrialists—capital which will be used for industrial expansion. The high profits which accompanied inflationary policy (greenbacks) and wartime prices apparently increased industry's share of the national income during the Civil War, and thus increased the sinews for industrial growth. Again, the industrial potential may be increased by the growth of industries producing materials which are necessary to increased activity in other industries. Some of the best-sustained increases during the Civil War were in the development of this kind of industrial capacity, such as coal, pig iron, and railroad rails, while one of the major segments in which production declined was cotton textiles which do very little to fuel other industrial activity. Still another aspect of industrial potentiality lies in the structure of the economy—that is, the extent to which (a) production is concentrated in large units, (b) mechanization is employed, and (c) the technology of mass produc-

As the postwar economy grew, a vast variety of consumer goods, accompanied inevitably by advertising, began to engage the attention of the country. Left: *reproduced from the collections of the Library of Congress;* right: *Warshaw Collection, Smithsonian Institution*

tion is applied. The Civil War tended to stimulate all of these tendencies, for the government ordered supplies for the Army in greater quantities than the market had ever seen. It required large-scale organizations to handle some of these orders efficiently, and the rapid increase of large corporations was recognized as one of the results of the war. Large-scale production also lent itself to mechanization—for instance, the shoe industry was mechanized to a great extent during the war. Where mechanization and the demand for goods in large volume were both present, mass production was the answer. The northern economy met the demand for more production, not by adding to the number of producers, but by increasing the productivity of plants which were already in existence.

New Issues in the Postwar World

The end of the war, therefore, saw the North in possession of an industrial system which was in many ways new, and which was supported by certain government policies such as the maintenance of tariffs, the use of federal subsidies in the form of land grants, and the creation of a national currency system consisting partly of "cheap," unredeemable greenbacks and partly of "sound" national bank notes which were based on government bonds payable in gold. To many political leaders the primary issues of the day related to the preservation of this new system, and to resolving the problems of a dual currency. They gave more attention, especially after Grant's election, to these issues than to the reconstruction of the South and the status of American Negroes. Very often, what they did about the South was done not with primary reference to the South itself, but with reference to their need for political support from the South to implement their measures for the protection of the new economic system. For President Grant, the question of greenbacks was more important than the local attitudes of whites toward blacks in Texas.

Some of the major events of the postwar years illustrate this diffusion of public affairs away from the issues of reconstruction. Two such events, both in the field of foreign affairs, were in a sense unfinished business from the war itself. One involved the French-supported empire of Austrian archduke Maximilian in Mexico; the other, the claims of the United States against Great Britain for having permitted the Confederate commerce raider, the *Alabama*, to be built in Britain, from which she went forth to ravage the American merchant marine.

Maximilian in Mexico. The Mexican situation arose from the fact that in July 1861, the Mexican government defaulted on its debts to Britain, Spain, and France. These countries agreed to take forcible steps to collect, though they also agreed that none would attempt to gain any "peculiar advantage" from the situation. However, the French emperor, Napoleon III, was not sincere in this self-denial, for he had already proposed to the Archduke to set up a French-sponsored government in Mexico, with Maximilian at its head. During 1862 and 1863 the creditor countries staged an invasion of Mexico, but soon disagreed among themselves, with the result that Spain and Britain withdrew, leaving the operations in the hands of the French. French armies occupied Mexico City a month before the Battle of Gettysburg, and shortly afterward a hand-picked group of Mexicans "offered" Maximilian the throne as Emperor of their country, which he accepted in 1864. He was not in control of Mexico, however, as large parts of the country were still supporting a republican resistance led by Benito Juarez. Meanwhile, the American Congress was voting angry resolutions, and Maximilian was still depending upon French military support. Secretary of State Seward refused to make any protests, for he asked, "Why should we gasconade about Mexico when we are in a struggle for our own life?" But he knew that the French invasion, plus the establishment of an empire, constituted a double threat to the Monroe Doctrine—the most serious threat which it had faced—and he was biding his time. After Lee's surrender he began to place pressure on France, gentle at first, but steadily mounting, until in February 1866, he virtually demanded that France set a date for getting her troops out of Mexico. In April Napoleon announced that withdrawal would be completed before the end of 1867. Aside from pressure by the United States, he had found the venture far more costly and unpopular than he anticipated. Maximilian could have withdrawn with the French troops, but he bravely chose to regard himself as a Mexican and to hang on, regardless of the French. For this decision he paid with his life at the hands of a Mexican firing squad in June 1867, while the southern states were in the first stages of military reconstruction. During all these developments, Seward had never mentioned the Monroe Doctrine, but Napoleon's withdrawal from Mexico was perhaps the most important victory that it ever scored.

The Alabama *Claims.* A second piece of unfinished business left after the war was the claim against Britain for damages caused by the *Alabama.* It ought to have been possible to settle this matter quite readily, for the British were in fact convinced that the building of the *Alabama* had been a violation of neutrality. Also, they were sensitive to the possibility that if they became involved in war, American shipyards might build commerce-raiders to be let loose against their merchant marine. But negotiations were complicated by a cluster of other issues: a dispute about the San Juan islands, off Vancouver; disputes about Canadian-American fishing rights; Irish-American aid to Irish revolutionists; and most of all, a lingering American desire for the United States to annex all or part of Canada—a desire which was stimulated by a limited measure of responsiveness in British Columbia. Because of these complications, it was 1869 before a negotiating situation could be reached. Then Senator Sumner blasted the opportunity for an agreement by a speech in which he held Britain financially accountable not merely for the American merchant ships which the *Alabama* had destroyed, but also for prolonging the war by two years. He proposed astronomical damages—far greater, in fact, than Germany was soon to impose on France at the end of the Franco-Prussian War.

Sumner's irresponsible behavior would not have mattered but for the fact that he was chairman of the Senate Foreign Relations Committee, which position provided a rallying point for everyone who preferred a quarrel with Britain—always popular in nineteenth-century America—to a settlement. The situation stood at an impasse for almost two years, until an event from another direction led to the removal of Sumner from his obstructive position. The bankrupt government of the Dominican Republic offered itself for annexation to the United States if this country would take over its debt. A treaty was negotiated, and President Grant threw all-out support behind the measure. No other question during his presidency ever engaged him so deeply. But Charles Sumner blocked the treaty in the Senate so Grant, roused to an intense fury, forced the Republican Senate to remove Sumner from his chairmanship, just as James Buchanan had forced the removal of Douglas from the chairmanship of the Committee on Territories at the time of the Lecompton Contest. These are the only two occasions in history when the chairman of a Congressional committee has been removed by his own party while continuing a member of the party. The removal of Sumner made it possible for Secretary of State Hamilton Fish to proceed with negotiations with Britain. An arbitration board of five members, with three to be chosen by and from disinterested countries, was agreed upon. What followed was the first important international arbitration—and one of the most successful—in history. In September 1872, two months before Grant's reelection, the arbitral tribunal awarded the United States $15,500,000 in damages.

The Purchase of Alaska. The other major event in the field of foreign affairs during these years was not recognized at the time as being very important. The purchase of Alaska was made possible almost entirely by the decision of the financially hard-pressed Russian government that it would do better to develop the region around Vladivostock in Siberia than to overextend itself in the more frigid area of Russian America. In response to a Russian hint, conveyed by a third party, Secretary of State Seward made inquiries which revealed that Alaska could be bought. A price was negotiated at $7,200,000. The American public and the Congress, both monumentally ignorant of the potentialities, or indeed even the existence of Alaska, took a highly negative view of the treaty for purchase, and some Congressmen had to be bribed to vote for the appropriation. The approval of the purchase was finally achieved largely through the tireless personal efforts of Seward, who made up in optimism what he lacked in exact knowledge, and who felt sure that some day, somehow, this "frozen waste" would be worth far more than the purchase price to the United States. The treaty was ratified in 1867, the payment was voted in 1868, and then Alaska was put away and forgotten, unexplored and unknown, until the Klondike Gold Rush of 1897. It did not even receive regular territorial government until 1912.

Currency Problems. These developments in the realm of foreign affairs claimed an appreciable share of the public's attention in the first seven years after the war, but economic problems provided most of the issues which really diverted attention from the questions of reconstruction. When the war ended, it left the country with a monetary system in which the largest component was $450 million in greenback dollars which had driven gold completely out of circulation. The status of this currency was highly uncertain: it had been issued only because of the emergency of a war which was now over; it was tagged with an indefinite promise that after peace returned it would be redeemed in gold; and it was even under a constitutional cloud, for though the Constitution gives Congress the power "to coin money [and] regulate the value thereof," it gives no power to require people to accept paper promises as if they had intrinsic bullion value. Yet that was what Congress had done.

A New Currency System. If it had then been simply a question of honoring the obligations of the United States by making good the greenbacks in gold, there would have been little opposition. But there was much more to it than this. Congress in 1865 had destroyed what had been the chief circulating medium of the country by placing a tax on the banknotes of state-chartered banks, and it had substituted a new circulating medium consisting partly of greenbacks and partly of national bank notes. So long as the war continued, this circulating medium was quite adequate, for the needs of the government forced it to issue greenbacks in heavy volume and to borrow freely, which meant selling more bonds to the banks, on the basis of which more national bank notes could be issued.

But peace raised at once a double threat of conversion and of contraction. Conversion would mean paying for the greenbacks in gold. Yet, since gold was, at current rates, worth substantially more than greenbacks, conversion would raise the value of the dollar, which meant that borrowers who were repaying their loans would have to repay with dollars worth more than those which they had borrowed. Greenbacks, it began to appear, were "the people's money"; gold was "the bankers' money." Were the people to be robbed of their cheaper dollars in order to enrich the already bloated bankers? Contraction would mean reducing the amount of money in circulation. This would result if the greenbacks were retired—i.e., withdrawn from circulation—as they were redeemed. Contraction would also result if the government began to pay off the Civil War debt, for such payment would mean a reduction in the outstanding bonds, and as bonds were reduced, the volume of national bank notes which could be issued against them would also be reduced. When contraction took place, the supply of state bank notes, now abolished by heavy federal taxation, could no longer flow back into the economy to provide an adequate circulating medium.

In short, what had happened was that the National Bank Act of 1864 had destroyed the currency system of notes issued by state-chartered banks. It had been a ramshackle, decentralized system, with certain conspicuous faults, including the constant presence of some currency of dubious value, and the constant hazard that, in times of crisis, the banks would stop redeeming their notes in gold. It had been a chaotic, irrational system. But it had had the virtue of a flexibility which enabled it to respond to the fluctuations in the country's economic needs for a circulating medium. At the moment when it was replaced, the supply of greenbacks and the potential supply of national bank notes was so copious that few people cared. But greenbacks were essentially temporary and the quantity of national bank notes was limited by the size of the national debt, for notes could be issued only to the extent that bonds were outstanding. The new system was integrated, uniform, and stable, but it was also rigid; the element of flexibility, of responsiveness to the needs of the economy was gone, not to be put back until the adoption of the Federal Reserve Act in 1913. Meanwhile, the forces of inflation and the forces of deflation were to fight with one another intermittently for almost fifty years.

Inflationists vs. Deflationists. By 1867 this sustained battle was already shaping up between the influential few who stood to gain by a steady increase in the value of the dollar, and the uninfluential many who stood to lose. The bitterness of the battle was much increased by the fact that during the war the government had issued certain bonds that could be bought with greenbacks, but that would be repaid in gold. Such a transaction, in effect, gave to the bondholder the premium of being repaid in dollars worth perhaps twice as much as he had lent. It was a very tidy arrangement—for those who had been able to afford to buy bonds.

The tug of war between inflationists and deflationists began with an act in 1866 authorizing the Secretary of the Treasury to retire $10 million worth of greenbacks within six months and not more than $4 million a month thereafter. But when the economy slumped in 1867–1868, Congress reversed itself and adopted a new law to stop further contraction. In 1868 John Sherman of Ohio secured the adoption of a bill which called for a policy of "resumption [that is, raising the value of the dollar by redeeming all obligations including greenback dollars, in gold] but no contraction" [that is, no further reduction by the Treasury of the number of greenbacks in circulation]. Although President Johnson vetoed this compromise proposal, it was enacted under President Grant in 1870, and became the basis of the policy of most moderates. But the question never rested for long. In 1869 the Supreme Court, with Chief Justice Chase voting with the majority, decided that the greenbacks, which Secretary of the Treasury Chase had sponsored seven years earlier, were unconstitutional. By 1871 President Grant had appointed two new justices to the Supreme Court. The Court looked again, and decided this time that Secretary Chase had been right all along, and it was the Chief Justice who was in error. The greenbacks were constitutional after all. In 1873 the country experienced a severe economic depression, to which Congress responded the following year by voting to increase the supply of greenbacks to $400 million. This was vetoed by Grant, and by 1875 Congress itself had a change of heart in which it voted that, as the supply of national bank notes increased, the volume of greenbacks should be cut back to $300 million. It also voted that on January 1, 1879, the Treasury should start exchanging greenback dollars for gold dollars on demand. Thus, Sherman's goal of resumption was accomplished. His desire to do this without contraction was almost accomplished also, for in 1878 the reduction of the supply of greenbacks was stopped where it then stood—at $346,000,000.

In themselves, the details of this running battle hardly matter. The point is that there were many problems to engage the attention of the citizen beside Reconstruction, and many things to wonder about besides what the former rebels were doing to the former slaves, or *vice versa,* way down in that not-quite-credible country below the Potomac.

The 1872 Election. If the public had other matters to take its mind off Reconstruction before 1872, it had even more urgent matters after that. Before Grant's reelection, his administration seemed reasonably successful and the country was prosperous. The sense of accomplishment and growth was symbolized in 1869, when the Central Pacific and the Union Pacific met at Promontory Point in Utah and a golden spike was driven to celebrate the fulfillment of the long-cherished dream of a transcontinental railroad. In 1872 Grant was triumphantly reelected over a Democratic party so distracted that it had nominated a lifelong Whig-Republican and antislavery man, Horace Greeley, to be its candidate. But shortly after the election, things began to turn sour, and the public was treated to a series of disillusioning revelations about the ethical standards of the nation's economic and political leaders.

Scandals Under Grant. The first of these disclosures did not involve the Grant administration at all, but did involve the building of the Pacific railroad. When the railroad company was organized, it did not manage the construction of its own line, but had the line built by a construction company named somewhat fancifully the Credit Mobilier of America. Although in itself this arrangement was quite legitimate, what had really happened was that directors of the railroad company had organized the construction company. Then in their capacity as railroad directors they had awarded to themselves, as contractors, the contracts to build a cheaply constructed road at exorbitant prices. In this way they could easily siphon off the grants made by the government, leaving the railroad company almost bankrupt and themselves wealthy. To avoid interference by vigilant Congressmen, they had distributed shares of construction company stock to strategically situated members of the House of Representatives. This was the first clear illustration which the public received of what may happen when a group of insiders gains control of a wealthy enterprise which they do not own. The separation of ownership and control was just beginning in the American economy at this time.

Later revelations filled out other dimensions of a picture of economic corruption widespread throughout the country, even reaching into the inner councils of the administration. In one scandal it was proved that the Secretary of War had been accepting bribes from men whom he had appointed as agents on Indian reservations—in effect selling government posts at a price which the agent would recover by cheating the Indians. Other evidence proved that the President's personal secretary had connived at the schemes of a "ring" which was amassing fortunes by evading the excise tax on whiskey. Grant himself appeared to have an indiscriminate reverence for wealth, and he seemed quite blind to the effect of associating as President with rich men like James Fisk, Jr., and Jay Gould, who were notorious looters, market manipulators, and corruptionists. Yet the low tone of the era was far too pervasive for Grant to bear any major responsibility for it. The most outrageous stealing of all, for instance, was done by the Democrats of the Tweed Ring in New York, who used the simple device of taking whatever funds they wanted from the municipal treasury, on the pretext of paying for goods and services which were never ordered and never received. In one day they helped themselves to $14 million by this uncomplicated method.

It is a regrettable fact that, during times of prosperity, the American public seems to have a high tolerance for graft and corruption, but amid scenes of distress, such behavior seems more callous and reprehensible. The scene of distress came in 1873, when the failure of Jay Cooke and Company, one of the largest investment banking houses in the country, precipitated a crisis in the securities market. The crisis soon caused business failures, the collapse of some prices, and widespread unemployment. The Panic of 1873 marked the beginning of the severest economic depression which the country had witnessed up to that time.

Farmers organized to protect their interests; this picture shows a meeting of the Grange in Illinois in 1873. *Reproduced from the collections of the Library of Congress*

Problems of Farmers and Workers. The 1874 elections gave control of the House of Representatives to the Democrats. By that time a great many Americans were deeply concerned about a great variety of problems. By 1875 there were 850,000 farmers who had joined the Patrons of Husbandry, or "Grange" as it was usually called, partly to bring about a correction of the discriminatory railroad rates which, they believed, threatened the survival of the farmer as an independent producer. Illinois, Iowa, Minnesota, and Wisconsin had adopted laws as early as 1874 to regulate railroad rates, and other legislation was in the offing. Between 1866 and 1872, another 600,000 Americans had joined the National Labor Union, which secured the adoption of an eight-hour day for employees on government works before the Union went to pieces in the depression that followed the Panic of 1873.

By this point in history an uncounted number of farmers thought that the railroads were the primary threat to American democracy while an uncounted number of industrial workers thought the primary threat was the economic tyranny of large-scale employers, who could reduce wages or discharge workers without any negotiation whatever. On the other hand, great numbers of employers and property owners thought the allegedly socialistic ideas of farmers and workers to be the greatest threat. All of these people grew steadily less responsive to questions of Reconstruction. After the withdrawal of the military governors in 1868 and in 1870, therefore, developments in the South were controlled less and less by national policy and more and more by local conditions. The essence of these conditions in 1868 was that the Negroes, through their place in the Republican Party, could expect to have the law and the initial control of the state governments on their side (though not by any means to dominate the party). But the whites still had the control of property and the knowledge of how to organize and execute a political or military program on their side.

The Southern Economy in the Postwar World

One difference between public policy and human living is that Congress could wait for two years after the collapse of the Confederacy before deciding that the affairs of the South must be settled by a program of military reconstruction, but the people of the South, both white and black, had to find ways to get along from day to day. This was true from the moment of Lee's surrender.

Wartime Devastation. The situation within which they had to operate narrowed their opportunities to a pitifully restricted range. Some of the evils that developed were caused by the devastation of war and the inherent evils of the cotton economy more than by the villainy of either vile carpetbaggers and riotous Negro rule (as traditional historians insisted early in the present century), or by the infamy of white racism (as revisionist historians have asserted with equal fervor more recently). The basic facts in the South in April

1865 were grim. The Confederacy had been defeated and its government had very unwisely kept on fighting for more than a year after defeat was certain. As a result, money was worthless and there was no banking system. Further, the transportation system had been completely worn out by the Confederate armies and then destroyed by the Union armies, which often tore up the rails, heated them over a fire until they were red hot in the middle, and then wrapped the ends around the nearest tree. (However, during the last year of the war and immediately after, many of the rail lines were restored by the Union Army.) Food supplies were exhausted, and many people, both Negro and white, would have starved to death in 1865–1866 if the Freedmen's Bureau had not dispensed scanty but vital supplies.

Problems of Reestablishing the Cotton Economy. Almost the only item that might give cheer to Southerners was the fact that the price of cotton was incredibly high after four years of almost no cotton crop. By the time the soldiers came home in 1865 it was quite late in the season to plant. Now, the dominance of cotton was a part of the creed which no one of either race challenged, so there was no question that cotton must be raised; the only question was *how* it should be raised. Before the war, planters, owning both slaves and land, simply put gangs of slaves to work on the land. But since the war the slaves were free, whatever that might mean, and the ownership of land was uncertain. Though the planter families were trying to hold on, their ownership was jeopardized by their inability to pay taxes, as well as by the confiscation policies, both actual and threatened, of the government. The Negroes were pathetically hoping to receive the forty acres that had been promised by the act creating the Freedmen's Bureau. Neither ex-Confederates nor exslaves had any money, and some of the most desirable land was bought up at extremely low prices by northern enterprisers who began moving into the South in substantial numbers, sometimes with a philanthropic intent to educate or help the freedmen, but very often with the intent to make the maximum profit by taking advantage of the distress of both insolvent landowner and helpless freedman.

First Negro Reactions to Freedom. Subsequently, the conduct of Negroes in 1865 and 1866 was harshly condemned as irresponsible, childlike, and unrealistic. They were especially blamed for roaming aimlessly about the country, for refusing to accept steady employment, and for congregating in towns, around military bases, or near Freedmen's Bureau offices. Undeniably, many of them were naive. Nevertheless their conduct was considerably more realistic than their critics have been willing to admit. Slavery had required them to stay on one plantation and to obey the orders of one master. Freedom, when it came, offered them little of a tangible nature. It did not feed them, clothe them, endow them with money or property, or gain them any recognition from the whites. Since it did permit them to go about wherever they pleased, they perhaps naturally proved migratory in their fondness for exercising this one tangible attribute of freedom. As for their reluctance to work, this could be

At first many Negroes simply wandered around, sometimes to try to reunite their families. *Reproduced from the collections of the Library of Congress*

stated in other terms: hoping to acquire land of their own, they did not want to accept the necessity of becoming agricultural laborers on the land of others. In this reluctance, they showed a realistic grasp of the vital fact that the essence of slavery is the involuntary dependence of one person or class of people upon another. Before the war the legal condition of the Negroes as chattels had imposed this kind of dependence. If after the war the whites monopolized the land whose cultivation was the only kind of work the Negroes knew, then a dependent condition could still be forced upon them by imposing the terms on which access to the land would be allowed. Thus they felt that freedom required the ownership of land. White landowners, on the other hand, felt that the point in owning land was to grow crops on it, and if they were deprived of the labor supply to grow the crops, they might as well have their land confiscated directly. If they could still control the labor supply the southern white society could survive the abolition of slavery, though individual slave-owners might be ruined, but if they lost control of the labor supply, the basic social and economic structure of the South would be utterly destroyed.

The Negroes Become Agricultural Laborers. During 1865 and 1866, the whites and the Negroes engaged, perhaps unconsciously, in a kind of tug-of-war to determine the basis on which Negroes should cultivate the soil. The

Negroes were utterly determined that they would not return to the old system of gang labor, and in fact, they never did. The whites, on the other hand, were determined to prevent them from escaping the necessity to labor as plantation workers. This meant that they must be prevented from owning land, which would have provided escape. In this contest essentially the Negroes lost, as proposals of land-confiscation and redistribution faded away. Even the Freedmen's Bureau told them that they must make contracts as agricultural workers, and though the Bureau promised to oversee the arrangement and to safeguard them against unfair terms, it put strong pressure upon them to go to work. Though the Bureau was hated by southern whites as an instrument of Yankee oppression cultivating discontent among the freedmen, some of its local agencies' activities justify the interpretation, which was not made until long afterward, that it was more a planters' bureau than a freedmen's bureau.

The Sharecropping System. When contracts were made, two controlling factors came into play. First was the condition that no one had any money. Agriculture has traditionally operated on credit in many countries, at many periods of history. This is partly because, unlike other enterprises, it produces revenue only at harvest time. It is almost the only kind of enterprise where payday comes only once a year. But the natural predisposition to rely on credit was greatly enhanced in the post-Appomattox South by the bankrupt condition of the country. The landowners could not pay cash wages, but would not have dared to do so if they had had the money, for they believed, no doubt correctly, that many freedmen would quit work if they had money in their pockets.

Human power and a wooden plow were all many Negroes had to maintain their existence. *The Lightfoot Collection.*

Therefore the contracts soon began to take the form of agreements that the freedman would cultivate a specified tract. As compensation for his labor, he would be provided with a dwelling (usually a rickety cabin) and he would receive either a fixed amount of money wages (perhaps $15 a month, though sometimes no more than $8 per month), or else a fixed proportion or share of the crop. Usually one half, but varying widely, the share would be larger if the worker had his own mule and farm implements or smaller if rations were furnished. This so-called sharecropping system became prevalent in 1868 and continued to be a dominant basis for labor in the South until the 1940's.

The Unprofitability of Cotton. Theoretically, there is nothing wrong with a system of labor on shares. In a bad season it protected the landowner against paying wages in excess of his revenue—a contingency that almost ruined some owners in 1867, when the crop was small. In a good season, it permitted the cropper to participate in the profits, and it might even be called an incentive system or a profit-sharing system. It made the worker more independent than he would have been on a strictly wage basis. All these theoretical advantages were nullified by the second controlling factor. This was the simple condition that cotton culture produced a very low revenue per worker, and hence it could not yield compensation adequate for the economic welfare of those who cultivated it, whether as landowners or croppers, whether Negro or white.

To understand the extremely low ceiling which the cotton economy placed upon southern economic welfare, one must recognize that the average able-bodied, full-time cultivator could hardly produce more than 2000 pounds of cotton. At the high prices which prevailed in the late 1860's (when production ran below these amounts), such a production would have yielded a market price of perhaps $600. But prices fell in the 1870's and 1880's to a point where the return would have been of the order of $220. This was the *total* return, before taxes, payment for feed for animals, payment for fertilizer and equipment, or any other expenses. Though it might be supplemented by the production of some other crops which provided food for the table or fodder for the mules, the *total* money income was likely to be not more than $220 per year. Under the sharecropping system, the tenant received only half of this, and the landowner received half, out of which he paid taxes and other expenses. *But even if the cultivators had owned the land and received the full amount clear,* their annual money income would have been around $220; their monthly income less than $20 a month.* What this means is that the South's economy had only a small fraction of the productivity per worker which prevailed in the North. Cotton was an exploitative crop and, while race prejudice was primarily responsible for the subordination of the Negroes, it was cotton which was primarily responsible for their impoverishment. In racial terms, the cotton culture was not especially discriminatory. It victimized white and Negro sharecroppers

*Another way of looking at this is to note the estimate of one planter, during slavery, that he made an average profit of $83 per hand annually for a period of eighteen years (1830-1847). Not allowing for changes in the value of money, this would mean that a freedman cultivating cotton and working as hard as a slave would not improve his standard of living above the standard of living of a slave by more than $83 per year.

alike, and ultimately it reduced more whites than Negroes to tenancy. It even victimized landowners who remained a relatively impoverished class.

Indebtedness. One further disastrous feature of the cotton economy was the fact that cultivators could not meet living costs out of accumulated income, and as a result they had to buy the necessities of life—which for them were cornmeal, fatback pork, and molasses—on credit. Lending to such insolvent people was highly hazardous, and the merchant who extended credit had in turn to borrow from someone else. He added interest for his loan to the cultivator to the interest which he had to pay for the loan to him, so interest ran to inordinate heights. Exact amounts are difficult to calculate, and have been estimated as high as 70 percent, but even if we accept conservative estimates of about 25 percent, it meant that men whose annual money income was usually less than $200 per year were paying $50 a year in interest charges. The accumulated debts and interest charges were frequently more than the annual revenue from the sale of four or five bales of cotton, and in such cases the cultivator received very little cash, or even none at all, but merely had his debt reduced by the amount gained from the sale of his cotton. Thus he could continue in debt year after year, not free to move to another landlord or to buy from another store because he was tied down by his indebtedness. Chronic debt, more than the obligation to turn over a part of the crop to the landowner, made the cotton system a curse to the South.

The South Under the Radical Governments

By the time that Congress had passed the Military Reconstruction Acts, the military governors had held elections, new constitutions had been drawn, new state officials elected, and the new governments recognized by Congress, the South was well into the fourth season of growing cotton since Lee's surrender. The southern whites had held on to their land; the system of sharecropping had evolved and was in 1868 almost a standard part of the cotton economy. The South was still producing less than half as much cotton as in the bumper year, 1860, but the volume was rising. In spite of bad weather conditions the crop reached 2,346,000 bales in 1867, from which point, it would rise to 4,025,000 bales in 1870. To white Southerners, the new state regimes seemed a pointless or detrimental interference with an economic reorganization and recovery that was still precarious. They were prepared to resent and resist these new governments, even before the governments began to function.

Negro Participation. By any objective measure, the new governments proved less drastic than the southern whites had feared. Because of the majorities of Negro voters who were registered and the large numbers of former Confederates who had been disfranchised, it had been anticipated that Negroes might dominate the new governments, monopolize the political offices, and treat the South to an indefinite period of tyranny by ignorant, illiterate, barbarous exslaves. What happened in fact was that Negroes formed a majority in only one constitutional convention (South Carolina), exactly half of the membership in one other (Louisiana), and a minority in eight others. In only three states altogether (Florida being the third) did they constitute as much as one fourth of the membership. After the governments had been organized, Negroes never formed the majority in both houses of the legislature of any state, and only in South Carolina, for six years, did they hold a majority in one house. They never elected a state governor;* they sent two Negroes to the United States Senate and 14 congressmen to the House of Representatives. "Negro Rule," as traditionally pictured, never existed. In asserting their equality, Negroes did not press for desegregated schools, except in South Carolina and Louisiana, and they did not offer serious opposition to laws forbidding the intermarriage of Negroes and whites. In Arkansas the Republican legislature enacted a bill for equal access to public facilities, but neither this measure nor the attempts in other states to secure desegregated schools was followed up vigorously. To the immense but unspoken relief of southern white landowners, Negroes did not raise the question of land confiscation and redistribution in any of the states.

Changing Interpretations of Radical Governments. In the perspective of time, historians have recognized that the Negro officeholders of the Reconstruction era behaved in a creditable and responsible way, and that they, with their white allies, adopted a number of desirable governmental innovations in the new state constitutions. Notable features included a more equitable apportionment for back-country districts in the state legislatures, a shift from appointive offices to elective offices, a recognition of some of the basic rights of women, reform of the penal codes, and especially the establishment of broad systems of publicly supported education.

In spite of these constructive aspects of Radical Reconstruction, a school of historians sympathetic to the southern position succeeded in creating a stereotype which was accepted for several decades, depicting Radical Reconstruction as a carnival of corruption, extravagance, waste, fraud, and African barbarism. Writers of this school argued that the Radical governments practiced corruption—looting and plundering the treasury to a point which marked a complete "blackout of honest government," whereupon southern whites rose in righteous indignation and reclaimed their native country from the ignorant exslaves, the political turncoats or "scalawags," and the predatory outsiders or "carpetbaggers" who had come winging in like vultures. Over the years, careful scholarship has demonstrated that this picture is a caricature of reality. A good many of the "scalawags" were reputable and conscientious men who believed in the recognition of Negro rights. Some of the carpetbaggers were indeed looters, and some, like Adelbert Ames and Daniel Chamberlain, governors of Mississippi and South Carolina, were high-minded men attempting to develop constructive policies. This correction has resulted both from a more careful

*One Negro Lieutenant-Governor, P. B. S. Pinchback of Louisiana, became governor for 43 days when the Governor was ousted from office.

evaluation of the evidence and from a change in public attitudes about who were the "good guys" and who were the "bad guys" in the Reconstruction contest. The whites were once regarded as good guys—as "redeemers," fighting to defend civilization from a descent into barbarism; they are now regarded as bad guys—racists and white supremacists. The Radicals, who were the bad guys—looters and despoilers—are now the good guys—champions of equality and Negro rights. In itself this reversal seems to be justified to the extent that historians are entitled to make and to correct moral judgments. But a fallacious corollary to moral verdicts in history is the tendency to believe that the people on the right side will always be virtuous while those on the wrong side will always be wicked. This view makes history much easier, for it is no longer necessary to examine the evidence about how people actually behaved in a given situation. One finds out which side they are on and then attributes vice or virtue to their actions accordingly. This perversion of history has been practiced as much by one side as by the other, but it is a perversion, for the truth is that in life and therefore in history, men are frequently on the right side for the wrong reason or on the wrong side for the right reason. Even good men do evil, and evil men can do good.

Corruption in Perspective. Recognizing that the carpetbaggers and scalawags have been grossly slandered and maligned, often for no reason at all except that they advocated recognition for Negroes, it is still necessary to ask to what extent they did practice corruption. Part of the answer would be that they did an appreciable amount of the kind of stealing that was done by other political rings in taking funds out of the treasury on the pretext of paying for goods or services that were not actually received. It was estimated in South Carolina that payments were being made for three or four times as many militiamen as were actually serving in the state militia. Not only did the Republican government steal from the state, but what is somewhat remarkable, it actually stole from the Negroes. The circumstances were that once again the question of distributing land to Negroes was raised; once again a promise was made and once again it was broken. In 1868 the state legislature voted a fund of $700,000 for the purchase of land to be sold to the landless freedmen on long-term credit. At the collapsed prices of land then current in South Carolina, this sum might easily have bought enough good land to settle 10,000 freedmen. But instead, the men who controlled the fund bought worthless land at fictitious prices ten times as high as the true value, and pocketed the difference between the fictitious price and the amount actually paid. One thirty-thousand-acre tract which was purchased for $122,000 was disclosed to have been on the market before the purchase at a price of $15,000, and a witness described it as "almost an entire unbroken swamp, utterly worthless except for the timber that there is upon it." Another large tract which the state bought was, in the words of a witness, "one vast sand bed, and if sold for $1 per acre, no set of people under heaven could raise enough to pay for it."

A proper perspective will remind us that this was an era of corruption and that political dishonesty was, as one historian has observed, "bipartisan, bisectional, and biracial." But it struck the South with especially disastrous effects because the South had no economic surplus with which to cushion large governmental expenses. As we have already seen, no cotton cultivator, whether white or black, could expect to clear, by his own labor, as much as $220 a year in cash by cultivating cotton, and if the tax rate was increased to fourteen times what it had been previously, which is what happened in Mississippi, landowners were threatened with the loss of their property almost as much as they had been threatened by the Confiscation Act of 1862, or the expropriation policies of Thaddeus Stevens. Even if the previous tax rate had been extremely low and if the funds were used for such socially desirable purposes as public education, property owners were still threatened, and the threat became a reality in Mississippi when one fifth of the land in the state was advertised for public sale because of default in taxes. Far from regretting this consequence, the Radicals to some extent desired it. It was a new and indirect policy of land confiscation, but unlike Thaddeus Stevens' policy it was not primarily for the freedmen.

White Hatred of Radical Governments. The Radical governments soon became the objects of bitterness and hatred on the part of the great majority of whites—an animosity such as no other political regime in America has ever quite encountered. The reasons for this intense feeling cannot be determined with the precision of factual events, but it is clear that certain features were involved. To begin with, the whites resented and feared the threat of the Radical governments to the new and precarious system of white landownership and Negro tenancy which they had worked out with such difficulty. Further, ever since the Negroes were disappointed in the promise of land, the whites had been afraid of a really fatal race war, or an "uprising" as they called it, among the freedmen. Anything which aroused Negro discontent seemed to the whites to make race war more likely, and the Radical governments were, without question, doing things to arouse Negro discontent. One policy which inflamed white indignation and fear most acutely was the policy of the governments in North Carolina, South Carolina, Tennessee, Mississippi, Louisiana, Arkansas, and Texas of organizing state militia consisting primarily of Negroes. The spectacle of Negroes organized as troops and armed for combat set off strong emotions of both fear and indignation among the whites.

Finally, it is evident that the South was seething with hostility to any sort of recognition of Negroes. Again, one cannot say with precision why this feeling was so strong. But the belief in the inferiority of Negroes was virtually universal. To the ancient ethnocentric impulses which have created social tensions all over the world, there were added, in this situation, certain factors which made the animosity to Negroes far more intense. The condition of slavery had placed a stigma upon the race that was enslaved. The fact that emancipation came as a war measure served to make the freedom of the Negroes a humiliating reminder to the whites of their bitter military defeat.

Apparently, the resistance of freedmen to becoming agricultural laborers on other men's land, and the devious ways in which they sometimes sabotaged the purposes of the landowners, by neglect, by quitting at a crucial time in the harvest, by damaging equipment or abusing work animals, had bred further ill feeling. But for whatever reason, the fact was that the whites almost universally seemed to regard it as intolerable that a former slave should show in any way a sense of his independence.

White Conservatives Recapture the South

For all these reasons, the white South set fiercely about the business of ridding itself of the Reconstruction regimes. Since the whites formed a majority of the population in all the southern states except South Carolina, Mississippi, and Louisiana, and since their overwhelming control of property gave them immense economic leverage, it is quite possible that they could have accomplished their purpose by sheer economic pressure without the use of violence. They did so in fact in the states where white majorities were largest. In 1869, the Conservatives gained political control in Virginia, without ever experiencing a Radical regime. In the same year, Tennessee also fell to the Conservatives after three years of Republican rule. In 1870, North Carolina made the transition after two years. Georgia followed in 1872, but in all the states of the deep South there were several years of struggle and violence.

Terrorism. Most of the native whites who had begun by cooperating with the Republicans now changed sides, either because of disillusionment with their allies or because of relentless pressure by other whites. By 1870, the southern whites were standing together with far more solidarity than they had shown during the war, and their unanimity added much to their strength. They attacked the Republicans by several devices. One of these was ostracism, so complete that one of its victims said "no white man can live in the South in the future and act with any other than the Democratic Party unless he is willing and prepared to live a life of social isolation." Another was economic pressure, especially against Negroes, who were warned that if they voted Republican, they would be excluded from employment and from access to land for cultivation. These pressures were supplemented by intimidation, violence, and terrorism. The earliest and most dreaded of the terrorist organizations was the secret Ku Klux Klan, which was organized with somewhat indefinite purposes in Tennessee in 1865, but which took on its real significance in the spring of 1867—that is, at the time of the Military Reconstruction Acts, when delegates from several states met and placed General Nathan Bedford Forrest at the head of the order. Along with the Klan there were many other secret organizations, but in all of them the strategy was the same. They used threats to intimidate their opponents, along with quite enough violence to give their threats a fearful credibility. This violence took the form of whippings, mutilation, or murder, and it was directed especially at Republican leaders, Negro officeholders, and

Negro militia officers, on the theory that the rank and file of Negroes would be frightened into submission if they saw that even their leaders were not safe. The actual number of killings or injuries inflicted is impossible to estimate, though it was large. Its significance lay less in the number of persons who were physically victimized than in the number who fled or submitted rather than face death at the hands of violent men who struck without a word in the dead of night. Most significant of all would be the number of those who were intimidated.

Both the states and the federal government enacted laws against the terrorists, but the state laws were largely meaningless, for all they could do was to outlaw men who had already outlawed themselves, yet who could rely on the support of the white community against the government. The federal laws, of which there were three in 1870 and 1871, were more serious; the severest of the three gave the President power for a period of one year to suspend *habeas corpus* and to declare martial law. Before this law was passed, however, President Grant had already shown that he did not like the idea of sending more federal troops back into the South, for he refused a plea by the Republican governor of North Carolina for military support in 1870. Later in the year, the Democrats took control of the state. Late in 1871 Grant invoked the law to suspend *habeas corpus* in nine counties in South Carolina and to initiate numerous prosecutions in Mississippi.

This Thomas Nast cartoon depicts the plight of the southern Negro, ignored by the North and terrorized by southern white supremacists. *Harper's Weekly, October 24, 1874*

THE TROUBLESOME ELEPHANT.

WHERE SHALL OLD SAMBO GO?

When white conservatives recaptured the South, thousands of Negroes fled north and west, despite attempts to prevent their departure. Then they discovered, with tragic irony, that they did not seem to be welcome anywhere. The basic issue of the place of the black man in America had not yet been faced. *Rare Book Division, The New York Public Library, Astor, Lenox and Tilden Foundations*

The Northern Mood. But Grant sensed correctly that the North was weary and disillusioned about Reconstruction, and that the public did not want to use armed force to protect the southern state governments if they could not protect themselves. Many respectable northern Republicans were embarrassed by the financial corruption of the carpetbag Republicans, and many conservative and business-oriented northern Republicans wanted political stability in the South as a prerequisite to the restoration of normal patterns of cotton production and intersectional trade. They realized that the Radical governments could not establish such stability, but the southern "Redeemers" could. Still further, they were by this time alarmed by what they regarded as the economic radicalism of northern farmers and industrial workers in the Grange and the National Labor Union, so they began to regard their political alliance with propertyless southern Negroes against property-holding southern whites as a mistake. Back of all these second thoughts about the Radical program lay the basic fact that the majority of the northern public—almost all the Democrats and many of the Republicans—did not believe in Negro equality and never had believed in it. They had fought the war more for the cause of Union than of emancipation. After the war they had held back from giving Negroes political power; they had done so finally, not because they believed in it in a positive way but for lack of southern white Unionists to base a government upon, so that Negro rule seemed the only alternative to giving the defeated Confederates a free hand to undo the results of the Union victory and the Republican ascendancy. So marked had been their reluctance that they did not establish Negro suffrage in the South until two years after the war, by the Military Reconstruction Acts, and they did not establish it in most of the northern states until four years after, at a time when they saw that the Republican Party urgently needed Negro votes in very close northern elections. In the Congressional election of 1874, the Republicans lost control of the House of Representatives, and the Democrats gained a sixty-vote majority.

Further Gains by Southern Conservatives. The southern resistance leaders were quick to sense that the tide was turning and after 1872 they began to make rapid gains. In 1874 they came to power in Texas, Arkansas, and Alabama. That left only four states still under Radical control—Florida, Louisiana, South Carolina, and Mississippi—of which the latter three had Negro majorities in their populations. Of these four, Mississippi was the next to be captured by the whites—and one may properly say "the whites" for the political alignments were almost completely racial. There the tactics of intimidation and terror were practiced in their most open form. Whites especially employed the device of provoking an incident of violence, and then using it as a pretext for a "riot" in which Negroes were hunted and shot almost indiscriminately. In many ways the whites made it clear that they would go to any lengths to keep Negroes and Republicans away from the polls at the state election in September 1875. Governor Adelbert Ames was deeply aware that large-scale violence was imminent, and he dared not call out the Negro militia. Instead he appealed to Washington for military support. The response of the Grant administration was negative: "The whole public," said the Attorney General, "are tired of these annual autumnal outbreaks in the South." After this Ames in Mississippi was as helpless as Maximilian had been after Napoleon abandoned him in Mexico, though Ames did leave the state alive. The election was only a formality. The Democrats carried sixty-two of the seventy-four counties, and won the only statewide office by a vote of 96,000 to 66,000. When the Democratic legislature met in the following January, Governor Ames resigned and the Democrats took complete political control of the state.

The Election of 1876 and the End of Radical Reconstruction. In 1876–1877 a process which by this time appeared irreversible, at last came to an end. Although radical governments still survived in Florida, Louisiana, and South Carolina all three depended heavily on the presence of federal troops. All of these states held elections in 1876. The Democrats won in Florida, but the Republicans remained in office, since their terms did not expire until 1877. In Louisiana and South Carolina both sides claimed to have won the elections, and they set up rival "governments," each claiming to represent the legitimate authority of the state. At the same time the country was also having a Presidential election, in which Governor Rutherford B. Hayes of Ohio for the

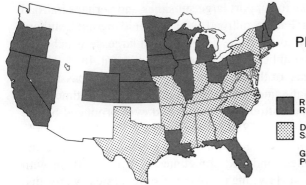

PRESIDENTIAL ELECTION:
1876

	Electoral Vote	Popular Vote
REPUBLICAN Rutherford B. Hayes	185	4,036,572
DEMOCRATIC Samuel J. Tilden	184	4,284,020
GREENBACK Peter Cooper		81,737

Republicans opposed Governor Samuel J. Tilden of New York for the Democrats. In the election, Tilden won a popular majority of about 200,000 and 184 of the 185 electoral votes needed to make him President. But one electoral vote in Oregon was disputed on a legal point, and in each of the three southern states where Republicans still held office, two conflicting sets of returns were submitted. If Hayes should receive every one of these twenty disputed votes, he would win the Presidency by a margin of one vote.

The Constitution offered no guidance for a situation of this kind. Congress created an Electoral Commission of fifteen members—five from each house of Congress and five from the Supreme Court—to resolve the dispute. Since the Commission divided on strict party lines, eight Republicans to seven Democrats, in all its decisions, it lost any moral authority which it might have had. Democrats were convinced, probably correctly, that the Republicans were stealing the election. Because they controlled the House of Representatives, they were in a position to prevent the completion of the count by refusing to meet with the Senate in a joint session, which is constitutionally required for receiving the electoral votes.

For weeks it appeared that the Democrats would obstruct the completion of the count, and it was, in fact, not completed until March 2, 1877—two days before the inauguration. Actually, blocking the election was not a satisfactory tactic, for it would not bring about the election of Tilden. It would only throw the country into chaos, which no one wanted to do. The Democrats, and especially the southern Democrats, decided to acquiesce in the election of Hayes but to negotiate the best terms possible for their surrender. These terms included a promise, conveyed indirectly from Hayes through his managers, that he would withdraw the last remaining troops from the South, which meant that the Republican claimants to control in Louisiana and South Carolina would collapse. Hayes apparently agreed to this quite readily, as he had probably intended to withdraw the troops in any case. Southern Democrats gave great publicity to their action in "ransoming" the last two of the states which were still "unredeemed," but they said much less about the fact that they had also extorted from Hayes a promise to support large subsidies and perhaps railroad land grants for a Texas and Pacific railroad, which would permit southern financial adventurers to enjoy some of the governmental largesse which they had been denouncing the Republicans for receiving. In April 1877, Hayes withdrew the troops, and the last of the southern state governments passed into Democratic hands. During that same year, the South, for the first time since Fort Sumter, produced a larger cotton crop than it had ever produced before the war. After a period of nine years, Radical Reconstruction was at an end.

The Democratic Ascendancy. The Radical ascendancy had threatened the position of the southern whites, and had sometimes confronted them with economic ruin, but though a few high-ranking Confederates were disfranchised, whites were never actually subordinated. The whites had sat in every Reconstruction legislature, usually in the majority and usually asserting themselves vigorously. Now the Democratic ascendancy completely subordinated the southern Negroes. Some of them might continue to vote, at least until the end of the century, and a remnant might sit in seats in the state legislatures, or even in Congress. But they were not permitted to assert themselves. They were a subordinate caste, not yet legally segregated, but segregated in practice, and legal segregation would come soon enough. Meanwhile they were discriminated against in many ways, by the government, the society, the merchants to whom they were in debt, and the property owners whose land they tilled.

The Era in the Balance Sheet

The era from 1846 to 1877 was, in more ways than one, a tragic period. It began with fifteen years of bitter sectional strife, followed by four years of the most deadly warfare in American history, followed by twelve years of economic distress, social dislocation, and racial strife in the South. All of the pain and suffering which these experiences produced could be justified, it would seem, only by some great constructive advances. In any trial inventory of advances, the men of that era would have asserted emphatically that the Union had been saved and the slaves had been emancipated. Both assertions were true in the literal sense, and in fact the Union had been saved in spirit as well as in law, for there was a genuine reconciliation of the sections. At the time of the Civil War, the South had claimed a full-bodied southern nationality. If this claim had been genuine, the military triumph of the Union would have left a protracted, festering discontent among the southern whites. But southern nationalism was not deep-seated, and before the century was over men who had fought for the Confederacy were volunteering for service under the flag of the Union in a war against Spain. Yet while the American people had achieved what Lincoln called his "paramount object"—to save the Union—they had not been able to resolve a dilemma which was perhaps insoluble in any case—the dilemma of reconciling the sections without sacrificing the quest for a new life for American Negroes, or of creating the basis for such a new life without making the hostility between the sections permanent. They had equivocated at times between these objectives, and in 1867 it had appeared that a new system of race relations might receive the priority. But this was only momentary, for the great majority gave a priority to attaining harmony between northern and southern whites, and the evidence indicates that, even in the North, there was no preponderant support for the full acceptance of Negroes in American society.

Both sectional reconciliation and racial harmony, based on a fair and impartial system of race relations, were vital to the future, and it would be arbitrary to say that either one ought to have been sacrificed to the other. But one can say that the crucial misfortune was that the nation fought a civil war for four years, and sacrificed half a million men (probably one for every six slaves who were freed) without ever recognizing in broad terms that one broad goal for which it was paying this immense price was the development of a satisfactory system of race relations. Instead, from first to last, the issue was constantly viewed in excessively narrow and limiting terms. Failing to see that the intrinsic problem was that of the social subordination of four million Negroes, men before the Civil War thought only of the institution of slavery, or, even worse, they thought only of slavery in the territories. When the war came, the tactical necessity of avoiding the alienation of the border states led to something approaching an embargo upon the discussion even of emancipation, much less of the future life of those who were to be emancipated. The will-o'-the-wisp of colonization encouraged many people to avoid grappling with the hard facts presented by the addition of four million new citizens with an undefined role in American life. Then, during Reconstruction too many Northerners thought of Negroes in America simply as a local condition in the South, and considered policy for them simply as an aspect of protecting the program and power of the Republican party. Too many Southerners thought of emancipation not as posing a problem to be solved but as presenting a challenge to be repelled and symbolizing a defeat to be resented.

So little was the nature of the situation understood that when sectional goodwill had been restored, without any solution whatever of the future of American Negroes, most observers took the view that the reconciliation of the sections and the emancipation of the slaves had solved everything. Sectional conflict, resulting in division, had been followed by reunion. With reunion, the country could look forward to a future free of tension. For nearly three generations, the republic experienced such remarkable tranquility that this view appeared to be justified. But the restoration of the Union without satisfactory solution of the relations between the races created latent stresses which a century later were to impose severe strains upon the structure of American society.

In a sense the Civil War generation committed the colossal error of failing to recognize the major issue with which it was concerned. In another sense each generation must solve its own problems. The Civil War generation had saved the Union and emancipated the slaves. If this left to later generations the difficult task of giving meaning to both union and emancipation, at least it did leave a union to give meaning to, and a Negro population whose status was not paralyzed by the rigid and static institution of slavery.

SUGGESTED READING (Prepared by Carl N. Degler)

The literature on Radical Reconstruction can be said to begin with William A. Dunning, *Reconstruction: Political and Economic, 1865–1877** (1907) because Dunning's views provided the framework against which much of modern historical study directs itself. Yet Dunning still repays study, if his pro-South and anti-Negro biases are recognized. W. E. B. DuBois, *Black Reconstruction, 1860–1880* (1935) is a pioneer study to counter Dunning's influence by emphasizing the activities of blacks in the South. A briefer and more scholarly modern study that is more successful in answering Dunning is John Hope Franklin, *Reconstruction After the Civil War** (1961). An analytical and interpretive short introduction to changing views and bibliography is Kenneth M. Stampp, *The Era of Reconstruction, 1865–1877** (1965). A good collection of documents by Radical Republicans is contained in Harold Hyman, ed., *The Radical Republicans and Reconstruction, 1861–1870** (1967).

One of the earliest and still one of the best revisionist studies of Reconstruction in a single state is Francis B. Simkins and Robert H. Woody, *South Carolina During Reconstruction* (1932). William A. Russ, Jr., "Registration and Disfranchisement under Radical Reconstruction," *Mississippi Valley Historical Review* XXI (1934): 163–80 puts the issue of disfranchisement into perspective. The ambiguous attitude of northern Radicals on Negro suffrage is emphasized in William Gillette, *The Right to Vote: Politics and the Passage of the Fifteenth Amendment** (1965).

A handy summary of the role of the *Negro in Reconstruction** is by Robert Cruden (1969). Important state studies are Vernon Lane Wharton, *The Negro in Mississippi, 1865–1890** (1947), which was a path-breaker in its time, and Joel R. Williamson, *After Slavery: The Negro in South Carolina During Reconstruction** (1965). The fullest and most recent study of intimidation of blacks is Allen W. Trelease, *The White Terror: The Ku Klux Klan Conspiracy and Southern Reconstruction* (1971).

One of the ways in which Reconstruction has been reinterpreted has been to recognize that not all so-called scalawags or carpetbaggers were evil. Important in developing that revisionist view was David Donald, "The Scalawag in Mississippi Reconstruction," *Journal of Southern History* X (1944): 447–60. T. Harry Williams, "The Louisiana Unification Movement of 1873," *Journal of Southern History* XI (1945): 349–69, discusses black-white cooperation. Jack B. Scroggs, "Carpetbagger Constitutional Reform in the South Atlantic States, 1867–1868," *Journal of Southern History* XXVII (1961): 475–93, points to the genuine reforms introduced by carpetbaggers. One of the most appealing and successful carpetbaggers is analyzed in Otto H. Olsen,

Carpetbagger's Crusade: The Life of Albion Winigar Tourgee (1965). Richard N. Current discusses *Three Carpetbag Governors* (1967).

Changes in agriculture in the South during Reconstruction can be reliably followed in Fred A. Shannon, *The Farmer's Last Frontier** (1945). David Montgomery, *Beyond Equality: Labor and the Radical Republicans, 1862–1872* (1967) seeks to demonstrate a conflict between organized labor and Republican ideology. The standard work on the financial developments of the era is Irwin Unger, *The Greenback Era: A Social and Political History of American Finance, 1865–1879** (1964). The early history of the silver question is discussed in Allan Weinstein, *Prelude to Populism: Origins of the Silver Issue 1867–1878* (1970). An important article on land grants to railroads is Robert S. Henry, "The Railroad Land Grant Legend in American History Texts," *Mississippi Valley Historical Review* XXXII (1945): 171–94.

A very recent detailed analysis of the *Alabama* claims is contained in David Donald, *Charles Sumner and the Rights of Man* (1971). The indispensable, though not entirely convincing study of the ending of Reconstruction in 1877 is C. Vann Woodward, *Reunion and Reaction** (2nd ed., rev., 1956).

*Available in a paperback edition

INDEX

Hooker, Joseph, 137, 138
Howe, Samuel Gridley, 87

I

Immigration, 106–109, *graph,* 80; decade of
  1840's, 65; and political alignments, 78–81
Impeachment, 193
Impressment laws, supplies from farmers, 124
Imprisonment for debt, 62
Income tax (1863–1872), 203
Indebtedness, 219
Indentured servants, 19
India, 3
Indians, California and Oregon, 4; Latin America, 4
Individualism, 12
Industrialization, 9, 10, 34–39; impact of Civil
  War, 205–207; North and South compared,
  94, 115, 116, *map* 115; Whigs, 199
Inflation, 206, 211; Confederacy, 124
International arbitration, 209
Iowa, franchise for Negroes, 195
Irish, Democratic party, 78–81; immigrants,
  106; in Union army, 109
Iron foundry, 36
Ironclad vessels, 119, 131, 148

J

Jackson, Thomas J. ("Stonewall"), 128, 136,
  146, 149
Jefferson, Thomas, slavery, 22
Johnson, Andrew, military governor of Tenn.,
  134; congressional statement on rights of
  defeated states, 157; impeachment proceedings, 193; military governors, 191; Reconstruction, 166–187
Johnston, Albert Sydney, 134
Johnston, Joseph E., 135, 141
Joint Committee on Reconstruction, 173, 174

K

Kansas, contest between proslavery and antislavery forces, 69–76
Kansas-Nebraska Act, 69–76
Kearny, Stephen W., 41
Kentucky, battles for Union control, 134, 140;
  secession, 112
"King Cotton" doctrine, 118–120
Know Nothings, 80–82, 89, 92, 109
Ku Klux Klan, 223, 224

L

Land, abundance of, 5; Democrats, 199; grants
  to railroads, 201, 207, *map* 201; Homestead

Act (1862), 200; Negroes' need of, 161; postwar problems of ownership, 215
Latin America, 3
Latter Day Saints, Church of Jesus Christ of
  (Mormons), 56
Lawn mower, *illus.,* 206
Leaves of Grass (Whitman), 58
Lecompton Constitution, 75, 76, 90
Lee, Robert E., 122, 129, 135–139, 142, *illus.,*
  136
Liberator, The (newspaper), 26
Lincoln, Abraham, *illus.,* 113; nomination and
  election in 1860, 92–101; reconciliation and
  freedom, 153–166; slavery a national question, 71; war years, 111–144
Liquor, reformers, 57
Literacy, 8
Louisiana, Reconstruction and elections, 191;
  restoration attempts, 165; secession, 95
Louisiana Territory, 4, 28
Lyon, Nathaniel, 133

M

McCardle, William H., 192
McClellan, George B., 131–137
McCormick's Reaper, 11, 39
McDowell, Irwin, 130
Machines, 9, 10, 36
Manassas Junction. *See* Bull Run
"Manifest Destiny", 28, 65
Marshall, John, 14
Maryland, remained with Union, 112
Mason-Dixon boundary, 16
Mass production, 10, 11, 207
Massachusetts Bay Colony, education, 7
Maximilian in Mexico, 207, 208
Meade, George Gordon, 138, 139
Merrimack (ship), 131, 148
Mexican War, 29, 30, 40–42
Mexico, 3; Maximilian, 207, 208
Mexico City, Mexico, defeat of, 42
Middle classes, 2
Military courts, 192–193
Military Reconstruction Act (1867), 180, 186
Mill Springs, Battle of, 134
Milligan, L. P., 192
Minnesota, franchise for Negroes, 195
Missionary Ridge, Battle of, 141
Mississippi, admittance to Union after War,
  192; secession, 95; taxes and land, 222
Mississippi River, Civil War, 130, 134, 148
Missouri, Confederate defeats, 132, 133; secession, 98, 112
Missouri Compromise (1820), 25; Kansas-
  Nebraska Act, 69, 70
Money, Confederate, 123; pre-Civil War, 199;
  transformation of monetary system, 203–207,
  210
Monitor (ship), 131, 147
Monroe Doctrine, 208

Sherman, William T., 141, 142, 150
Shiloh, Battle of, 134
Singer Sewing Machine factory, 34
Slavery, abolition, 1, 22, 159, *maps,* 72–73; during Civil War, 116, 156–159; conditions of life, 19, 20; controversies after Mexican War, 1, 45–101; divisiveness, 16–23, 31; controversy cause of secession, 152; pre-Civil War reformers, 56–60
Sloat, John D., 41
Smith, Gerrit, 87
Social conditions, absence of hierarchy, 5, 94
South Carolina, secession, 95; legislature, *illus.,* 190; temporary settlement of land by Negroes, 183
Southern Homestead Act (1866), 185
Southern Pacific railroad, 202
Spain, Mexican debt, 207
Special Field Order Number Fifteen (Sherman), 183
Stanton, Edwin M., army supplies, 128; suspension by Johnson, 193
Staple crop agriculture, 23
Star Spangled Banner, Order of, 80
State militias, 222
States' rights, 15, 27; confusion of ideas after War, 162, 163; hardship within Confederacy, 125
Steam power, 9
Steamboats, 3, 9, 36
Stevens, Thaddeus, distribution of land among Negroes, 174, 185
Stowe, Harriet Beecher, 83
Strategy, defensive v. aggressive, 120–123
Suffrage, aliens, 106; manhood, 2, 3; Negroes, 25, 162, 165, 166, 171; Radical Reconstruction, 121, 122, 191, 195, 196
Sumner, Charles, 77; *Alabama* claims, 208; Negro citizenship, 174
Supplies, Army, 128
Supreme Court of U.S., Dred Scott decision, 84, 85; greenbacks, 217; Radical Republicans and military courts, 192, 193

T

Tactics, defensive v. aggressive, 120–123
Taney, Roger B., 85
Tariffs, 199, 207
Taxes, 222
Taylor, Zachary, Mexican War, 42; President, 49–52
Technology, 2, 9, 10, 34–39; Civil War impact on, 207
Telegraph, 146
Temperance movement, 57
Tenements, immigrants, 106
Tennessee, battles and return to Union, 134, 140; secession, 98, 112

Tennessee River, Civil War, 130, 134
Tenure of Office Act (1867), 193
Terrorism, 223
Texas, 26, 28, 46; admittance to Union after the War, 192; secession, 95
Textile industry, War years, 118
Thirteenth Amendment, 17, 159, 171
Thomas, George H., 134
Thoreau, Henry D., 87
Tilden, Samuel J., 227
Total war, 117
Transcontinental railroad, 68–70, 212
Transportation, 9, 10, 36; devastation in South, 215; unity of nation, 14
Trench warfare, 146, 150
Truth, Sojourner, 60
Tweed Ring, 213

U

Uncle Tom's Cabin (Stowe), 83
Underground railroad, 60
Union, The, 111–144; reconciliation and freedom, 152–187
Union Pacific railroad, 202
Utah, 43; Mormon migration, 56

V

Van Dorn, Earl, 140
Vicksburg, Battle of, 134, 139, 140, 150
Virginia, admittance to Union after War, 192; campaigns of war, 135–139; secession, 98, 112

W

Wade-Davis bill, 164
Walker, Robert J., 75
Weld, Theodore Dwight, 26
Whig party, collapse of party, 70; economic policies, 199; Republican party, 78–80
Whitman, Walt, 58
Whitney, Eli, 10
Willamette Valley, settlement, 4
Wilmot Proviso, 31
Wilson, Henry, 172
Women's rights, 60, 62
Wright, Elizur, 185
Wyoming, 43

XYZ

Yancey, William L., 95
Zollicoffer, Felix, 134